WITH CHRIST IN THE SCHOOL OF DISCIPLE BUILDING

CARL WILSON

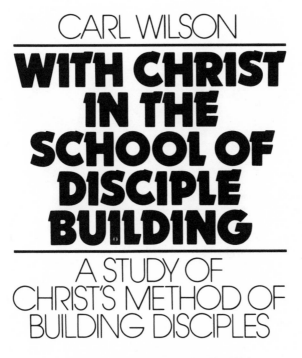

WITH CHRIST IN THE SCHOOL OF DISCIPLE BUILDING

A STUDY OF CHRIST'S METHOD OF BUILDING DISCIPLES

WITH A FOREWORD BY
Harold J. Ockenga

ZONDERVAN PUBLISHING HOUSE OF THE ZONDERVAN CORPORATION GRAND RAPIDS, MICHIGAN 49506

WITH CHRIST IN THE SCHOOL OF DISCIPLE BUILDING

Copyright © 1976 by The Zondervan Corporation
Grand Rapids, Michigan
Second printing 1977

Library of Congress Cataloging in Publication Data

Wilson, Carl W
  With Christ in the school of disciple building.

  Bibliography: p.
  Includes index.
  1. Christian life — 1960-   2.   Evangelistic
work.   I.   Title.
BV4501.2.W55   248'.4   76-13214

ISBN 0-310-34591-X

Unless otherwise stated, Old Testament quotations are from *The New American Standard Bible*
© 1971 by the Lockman Foundation, published by Creation House, Inc., and New Testament
quotations are from *The New International Version* © 1973 by the New York Bible Society,
published by The Zondervan Corporation.

Printed in the United States of America

Contents

IV. STUDY QUESTIONS

Diagrams and Charts

Acknowledgments

I wish to express my gratitude to the Lord for giving me the insights expressed in this book. I am increasingly conscious that everything that contributes to the fruitfulness of God's kingdom is motivated by Him and used in spite of our frailties and sin.

I am especially in debt to Miss Cyndie Heiskell, whom God sent to help me write this and to show me servant love. She freely gave months of her time editing and helping make it clearer. Graham Harvey, his wife Mary, and Jim Hancock helped in many ways. Nancy Richards, Brenda Dalton, my daughter Sharon, and Juanita Hawley, as well as others, labored hours typing and retyping. My dear wife also edited and helped in other ways. Bill Watkins, a faithful assistant, helped research various questions. The Worldwide Discipleship staff in Atlanta assisted and proofread the manuscript. Judy Moerlein, Janis Jones, and Don Richards especially helped in this. It is not possible to thank all who helped.

I could not have had more gracious cooperation and help from the publisher. I am thankful for the special blessing that has come from my contacts with the men of God who lead and edit for Zondervan. They have shown a desire to please Christ and help the author.

Foreword

Reading *With Christ in the School of Disciple Building* is like reading the four Gospels again, because Scripture is used so profusely. In this study, Carl Wilson has sought to discover and state the method used by Jesus to train and equip first the twelve apostles, then the seventy, and then succeeding groups of disciples.

This model contains seven steps that are traced in detail through the ministry of Jesus with supporting Scriptures. The repetition of the model leads Wilson to believe that it is applicable to disciple building at any age of the church and can be the secret of church growth today.

He emphasizes training church leaders to share the responsibilities of ministry with the pastor. With such leaders it is believed the church will grow geometrically, rather than arithmetically.

The evangelical convictions and evangelistic passion of the author shine through the entire treatment. His criticism of present church evangelism is constructive. He believes evangelism and discipling should go hand in hand. Those who take the time to master this discipleship method and put it into practice will be rewarded richly.

HAROLD J. OCKENGA

Introduction

Our Lord Jesus Christ rules from heaven over the affairs of men and especially over His body, the church. This book is a message that I believe He has given me to communicate to His people. I believe it is appropriate for our time and urgently needed.

My assertion that this is a message from Him is not derived from a claim to special prophetic insight or infallibility but from a diligent search of His Word in Holy Scripture and years of practical involvement in His work, both in local churches and interdenominational youth work.

I believe Christ wants to renew His church. The great need of the church lies in a renewal of the New Testament approach to building disciples and "teaching them to observe all things" that He commanded (Matt. 28:20). Many of us in the church have defaulted in our moral commitment to Him in the new covenant of grace, and therefore we are not honoring Him as we should. I believe the mission of the kingdom of God is at stake in this matter and this book can help rectify this.

I make no claim to having said the first or last word on the subject of New Testament discipleship. There are many who have written more brilliantly than I. But I believe Christ has given me an understanding of how He built His disciples and has enabled me to begin showing others how to do this, based on Scripture, in a way not set forth by any other author. Most books deal with principles of discipleship. This book delineates the biblical basis of the chronological steps for developing a disciple, from the first involvement with his teacher until he is sent forth on his own. It also includes insights into principles of discipling as these principles unfold through those steps.

This book is written as a biblical philosophy of discipleship and points the way for a person to go about doing it. The detailed "how to's" will be presented in subsequent works. I trust others also will use this book to write their own. Many will improve on what I have done, I am sure.

My practical application came out of the biblical principles presented in this book as they were applied to my work with college and high school youth. More recently I have applied them to the local church and have trained pastors in how to use them. Businessmen have used them in working with other businessmen and their employees with great effect in human relations as well as in forwarding the kingdom of God.

Many scholarly questions are involved in what has been said. Some scholars will be disappointed in the book. For years many Christian scholars were sidetracked down the road of the quest for the historical Jesus and into considerations of the origins of Pauline thinking. Those studies have run their course and have come very nearly to a dead end, in spite of efforts to revive a new quest. While that detour in thought was a perversion of the unbelieving epistemology (beginning with Descartes) and while it led through many desert and dry places, there were some things learned through critical studies that have been useful to the background for this work.

Scholars will be disappointed that I have not dealt with the critical problems opened, from Reimarus to present day redaction criticism. That would have perverted the usefulness of this book. Indeed, one of my purposes is to encourage scholarship to go back to using the revelation of Scripture to discover the mind of Christ so we may be led by it and involved in building the kingdom. The critical movement stepped aside to analyze the Christ and His kingdom from a distance rather than from an involvement. That applies even to Ritschl, Harnack, and all the ethical and psychological efforts of that movement as well, even though that will be denied.

I believe that the critical movement has been exposed as having been highly speculative and that it failed to separate the history of God's people from the supernatural, or the natural Jesus from the supernatural Christ. I believe that modern archaeology and textual criticism have given strong support to historical evidence about Jesus and His kingdom. Why should we continue on a detour when the world needs to be shown the way? The world is much in need of our acting on that which, I believe, is a revelation of God in history.

A side value of the book will be that those who study it will immediately gain an appreciation of the chronology of Christ's ministry in the Gospels. They will also gain a sense of the unity of the theology of Christ and that of the writings of His followers in the Epistles and Acts. These alone will make the book valuable for many.

I am not naive. I know this book may stir up a storm, certainly from many religious unbelievers, but some winds may also blow from earnest followers of Christ. I am not greatly concerned about the former, but of my brethren I ask for prayerful consideration and careful study. What you think concerns me deeply.

Spurgeon once said that even though a man's dog may have a few mangy hairs on it, it can still be recognized and appreciated as his pet and friend. Perhaps you will be able to grasp the main image of what I have sought to describe, even though you may see some faults.

Writing is not my gift, but a painful labor. This book would never have been written had not the Lord called me to write it. Its strength lies in the burden of urgency, the insights from careful efforts to understand the Scripture, and prayerful search of how to apply it to our world for Him. The first three chapters and the last will give the burden and vision; the rest will supply inspiration, guidance, and wisdom in doing the job.

If this book is a help to you, will you please recommend and give it to others to help forward Christ's work?

The material in this book is already being studied by students at two theological seminaries and several colleges. To enhance more careful study, I have included study questions for each chapter (see Study Questions, p. 279).

Before you read this book I want to remind you that successful building of disciples depends primarily on the love of a leader for his disciples and not on a program, no matter how good. If one cares about his children, he will spend time with them and find a way to help them grow. But understanding the best program of growth can make love more effective and give it its best and freest expression and its maximum opportunity for success. This book seeks to present such a program while not letting you forget the centrality of love in carrying it out.

I

The Need for Disciple Building

1

The Need for a New Approach

to Disciple Building

The crisis facing the United States and the world, especially the West, is directly related to the church's failure to fulfill her mission. Although the church has been the chief force of resistance to the growing evil of our time, she has not been the salt of the earth and the light of the world as our Lord intended. Salt stops corruption and light drives back and dispels darkness. It is the thesis of this book that the main cause of the church's failure is that she (unknowingly and unwittingly) has been trapped by certain historical developments and is no longer effectively building disciples as Jesus intended, and therefore many in the church are ignorant of, and disobedient to, His will. As a consequence, secular humanism has become the leading philosophy even in churches. We are now faced with the possibility of a clear rejection of Christian ethics in our so-called "Christian" America.

The church urgently needs to return to the New Testament method of training men to build disciples so that they obey the Lord. He commissioned her not only to "make disciples of all nations, baptizing them," but to "teach them *to observe all things*" that He commanded (Matt. 28:19,20). *This book is a study of how Jesus built His disciples.* It is hoped that from it many will learn how to train believers to build disciples in such a way as to multiply Christians who obey the Lord. It is only when the church is obedient to the Lord also in this basic command that she can expect her life to be characterized by vitality and growth.

THE CRISIS TODAY

The United States, with the entire world, is facing a crisis of gigantic proportions. Aleksandr Solzhenitsyn recently said,

> We are approaching a major turning point in history. I can compare it only with the turning point from the Middle Ages to the modern era, a shift of civilizations. It is the sort of turning point at which the hierarchy of values to which we have been dedicated all our lives is starting to waver, and may collapse.[1]

The present condition of our nation is critical. As we enter the fourth quarter of the twentieth century the darkness grows and the corruption spreads. Prophets of doom have always been with us, but now more prominent figures warn of disaster, and their warnings have become stronger and more frequent.

Moreover, the ordinary person cannot avoid the reality of the crisis. He feels it where he lives: the scandals involving government leaders and criticism about them, assassinations of leaders, the precarious economic problems, the continued rise in crime, the misuse of natural resources that portends a serious energy crisis, the possibility of lethal conditions caused by pollution, and the maldistribution of food and wealth as well as a growing shortage of the basic necessities of life. And the problems have all intensified.

Although short breathing spells of improvement have relieved and deceived us at times, basically the national conditions continue to worsen. And generally, we are stoically indifferent as we adjust to these evils. Most industrialized nations are experiencing these trends.

The crisis today is one of human values. It lies in the choice between man's enthroning himself as god and king of the world with a right to exploit creation for himself, and acknowledging himself as a sinful creature to be redeemed and remade into God's likeness to control the world for His glory. It is either putting Adam in the holy of holies to be worshiped as Antichrist or restoring Adam to his position of divine sonship. The crisis is that of choosing secular humanism or redemptive theism. The outcome of the issue lies in whether the church will allow God to use her in restoring Adam to the divine image as seen in Jesus Christ. The United States is now at a crucial turning point. Since she is a leading nation of the world the future of the world is also involved in her choice.

The work of the church involves teaching all that Jesus taught, applying this teaching to daily life so that it will be obeyed, interpreting the errors of secular humanism so that its errors can be avoided, and training leaders so they can do these three things with others.

Jesus forewarned His followers against professing to know Him without truly submitting to His lordship and obeying His will. He pointed out that security comes from true obedience and that tragic consequences follow hypocritical profession of a relationship with Him that is not attended by doing what He taught (Matt. 7:16-29). The church and the world need to heed this warning today.

HISTORIC DECLINE OF DISCIPLE BUILDING AND OF LAY MINISTRY

In the early church, following the death of the twelve apostles of Christ, the decline of the disciple-building ministry and the emergence of a separation between the church leadership (clergy) and the people (laity) are directly related. From apostolic times through the second century there was a college of presbyters or bishops, with one of them as leader, that governed the local church.[2] As Louis Duchesne has pointed out, each presbyter was "on an equality with their president" until about the middle or late third century, especially beginning with Cyprian.[3] According to Philip Schaff, the separation of clergy from laity began in the third century and became rigid and complete by the end of the fourth century.[4]

Generally speaking, a New Testament ministry that involves all the people of God and produces a normal and gradual flow from laymen to leadership has never been restored, nor has a fully effective disciple-building process. On a few occasions the lay ministry has emerged in part but has been hindered or destroyed. Ironically, the conditions that caused the demise of disciple building and lay ministry in those times are recurring in the modern church and pose the same threats.

THE CAUSES OF THE DEMISE OF NEW TESTAMENT DISCIPLE BUILDING IN THE EARLY CHURCH

Vacuum of authority. The manner in which Jesus and His apostles built disciples disappeared from the church between the second and fifth centuries A.D. There were several influences that caused this important change. The primary authority of the original apostles disappeared with their deaths and the deaths of those who had heard them preach. Before the writings of the apostolic community could be gathered together and circulated in an authoritative New Testament canon to take their place, a void of authority developed at a time when there were serious threats in the church.

Indifference of second- and third-generation Christians. Unfortunately this void of authority occurred precisely during the time when second- and third-generation Christians in the gentile world were growing up. For them the important distinction between paganism and Christianity was not so sharp. In many areas — such as Syria, Bithynia, Asia Minor, and Alexandria — Christianity had become the dominant force and paganism was not the same threat as when their grandfathers and fathers, as a part of a minority, were struggling to present Christ. Especially in areas where there were similarities to Christian thought, those who had received the Christian religion from their ancestors were more open to study and accept pagan religious and ethical ideas. During the second century, and perhaps before, Greek philosophical and religious views from the Hellenistic, Syrian, Egyptian, and other cultures began to infiltrate the church. This was especially true among the educated class. This void of authority and the open-mindedness or indifference of the second- and third-generation Christians left the door wide open to movements that caused a breakdown in the disciple-building process, produced a division between the leaders and the people, and introduced a new kind of ceremonial ministry that excluded the laity and minimized teaching and preaching the Word of God.

There were at least four movements involved: Gnosticism, emphasizing knowledge; Montanism, emphasizing emotional experience; Clericalism, emphasizing leadership authority; and Sacramentalism, emphasizing ritual and ceremony.

Special knowledge and learning – Gnosticism. About the turn of the second century A.D. the early church began to move away from the simple preaching of the cross toward the philosophy of men, against which Paul had warned (1 Cor. 2:2-5; Col. 2:8-10). A group designated Gnostics taught that a person had to acquire certain insights of philosophical and religious knowledge before he was a true Christian. It was a religious syncretism that denied the unique deity of Christ and redemption through Him, while giving Him the highest religious values. This movement appealed mainly to the educated and left out the masses of people who could not understand or appreciate it.[5]

During this period the committed Christian leaders responded by writing apologetical defenses and attacking heretics. This was the theme occupying the greater portion of the writings of the ante-Nicene church fathers. Thus, emphasis on simple, positive teaching and application of Christian truth to the life of the Christians was neglected. Even when the preparation of catechumens before baptism was gradually extended to include more instruction in schools, it was presented on a highly intellectual level. So Philip Schaff calls the most prominent of these teachers "churchly gnostics."[6] To a great many ordinary Christians, the thought in the church became cold, speculative, and controversial. The result was that the people left serious study of truth to the leaders. Training of disciples was neglected.

Emotional experience – Montanism. The Montanist movement was in part a reaction to this intellectualizing trend. They sought to reestablish apostolic and prophetic authority by claiming a renewal of the sign gifts and the experience of the inward working of the Holy Spirit. This at first brought to the people a new sense of the immanence or presence of God and a realization of Christ as alive and coming again. But with rare exception, it also minimized teaching and disciple building.[7] The leadership and people became preoccupied with the gifts of the Spirit and with emotional experience to the point that the teaching of Scripture and the apostolic traditions were neglected, and preaching and teaching became shallow. In the place of adequate discipling of its converts, this movement inclined toward an authoritative legalism to solve questions of the Christian life. Montanists often claimed a superior spirituality and at times were schismatic.

Legalizing authority – clericalism. These conditions spawned clericalism. There was the void of authority between the time of the apostles and the forming of the scriptural canon, and also there was the more-gullible and less-committed second and third generation. The committed leaders spent more of their time answering the heresies than teaching the disciples. To this was added the Montanists' preoccupation with emotional experience, sign gifts, and prophecy of the Lord's return, strongly tending to minimize Christ's command to teach disciples to obey everything He had commanded them (Matt. 28:20). As pagan morals began to take over in the absence of solid biblical training, there were growing problems and sin that demanded serious attention in the congregations. The need was that of renewing disciple-building efforts based on teaching apostolic traditions and claiming the apostles' authority as a corrective for sin and heresy. But the local leaders sought to help, unite, and cleanse the church by claiming they had the right to speak personally for Christ apart from His revealed word.[8] Thus the old depraved nature in church leaders found opportunity to claim power on reasonable grounds.

Since most of these leaders were godly men with apostolic background, this seemed, at the time, to be of little consequence, but eventually it led to setting the authority of men as church leaders above the Word of Christ. Also, since the leadership of the church had the answers for the congregation, there was little need or incentive for the people to seek the truth for themselves. Discipleship training thus receded farther into the background.

Ritual and ceremony – sacramentalism. The crowning blow to training disciples came when ritual and ceremony took the place of teaching. The last step in clericalism was that of claiming the priest-hood belonged primarily to the clergy who must lead the people in worship.[9] The celebration of the Mass more and more became the center, with proclaiming and applying the Word of God being made peripheral. Acceptance of God by faith was replaced by works as the way to be righteous. Thus, the separation between clergy and laity was complete. The clergy ministered and the people watched. This was the door into "The Dark Ages."

Evangelism without adequate discipleship training. As disciple building degenerated in the early church, valiant efforts in evangelism continued and Christianity was spread widely (cf. Pliny the Younger, Epist. X 96, 97, Tertullian, Apology XXXVII). The continued expansion without depth of teaching later left the church weak. And even though, under divine providence, the widespread persecution of Christians that began with Trajan early in the second century tended to remove many who would make a superficial profession of faith,[10] giving a purifying effect in many places from time to time, eventually the lack of teaching and application in depth was the church's undoing.

SIMILAR CONDITIONS AND SIMILAR DEGENERATION
OF DISCIPLE BUILDING TODAY

Loss of authority and acceptance of pagan thoughts. The church today finds itself confronted with some of the same conditions that existed in the second to fifth centuries. Secular humanism, which has its roots in ancient paganism, has invaded the church and has under-mined Christian morals and worship. The renaissance (rebirth) of pagan humanism occurred from about the thirteenth to the sixteenth centuries. Beginning with Descartes, each successive philosophical development has pushed the concept of God farther into the realm of *unbelief*. The challenge of secular humanism came into focus in about 1870, with a strong claim to be heard as the truth to save man. Intolerant of Christianity, it became the controlling philosophy in Germany during the twenty years before Hitler and continues to dominate much of Europe in the form of Marxism. Those who held these philosophies distorted scientific evidence and claimed modern science to be inimical to theism. In the last few years secular humanism has risen to a point of dominance in American life and is threatening the moral values of the church, much as pagan humanism did in the second century. One main objective and the most important result has been the deceptive undermining of the reliability of biblical truth, and today there is a vacuum of divine authority.

This vacuum created by the attack on biblical authority has allowed every conceivable kind of perverted religious authority to come into America. We are filled with philosophical speculation, Satanism, witchcraft, the teaching of Islam, and many Oriental cults. Transcendental meditation has deceived multitudes into thinking it is based on modern science, but its initiatory puja is based on idolatrous Hindu worship, as is the whole movement.

Special knowledge and learning. As the Gnostic movement intellectualized Christian thought and synthesized it with other philosophical and religious ideas, so have modern liberal theology and existential theology. Modern theology, especially as taught in the old-line denominations, has demanded that Christians have certain knowledge and insights to understand truth. The pastor and his theology were often "over their heads." Thus, many laymen have left the study and application of Christian teachings to the pastor and theologians. Like Gnosticism of old, these modern theologies have denied the unique deity of Christ while often attributing the highest religious and ethical values to Him.

Emotional experiences, spiritual gifts. In reaction to the emphasis on intellectual teaching in the old-line denominations, the charismatic movement began in the early part of the twentieth century to emphasize the gifts of the Spirit, supernatural experiences, and emotional involvement. Like the Montanists, this movement has brought warmth and meaning for many Christians. But the modern charismatic movement has, generally speaking, also been more preoccupied with emotional experience, the gifts, and the Lord's return than with building disciples. Many leaders of this movement are awakening to this failure and are beginning to be seriously concerned.[11] This movement at times has also produced unhealthy emotional excesses and grew by schismatic efforts.

Clericalism. Clericalism began to be obvious in the old-line denominations by the second quarter of the twentieth century. By about the middle of the century even ecclesiastical moderates like Dr. John Mackay, president of Princeton Theological Seminary, and others were warning against it. Even in the evangelical churches the authority of the pastor became increasingly strong. In recent years the "body-life" movement has sought to reinvolve laymen in church ministry in such a way as to participate in ministry along with the pastor. Probably the charismatic emphasis on gifts has been partly responsible for this.

But the charismatic groups themselves are now becoming

embroiled in a battle over clericalism.[12] Because secular humanism has so affected the lives of the people in the churches, causing sin, division, bitterness, breakdown in home unity and government, and the like, there is a desperate need for members of the churches to know what to do in a multitude of situations. The counseling movement has been of some help, but it has not been adequate. Hence, clergy within the charismatic and certain other groups are beginning to claim the right to speak for Christ in telling the people what to do, without having clear scriptural authority for what they say. Some leaders in some evangelical groups are claiming an authority that actually puts them between Christ and the people. They tell them when to marry, divorce, go to school, and the like. Some of these are even appealing for their authority to the statements of the early church fathers who established the clericalism of the second to fifth centuries.[13] The claim of the title of "apostles" by some may not go beyond that of "missionary," but it could lead to great abuse of authority. If the people of the churches concede to the clergy the right to make decisions of life and doctrine apart from the clear teaching of Scripture, it will inflict the deathblow to disciple building in the churches, even as it did in the early church.

SUCCESS IN EVANGELISM IS THREATENED
WITHOUT DISCIPLE BUILDING

Twentieth-century rapid expansion in evangelism. While secular humanism has made inroads into the church and created these movements affecting disciple building, the church has in the twentieth century enjoyed perhaps its greatest period of evangelistic expansion since apostolic days. At the 1974 Conference on Evangelization in Lausanne, Switzerland, Billy Graham stated in his keynote address, "God is at work in a remarkable way. Never have so many people been so open to the gospel." Dr. Graham then proceeded to tell of the amazing expansion of the church in Asia, Latin America, North America, and other parts of the world.

Dr. Graham's statements agree with the reports of missionary statisticians. In 1964 R. Pierce Beaver cited statistics showing that in the first sixty years of the twentieth century Protestantism increased eighteenfold in the non-Western world. During this period the population increased only twofold. Ralph Winter, referring to the study of Beaver and others, wrote, "In almost every place, the Christian community was growing as fast or faster than the population — not in absolute numbers per year, but in growth rate and therefore in percentage of the population."[14]

Continued success in evangelism dependent on disciple build-

ing. Evangelistic organizations and efforts should be strongly encouraged to continue. However, unless an unusual effort is made to train men to build disciples in the days immediately ahead, this evangelism growth is not likely to continue. There are two reasons for this. First, unless disciples are adequately built, there will not be enough competent leadership to carry on the work of the church. Secondly, the quality of life of the Christians will be lowered. Any good businessman knows that if a product's quality decreases, the sales of that product will also fall off. There is much clear evidence that the moral quality of Christians within the church has declined considerably in recent years.

In many cases around the world, converts have fallen away because they have not been adequately taught. Dr. Clyde Taylor cited a number of examples in an address for Campus Crusade for Christ at Purdue University in July, 1973. He said that in 1971 in one central African republic with a population of 1,600,000, the six main denominations of the church cooperated in training their 200,000 members to participate in an evangelistic outreach to every home in the country. That year 126,000 new members were added to the church — a growth of over 60 percent in twelve months. Because of the lack of leadership, the church authorities had to try to stop evangelism lest chaotic conditions result. While this example is extreme, similar situations have occurred elsewhere.

In cases of explosive growth, such as this, almost everyone agrees that disciple building is an urgent matter. However, today the church has consistently grown in most places throughout the world, though not with such an explosive rate as to attract attention (see Addendum 1), yet all too often an adequate effort at building disciples has not accompanied the growth. In the United States there has been a marked loss of effectiveness in Christian nurture.

THE LOSS IN EFFECTIVENESS IN BUILDING DISCIPLES
IN THE UNITED STATES

The church has lost its effectiveness in disciple building in two sectors. It has lost its strong influence in public education, especially at the college and university level. Also, it has been greatly weakened in its internal educational program. These things have happened slowly as a result of trends over a period of time so that the church has gradually and almost unconsciously given up much of its ability to communicate with and build its people.

Loss of colleges and universities to secular humanism. The churches of the United States were the primary force originating the educational system of our nation and of the Western world. Dr.

Charles Malik, former president of the United Nations General Assembly, former minister of foreign affairs for the Republic of Lebanon, and professor at the American University of Beirut, in speaking to the legislature of the State of Texas said:

> Now all universities arose in the womb of the Church, and without Christ no Western university would ever have arisen. And yet today, they are all moving away from their origin and their source, with the result that if Christ came to the world today, there is one place where He would never feel at home, one place where He would be a total stranger, and that place is the university campus.

Of the first eighteen colleges and universities in the United States, all but one (the College of Philadelphia) were founded by the church or by the church and state together. The church in the United States at first heavily relied on higher education to communicate Christian teaching. In 1750 about 95 percent of the students in colleges and universities were in institutions established for teaching Christian truth, either by the church or by the church and state together. Today the situation is reversed, with at least 90 percent of the students now being enrolled in colleges and universities that are purely secular and dedicated to humanism, or that are anti-Christian.[15] Moreover, a far larger segment of the population goes to college than in 1750, and so many more are now being indoctrinated in secular humanism. Graphs A and B indicate the loss of Christian influence in the colleges and universities in America in the past two centuries.

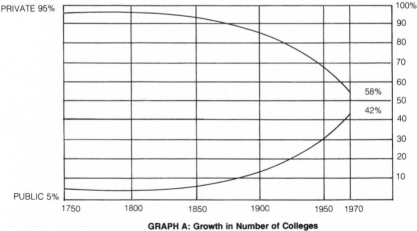

GRAPH A: Growth in Number of Colleges and Universities

Graph A shows the decrease in the number of private or quasi-privately controlled *colleges* as compared to the increase in the number of completely government-built and government-operated ones.[16]

Whereas 95 percent of the colleges were privately controlled in 1750, by 1970 only 58 percent were privately controlled. Correspondingly, the percentage of publicly controlled schools rose from 5 percent to 42 percent (Graph A). Moreover, many of those established as Christian colleges have become secular or even anti-theistic in thought.

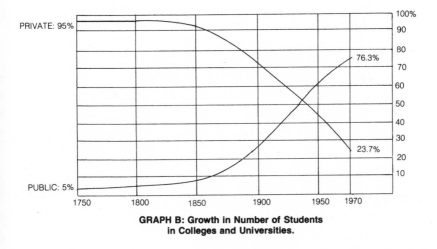

GRAPH B: Growth in Number of Students in Colleges and Universities.

Graph B contrasts the number of *students* attending the two types of schools today.

In 1750 95 percent of the college *students* attended private institutions, whereas only 23.7 percent were enrolled in private schools in 1970 (Graph B). Correspondingly, the 5 percent of the students in public institutions in 1750 had increased to 76.3 percent by 1970.

Besides all this, many church-related colleges have in recent years adopted a secular humanistic view without the knowledge of the general public. A preliminary report of an extensive study of American colleges funded by the Danforth Foundation sought to put the facts straight in this regard. It stated:

> In this connection we must comment on the widespread impression, especially among educators who are not personally acquainted with church-affiliated colleges, that these institutions are narrowly sec-

tarian, they are engaged primarily in religious indoctrination, and that their faculties are selected only for their evangelistic zeal. This impression is very far from the truth. It would accurately describe not more than 10 percent of the church institutions in the United States . . . . Many faculty members and students in church colleges and universities share the secular view that religion does not really belong in an educational institution. There is widespread feeling, often unconscious, that religion is not genuinely concerned with truth.[17]

Thus, the estimate that 90 percent of the students today are in secular institutions, is obviously conservative and is probably not high enough. And though it must be acknowledged that there are some good Christian teachers in public institutions, my experience on many campuses indicates they are not very vocal.

This shift resulted from a growing acceptance of the secular world view. Basically, men believed that education would increase human wisdom and a glorious material culture would result. There are two immediate causes for this shift, both of which express this secular world view.

1. Beginning in the last part of the nineteenth century, men's confidence in human intellectual abilities grew, and there was a corresponding loss of confidence in the validity of supernatural revelation in the Bible.

2. American government and business also accepted the humanistic idea that man's hope lies in education, and they began to help many more persons earn a college degree, especially through the G.I. Bill and various scholarship programs. Many colleges and universities were built and functioning schools were expanded to absorb the growing number of students.

The following figures give an approximate idea of the increasing number of students in our higher educational institutions:

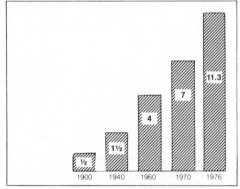

GRAPH C: Growth of College Enrollment
Showing Millions of Students

The effect on the thinking of college students may be seen in the results of recent studies. The Yale Daily News surveyed four hundred of their graduating seniors in 1974 and found the following:

54 percent said they didn't believe in God.

33 percent considered themselves "capitalists."

24 percent considered themselves "socialists."

10 percent considered themselves "anarchists."

33 percent were indifferent.

Oklahoma Christian College recently conducted a Gallup Survey on student outlooks in fifty-seven colleges with these results:

30 percent of the freshmen considered themselves "left" or "far left" in political philosophy.

53 percent of the seniors considered themselves "left" or "far left" in political philosophy.

41 percent felt their political views were influenced by the courses they took.

29 percent acknowledged influence by individual teachers.

There was a larger number of students who approved smoking, drinking, abortion, premarital sex, and legalized marijuana as the class status increased.

The editor of *Christianity Today* has made the following observations about these studies:

> The very least that can be inferred is that, one way or another, colleges and universities play a significant role in determining the world and life views of their students. Quite obviously the drift is leftward, theologically, ethically, and politically.
>
> The question this poses for America in general and the Church in particular is whether this state of affairs can be tolerated. If the leftward movement succeeds, America as we have known it will disappear. The question appears more acute when one realizes that most of the nation's higher educational institutions are dependent on tax money. The American public, which includes multitudes of Christians, is financing through its government an educational system that promises to bite the hand that feeds it, and to undermine many things that most Americans, and particularly Christian Americans, hold dear. Do American citizens really want it that way, or are they simply ignorant of or indifferent to what is happening?[18]

Secularization spreads to lower education. The secularization of higher education has determined the present trends in elementary and secondary education. The first elementary and secondary schools were primarily Christian in their orientation. In 1647 Massachusetts became the first state to require a public school system. Both spiritual and social motives brought this law into existence. But today with the secularization, or more properly, the paganizing of higher education, the secondary school system and the elementary school system have been rapidly engulfed by the secular camp.

The secularization of secondary schools has followed the secularization of colleges. A few years ago a scientific study done by the Gallup Poll for the *Saturday Evening Post* (vol. 234, no. 51) indicated the trend of religious thought among American youth. While two-thirds (66 percent) of the high school and working youth believed in biblical authority, only 22 percent of the college youth did. Since that time, the college graduates have moved into the teaching positions of the secondary and elementary levels. Their influence has had a paganizing effect. Today textbooks and reading materials of public schools militate against Christian views.[19]

Government-sponsored secularism. The original objective of separating the church and state (as expressed by Thomas Jefferson) was to prevent the abuse of specific religious views. But this original intention has been turned around, and now pagan views that discredit Christianity are being taught. Christianity is now being denied a voice. A spokesman for the Catholic League for Religion and Civil Rights located in Milwaukee has said, "In recent years secular humanism has moved from seeking merely tolerance for itself in a basically religious society to seeking to make its philosophy the only acceptable one in American life."[20]

The Supreme Court has consistently affirmed that the government *"may not* establish a 'religion of secularism' in the sense of affirmatively opposing or showing hostility to religion, thus 'preferring those who believe in no religion over those who do believe.' "[21] But the state is obviously doing so.

Not only is much that is contrary to Christian thought being taught in the public schools, but through taxation Christians are required to help pay the bill for this pagan indoctrination. This situation is producing a growing conflict in school boards and in government. One of the earliest confrontations was in California where Christians demanded the opportunity to present data in the science classes for the biblical creation account as well as for evolution. The public's attention has also been caught by the protests in Charleston, West Virginia, in the Kanawha County demonstration.[22]

Future of private schools. Christians have realized that the public education system is destroying Christian truth and producing non-Christian behavior, an undisciplined environment, and academic laxity. Therefore, in the last several years there has been a movement to create Protestant Christian day schools all across the country, though Roman Catholic day schools have been closing because of lack of funds. Also, new Christian colleges have been founded in the last two or three years, while at the same time some older Christian colleges are being hurt or are closing because of lack of funds.

The opinion of some authorities is that the picture is extremely bleak for private schools. Peter Pouncey, president of Columbia College of Columbia University, recently predicted that because of rising costs, there would be no private colleges, including Harvard, within fifteen years.[23] As a result of a study by Pioneer Western Corporation, a financial services organization, the chairman of that group, W. Scane Bowler, predicted that by 1980 the cost of a four-year course in a private institution will be $50,000.[24] Subsidies by taxes keep the cost of public colleges down. While it is unlikely that private Christian colleges will all die, as Pouncey predicts, they will most likely become the privileged place for only the most wealthy.

WEAKENING TRENDS WITHIN CHURCH EDUCATION

Not only has the church lost its voice in higher educational institutions and more recently in the lower public school system, but its own educational program has also been weakened. Several trends have caused this erosion of influence.

1. *Population explosion.* It is important to examine the startling growth of population in our nation since 1850 as shown in Graph D (page 32).

In 1850 there were only 23,261,000 people in the United States, whereas in April 1973 there were over 210,036,000. The population growth has been consistent (with an added upswing in the 1950s and following). In the last few years the birth rate has approached the death rate, so that there is a trend toward stabilization, at least temporarily.

This growth in population has profoundly influenced the church. The graph also shows the increase in church membership. Until the 1960s this increase was in proportion to the population growth. Because of this explosion in membership, the churches gradually lagged behind in producing a comparable number of pastors, perhaps by 20 percent. Larger churches perhaps had the advantage of attracting more capable men to their pulpits, but the intimate association between the pastor and the people was lost.

2. *Migration from rural to urban and suburban areas.* During these same years more people have moved from rural areas to the

more urban areas. William Warren Sweet points out that during the last two decades of the nineteenth century the number of rural churches decreased, and by the end of the century the large Protestant

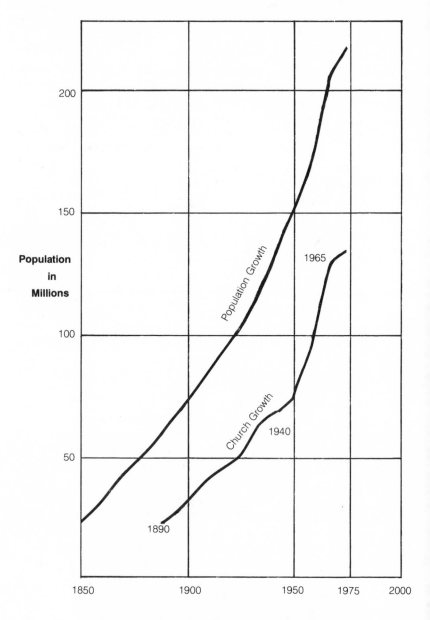

GRAPH D: Population Growth and Church Growth

denominations were fully aware of the seriousness of the situation.[25]

According to page 18 of the Statistical Abstract of the U. S. Department of Commerce, the percentage of the population in the urban areas of the United States rose from 45.6 percent in 1910 to 73.5 percent in 1970. What is happening in the United States is happening in the entire world. In 1875 there was only one city in the world with three million or more people; in 1968 there were thirty-two. This affects the size and stability of the churches and therefore directly influences disciple building.

People in rural communities tend to stay in the same place for longer periods of time. Rural churches are usually smaller and more intimate. The pastor can get to know his people and build a close relationship with them so that there can be effective application of the truth. He also has a more stable group of leaders he can train to disciple others.

Urban populations tend to move about more from one house and/or city to another. Studies show that almost one-third (31.8 percent) of the population of the United States in 1970 were living in a different dwelling by 1973 (Statistical Abstract, 1974, page 37). Such transience makes continuous teaching and disciple building very difficult.

3. Shift of responsibility for education from local to organizational boards. A third trend that has greatly influenced the Christian education program within the church has been the shift of the responsibility for Christian education from the local pastor and local leadership to organized committees and boards of Christian education. The organizational trend began with the Sunday school movement and westward expansion in the early nineteenth century. In the late nineteenth and early twentieth centuries the structured organizational systems of the various denominations were formed. As the industrial revolution produced large business organizations in America, businessmen began to have a profound influence on the church itself. Pastoral involvement in more administration began.

Although formerly the local churches had used some outside materials produced by Sunday school groups, they had controlled their own Christian education programs. With the growth of Christian education boards, however, personal involvement at the local level was gradually severed. Churches were asked to teach what was handed down to them by the boards and had little or no part in producing the material. Because of a lesser involvement, Sunday school teachers often had a lesser interest in communicating the lessons.

The organizational boards tended to select the most highly

educated persons to take over Christian education functions and these individuals were influenced by the secularization of higher education. Thus, the boards themselves became more secularized in their thinking and in their Christian education.

4. *Home education to institutionalized classes.* There has also been a shift from biblical teaching in the home to education in the local church. In Deuteronomy 6 Moses instructed God's people to teach the will of God to their children in their "sitting down," and their "rising up," and in their "walking in the way." That is, in every situation, parents were to take the opportunity to apply truth to their children's lives.

By the 1830s the Sunday school movement had spread throughout America. The original American Sunday school movement helped provide information and material for parents to use in the home in conjunction with the church. Only in more recent years has the full focus of Christian teaching been shifted outside the home to the church building in one-hour-a-week institutionalized classes.

When this shift occurred, most parents felt that they had done their duty in Christian education by taking their children to Sunday school. Therefore, the children got only one hour of instruction each week, and this was in the Sunday school, not in the home. Often the teachers knew the children only slightly. Thus, they were unable to apply truth to the children's life situations. Teaching became irrelevant and impersonal.

RESULT OF TRENDS

All four of these trends in America had a twofold effect. *The pastor* (and usually the Sunday school teacher) *became a lecturer* who did not have close contact with his congregation. Also, by 1956, research showed that pastors had come to be occupied much of the time with administration, even though they did not rank this as a high priority.[26] Thus, they had fewer opportunities to develop personal relationships with the church members. As a result, *the individual application of truth was not explained* or stressed in most of the teaching situations that existed in the institutionalized church.

The difficulties of the modern church schools were voiced on January 27-30, 1975, at a four-day meeting of United Methodist educators and others of the Christian Educators Fellowship and the Center of Continuing Education at Scarritt College. An Associated Press article entitled " 'Sick' Sunday Schools Giving Up the Ghost" quoted John Westerhoff, III, associate professor of religion and education at Duke Divinity School, as saying, "Denominational programs bring on feelings of inadequacy and failure."[27] His statement was supported by the following statistics: (1) From 1959 to 1974 (fifteen years) Sunday school attendance declined nearly 23 percent. (2) Of all United Methodist church schools, 77 percent have fewer than one hundred persons in attendance. (3) Only 3.1 percent have more than three hundred people attending.

Robert Lynn, co-author of *The Big Little School,* according to Associated Press, argued, "Wherever evangelical Protestantism is strong, there you will find a vibrant Sunday school." Attendance is stronger where the Bible is taught as the Word of God. But even there the attrition is great for teenagers and adults — the ones who should be the most actively involved in disciple building. And usually the teaching is not applied to the individual. As a result, many of these church people have the same moral problems as are found among non-Christians.

Through His intimate relationship with a small group of men, Jesus Christ built them into effective leaders who could build disciple-builders. It is important that the church get away from the strictly lecture-type, administrative-type Christian leader. It needs leaders who will train small groups of people (giving personal application) who will in turn train many others, producing a multiplying effect in the congregation. Only in this way will Christianity become relevant to the times in which we live, and only in this way will people take seriously the things they are taught. If such changes are made in the church, there will be a radically different approach to Christian education — an approach long overdue.

CLERICAL CRISIS REFLECTS NEED FOR NEW APPROACH TO DISCIPLE BUILDING

The Catholic Church is struggling with a general unrest among its clergy. In recent years the number of United States priests has dropped by 3,000, and seminary enrollment is off 61 percent. The National Conference of Catholic Bishops made a $500,000, four-year study of priestly life. The study has been said to be the most massive single examination of the priesthood in history. The 1971 report of this study greatly concerned the Catholic bishops, for it showed very unpleasant attitudes and trends, especially among younger clergy.

The frustrations of the Protestant clergy can be well illustrated by statistics from the Southern Baptist Convention (one of the most conservative of all the traditional Protestant denominations in America). In this one denomination approximately 1,000 pastors (3 percent of the total) leave the ministry every year. A survey indicated that three-fourths of the convention's ministers experience "severe stress in their work" and about 11,500 have seriously considered quitting in the last few years.

The fact that the people do not feel their spiritual needs are being met is possibly evidenced in the low average salaries they are willing to pay their pastors. Of nineteen denominations surveyed in 1974 by the National Council of Churches, the average salary was placed at $7,703 plus $3,600 in housing allowances. About 84 percent of the ministers felt that they were underpaid compared with other professional men of equal education.

Another indication of the crisis in the clergy is seen in the fact that people are turning away from their ministers and seeking other professional help. In the past twenty-five years the number of mental health workers has jumped more than 600 percent, whereas the ranks of the clergy have shrunk by 20 percent in proportion to the population. A recent national poll ranked the clergy only twenty-ninth among professions "most respected by the public."[28] Although some clergymen do indicate that they are slightly happier with their jobs now than they were a few years ago, the overall trends point to growing frustration.

This crisis indicates that the clergy themselves are ready to find a new approach for their ministry. The more liberal pastors are disillusioned because their optimistic humanitarian social programs have failed. The fundamentalists have found that orthodoxy and the defending of the faith, however good, do not by themselves breed love and vitality. Successful evangelism can often only generate more spiritual children who need caring for. As has been pointed out, the charismatic groups have *inserted* a consciousness of an experiential relationship to God through the Holy Spirit, but these groups tend to be shallow on biblical content and often need more understanding to accompany emotional experience. (For more consideration on these points see pp. 309,310, Addendum 2.)

The frustration of the pastors is linked also to the failure of many seminaries to train their students how to minister to people. Many have become completely secularized, and the graduate can offer his congregation no more than unauthoritative opinions on social, economic, and psychological problems. Hence, he has no spiritual ministry to offer — only chaff without any grain. Souls are not fed and hope is not given. Enrollment in these schools is declining.[29]

Conservative seminaries usually offer good teaching and equip students to fit into the traditional role of lecturer, administrator, and counselor but not necessarily that of disciple-builder. A moderator of a large Protestant denomination recently complained to me, "Graduating seminarians don't seem to know how to minister to people in such a way as to help them really live the Christian life.'' I have visited a number of evangelical seminaries and have found discerning professors who are searching and struggling to lead their students in new directions to meet these needs. The seminarian needs to be trained to work with small groups and individuals personally so that the people can experience dynamic growth.

For a number of years I was a pastor with an evangelistic heart. Most of my churches experienced both numerical and financial growth, as well as the addition of church facilities. But my job was burdensome, for there was little evidence of spiritual growth among the people.

In recent years, however, I have concentrated on building strong lay people who can minister, and now my congregation is experiencing exciting growth in quality and quantity. Also, men whom I have trained to work with youth and who have been applying these principles and this basic approach to disciple building are saying that it works. They are having the most fulfilling ministries they have ever had.

We need a fresh approach to the ministry and new models to follow. Unless models based on Jesus' ministry are established, people will continue to follow the old models. Jesus' approach offers relief to the pastor and strength to the church.

THE CHURCH IN THE UNITED STATES NOW AT A TURNING POINT
THAT POSES A THREAT BUT ALSO OFFERS OPPORTUNITY

The church in the United States has just reached a crucial turning point. *For the moment* the forces of secular humanism have reached the point of dominance and may unleash a serious attack on the believing church. At the same time, conditions are ripe for the forces of Christ to regain the initiative and return in great strength in extending the kingdom of God. I believe the key lies in whether the church will return solidly to a New Testament program of disciple building, and that does not necessarily mean my view of this.

The turning point and threat. It has been shown that secular humanism seems to have reached a point of controlling influence in education and has made serious inroads into the church. Moreover the vacuum in adequate Christian teaching and application left by the intellectual movement in the church and by the charismatic movement offers an opening for ingress of further secularization unless it is filled. The discouragement in the ministry poses real problems. Moreover, the drop in morals within the churches threatens the future of evangelism.

There are many indications that the church is losing ground now and is headed for opposition. Until recently, the total membership of the churches has consistently increased through the years. But in 1974 the church registered only 131.2 million members, a decrease of 180,000. *"This is the first time a decrease in total membership has ever been reported."* [30]

Christianity Today reported on a 1969 poll of American youth.[31] When asked, "Is religion very important to you?" 59 percent said yes. In 1974 the same poll was taken, and only 39 percent answered yes. Interest had *decreased* by 20 percent in only five years. In 1974 I instituted a study of the youth in America — a study that was carried out by Clyde Elbrecht in conjunction with the Graduate School of Marketing of Wheaton College. We found the same trends.[32] These findings are significant, for the youth are the most responsive to the gospel and the most strategic group for the spreading of the gospel. One of the reasons for the decline in interest is the lack of moral integrity and moral quality found in professing Christians.

These trends have been observed by other alert scholars.[33] James Hitchcock, historian of St. Louis University, warns that "a religious downswing is coming. Christians must accept being a defined minority for the time being." Ted Ward, research specialist of Michigan State University, sees similar trends that will produce opposition to Christian teachings in the days ahead, with only committed Christians continuing in their faith. Unless the evangelical churches rebound with vigor soon, the future may not be bright.

THIS IS A DAY OF OPPORTUNITY FOR RENEWED DISCIPLE BUILDING

There are many indications that the time is ripe for the restoration of the New Testament method of disciple building for the first time since its degeneration in the fourth century. There are both positive and negative factors that can contribute to this.

Movements in history that have prepared the way for a movement in discipleship. Since the demise of disciple building in the fourth century, God has been gradually working to restore the church to her New Testament ideal. This ideal will be reached when ministry becomes the responsibility of all the people. In Ephesians 4:11,12, the official leaders are said to be gifts to the church for the purpose of training and leading people to minister. Through successive movements the Holy Spirit has been making changes in the body of Christ so that today things are ripe for a movement in disciple building.

The church seems to have two functional dimensions that may be said to resemble the warp and the woof of a piece of cloth. The stationary threads (the warp) are illustrative of the local churches, and the threads (the woof) that the shuttle moves through these illustrate the movements that go through the churches. The tapestry of God's church is woven by both of these. Scholars who have observed these two dimensions of the church have otherwise identified the local churches as the vertical dimension and the voluntary movements as the horizontal one.[34]

Many organizational leaders and even laymen are not aware that most local churches with their denominations were the products of past movements. The Reformed movement produced the Presbyterian and the Reformed churches, the Lutheran movement produced the Lutheran churches, the Anabaptist movement produced the Baptist churches, the Wesleyan movement produced the Methodist churches out of the Anglican Church, and so on. The horizontal movements are just as much a part of the body of Christ by which He works as are the local churches.

Through the centuries God the Holy Spirit has raised up successive movements through which the laity have gradually become more and more involved in the church's ministry. It is hoped that this book will better outline the direction a movement toward building disciples is beginning to take and should take. The operation of the two dimensions of the church through the centuries may be illustrated as follows[35] (Read from bottom to top, as a tapestry is woven):

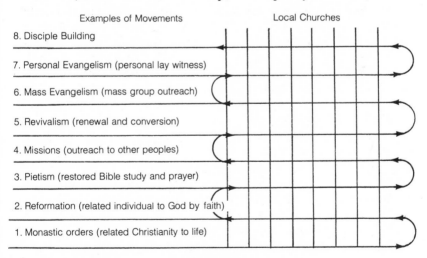

THE CHURCH

TODAY

God is not asleep. The Spirit is making some important changes in the modern church. In recent years more and more laymen have become actively involved in a movement of personal evangelism. Campus Crusade for Christ, the Coral Ridge program, the Navigators, and many denominational and interdenominational organizations have been instrumental in getting laymen involved in this movement.

But laymen also need to be trained to share both the responsibilities of teaching and training others and the responsibilities of evangelism. The growing number of home Bible studies is another step in the right direction, and through them the needs of many have been met. But these home Bible studies have often lacked a well-thought-out and easily transferable program for building disciples.

The current interest in ''body life'' stimulated by Ray Stedman, Gene Getz, Larry Richards, and others (another step toward a fully lay ministry) is wholesome and needed. Every Christian needs to discover his gift or gifts and exercise them for the benefit of the whole church. The new types of meetings that allow individual sharing have given new vigor to the body too.

But if men and women are not properly discipled, the exercise of gifts and the open sharing in meetings will soon cease to give new impetus to growth. Immature sharing and the immature use of one's gifts *can be a liability* as well as an asset. The gifts are not a shortcut across the long period of time it takes to build disciples personally. Jesus spent three years pouring His life into His men. The Holy Spirit works by means of the Word implanted in the heart. Pentecost would have done little without the three previous years of preparation.

Desire for new approach to ministry by pastors and people. So much of what has been happening in the church seems to have been leading up to and preparing the way for laymen to participate in a disciple-building program that shifts the burden of the ministry more on the lay men and women.

The present situation in most churches puts an undue burden on the pastor. When one man is called on to bear the burden of the entire ministry of the church, the people themselves do not have their needs met and the movement does not grow with an increasing momentum. Only as members are trained to train others how to have a ministry can the burden be shifted.

The present approach to Christian education is not adequate. In far too many churches it is impersonal, unrelated to the individual, and not clearly applicable to needs. Both clergy and laity are often frustrated, missing the power of the risen Christ in their lives. Many members don't know how to serve in a real spiritual ministry, thereby limiting those interested in and available to the ordained ministry. The church is ready for another approach to Christian nurture.

Encouraging attitude of high school leadership. Moreover, there is a point of encouragement among youth. While the mass of young people, especially at college age, have shown a decrease in feeling a personal relevance of religion (see p. 29), the *leadership* in our high schools has shown an increase in belief that religion is relevant in United States society. A poll of 22,300 students by ''Who's Who Among American High School Students'' showed that in 1973, 73 percent thought religion was relevant, while in 1975 the percentage was 86 — a growth of 13 percent in two years. This poll of juniors and seniors shows that youth leaders graduating from high school are ready to respond to the challenge of Christian teaching.

A more conservative Supreme Court. With the appointment in 1975 of Judge John Paul Stevens, the Supreme Court is more decisively inclined in a conservative direction than it has been in many years. This should open the possibility of giving Christianity a fair chance to be heard in public education again. His appointment probably shifted the balance of thinking of the court.

The philosophy of secular humanism vulnerable today. In addition to the fact that conditions in the nation and the church are ripe and the need is urgent to return to the New Testament way of building disciples, secular humanism has reached a point of great vulnerability today. The philosophy is like a great, tall building whose foundation is crumbling so that if strong pressure is exerted, the building could begin to come tumbling down. It has become increasingly clear that secular humanism is based on a great many distortions of the truth. It is therefore possible today to assure Christians that the biblical revelation has historical reality as a basis for believing the things Jesus taught.

The deistic philosophy that taught that science had demonstrated nature to be a closed system of physical laws that excluded the miraculous can no longer be held. Vannevar Bush, one of the most respected of America's scientists, presents a strong case against scientific absolutism on the basis of modern discoveries.[36] Einstein showed that Newton's physics was but one way of looking at things. Heisenberg's theory of indeterminacy shows that some questions must go unanswered. The uniformitarian theory of geology that was the basis for the evolutionary hypothesis has been thrown into question by strong scientific support of cataclysmic views presented by Immanuel Velikovsky and others. Hebrew and Christian history, which was once taught to be fraudulent by the higher critics, has now been supported by archaeology. The literary criticism against biblical authenticity has reduced itself to absurdities for any who will carefully trace its developments. Anthropological research in Africa in recent months and years has shown that man's existence preceded all known possible connecting missing links to other animals. The two most popular secular philosophies of our time find themselves in embarrassing contradiction. Logical positivism holds that only empirical facts are real, while existentialism teaches that only values are real. Their contradiction is derived from the faulty epistemology (way of knowing) that both hold and that leads to the rejection of supernatural revelation. Modern scientific technology has produced tremendous sociological, ecological, economical, and other problems that now expose the sinfulness of man in his great learning. These are causing a demand for some guide for human conduct at the personal and corporate level. It is time to expose the lies against Christianity for what they are.[37]

Danger warning. There is a great danger that the church leadership will do what the early church fathers did, namely, direct their attention almost entirely toward an apologetical defense and refutation of secular humanism rather than primarily at disciple building. There is a growing number of young Christian scholars and seminarians who are becoming seriously concerned about giving an answer to secular humanism. Although this can be good, it can also lead to pride and combat with the secular world that breeds only heat and no light. "Knowledge puffs up, but love builds up" (1 Cor. 8:1).

The chief objective must be to build men up into the image of Christ in love. Jesus said, "Love one another. As I have loved you, so you must love one another. All men will know that you are my disciples if you love one another" (John 13:34,35). A community united in sacrificial love is the witness that will make men believe (John 17:21). This can come only by patient teaching and application of the truth in a meaningful discipleship relationship.

Our battle must be focused on our captain, the living Christ, not on the adversary. We cannot win the battle with our fleshly minds, but by obediently following Him and drawing on His power. He will show us how to slay the Goliath of secular humanism and all other heresies. "Through *God* we shall do valiantly" (Ps. 108:13).

CONCLUSION

The sum of the matter is that *the church is urgently in need of a new biblical philosophy of ministry* and is faced with an unusual opportunity to renew the New Testament approach.

Without a revival of the moral influence of the church, political corruption, economic chaos, and a surging wave of crime may well usher in totalitarian government. Our world is so urgently in need of authority and so ready to worship man that it could easily be deceived into accepting an anti-Christian dictator or a government that advocates the revolutionary Marxist theology of liberation. In such an event, we could lose our freedom to preach Christ and His kingdom. Economic troubles from American greed alone could greatly hinder the growth or even the continuance of the Christian witness in many places.

Can the church fail to consider a new approach to disciple building as an urgent priority?

Notes

[1] Aleksandr Solzhenitsyn, "Wake Up! Wake Up!" *The Reader's Digest,* vol. 107, no. 644 (December 1975): 72.

[2] The early church organization was composed of a group of elders (presbyters) who were also called bishops or pastors. One was the leader but he was considered equal with the others, and they functioned as a team. They were assisted by deacons. Cf. the Jerusalem Church (Acts 15:4,22), Philippi, A.D. 63 (Phil. 1:1), Ephesus (Acts 20:28), all churches (1 Tim. 3; Titus 1:5-9; James 4:14; 1 Peter 5:1-5); see also Polycarp's letter to Philippians, A.D. 115 (5:6), Hermas on Roman church (Vis. 3:5; Sim. 9:27); Second Epistle of Clement, et al.

[3] Monsignor Louis Duchesne, *Early History of the Christian Church* (London: John Murray, 1950), 1:69.

[4] Philip Schaff, *History of the Christian Church* (Grand Rapids: Eerdmans, 1950), 2:125-128, 150.

[5] Ibid., p. 449.

[6] Ibid., p. 779.

[7] Tertullian, who *later* joined the movement, was an able teacher. He eventually separated and formed his own group.

[8] Ignatius, Bishop of Antioch (A.D. 110), made the first strong statements about clerical authority. While Clement of Rome draws a parallel to God's choice of Aaron to that of church officers, he clearly held to the priesthood of all believers and a ministry of all the people. Cyprian (d. 258), a new convert who was hastily made the presiding bishop, made the first clear claims demanding absolute obedience to one leader as bishop. "The bishop is in the church, and the church in the bishop, and if any one is not with the bishop he is not in the church" (Epist. lxvi. 3; lv. 20). While these Fathers quoted Scripture, they often established decisions on their own apart from Scripture.

[9] Some have said that the ingrained worship system with its priestly authority both in Jewish and pagan religion reasserted itself and was the primary reason for the growth of clerical authority. I see it as a final claim more than a cause. One of the basic foundation stones to the churches which Paul established was the rejection of legalistic and ceremonial Judaism (cf. Gal., Rom., Col., et al.). Moreover, there was a bias against the idolatrous sacrificial system of paganism as sin (Acts 17:23,29; 19:24-27). Throughout the second and third centuries the evidence is that the turning to Christianity by many left the temples almost abandoned and sacrificial victims without sale (Plinius, jun.: Epist. x. 96ff. Tertullian, Apology, et al.) Tertullian

(early third century) still held to the priesthood of all believers, each one having the right to baptize or serve the elements of the Lord's Supper. But he limited the layman's functioning in this capacity *only in emergencies (Exhortation to Chastity,* chapter 7). By the time of the Apostolic Constitutions (probably in fourth century) the laymen were prohibited from any priestly functions (book 3, sec. I, x.) The Lord's Supper was only a thank-offering and not a sin-offering throughout the second century and beyond. (Schaff, *History of the Christian Church,* p. 246).

[10]The earlier persecution under Domitian was limited and not a threat to all of Christendom. Cf. Duchesne, *Early History of the Christian Church,* pp. 78, 79.

[11]Cf. Juan Carlos Ortiz with Jamie Buckingham, *Call to Discipleship* (Plainfield, New Jersey: Logos, 1975) and writings of Christian Growth Ministries of Ft. Lauderdale, Florida.

[12]"The Deepening Rift in the Charismatic Movement," *Christianity Today,* vol. 20, no. 1 (October 10, 1975): 52 [44]–54 [46]. Some leaders, called "shepherds," "forbid marriages, reject school and vocational plans, demand confession of secret sins."

[13]"Whatever Happened to the Jesus Movement?" *Christianity Today,* vol. 20, no. 2 (October 24, 1975): [103] 47.

[14]Ralph B. Winter, *The Twenty-five Unbelievable Years, 1945-1969* (South Pasadena: William Carey Library 1970, p. 14.

[15]*Christianity Today* gave a figure of 95 percent but called it "ominous," vol. 11, no. 4 (February 17, 1967): 28 [508]. That figure would certainly be larger today.

[16]Some schools were founded entirely by the church while others were founded by the church and state together. In some colonies there was little distinction between the church and political spheres. Therefore, the distinction of "private" is dubious in the early colonial years. By private I do not mean individually owned but not controlled by public government alone. But since our purpose is to show decline of religious influence, this factor does not affect the main object. By 1750 deism had made inroads in some colleges, but religious revival reversed that.

[17]Manning M. Pattillo, Jr. and Donald M. Mackenzie, *Eight Hundred Colleges Face the Future,* 1965, pp. 40,44. Quoted from Larry Poland, "The Day Jesus Christ Left College," *Worldwide Challenge,* vol. 2, no. 11 (November 1975):8.

[18]"One More Time: The Crisis in Higher Education," *Christianity Today,* vol. 19, no. 21 (July 18, 1975): 20 [1022]. Campus Crusade for Christ interviewed 9,000 students on 48 campuses and found 51 percent held to a relative view of truth and 34 percent held pantheistic occult ideas.

[19]Noel F. Bush, "The Furor Over School Textbooks," *Reader's Digest,* vol. 108, no. 645 (January 1976): 125-129.

[20]"Scholars: 'Believer' will be U. S. Minority," Associated Press writer, George Connell, *Atlanta Journal* (November 1, 1975), p. 8A.

[21]Zorach V. Clausen, 343, U. S. Supreme Court; cf. also Justices Goldberg and Harlan concerning Engel v. Vitale, no. 468. Justice Clarke made a similar statement in a recent case.

[22]"Parents Versus Educators: Split Widens Over Schools," *U. S. News and World Report,* vol. 78, no. 4 (January 27, 1975): 30 ff.

[23]William Murchison, "America's Dollar Starved Colleges," *Atlanta Journal* (March 18, 1975).

[24]"Soaring College Costs Worry Business Executives," *Atlanta Journal and Constitution* (May 18, 1975), p. 6G.

[25]William Warren Sweet, *The Story of Religion in America* (New York: Harper and Brothers, 1950), p. 353.

[26]Henry Willard Quinius, Jr., "The Emerging Role of the Pastor as a Church

Administrator," *Austin Seminary Bulletin,* vol. 73, no. 12 (September 1957): 3-16.

[27]The addresses of the entire meeting are recorded in *Duke Divinity School Review,* vol. 40, no. 3, Fall 1975. The complete text of John Westerhoff III's address was published on pp. 183ff.; cf. also pp. 213ff.

[28]"Another Wave of Unrest in U. S. Clergy," *U. S. News and World Report,* vol. 77, no. 22 (November 25, 1974): 101ff.

[29]McCormick Theological Seminary abandoned its campus and merged with the University of Chicago Divinity School. Columbia Theological Seminary has less than one-half its former enrollment. So it is with other schools.

[30]*The Church Around the World,* vol. 5, no. 12 (November 1975).

[31]"Youth and Religion: A Rare Change," *Christianity Today,* vol. 18, no. 25 (September 27, 1974): 37.

[32]Dr. Jon Alston, sociologist at Texas A & M, did surveys in 1971 and 1975 from the point of view of impressions of youth as to whether the influence of religion on the American way of life had increased or decreased. The increase of "Yes" on this does not necessarily contradict the other studies. A Gallup Poll through 1975 shows the decline in church attendance by youth is leveling off.

[33]Cf. George W. Connell, "Scholars," p. 8A.

[34]Ralph D. Winter and R. Pierce Beaver, *The Warp and the Woof* (South Pasadena: William Carey Library, 1970), p. 63.

[35]The movement is raised up to effect changes in the local churches and should lose itself as a servant of the local churches. Because the movement is called to change the local church, it is often seen as a threat to the local church and is denied as a part of the church by some theologians. Although most uses of the word *church* (*ekklēsia* in Greek) refer to the local congregation, the Scriptures show that these local churches were produced by traveling laymen and apostles and were therefore a product of a movement: even in the Old Testament church these two dimensions are seen. There the Law was represented in the temple and the priestly teaching throughout the land, and the prophets were raised up and went about rebuking the people for departure from the Law.

[36]Vannevar Bush, "Science Pauses," *Fortune,* vol. 71, no. 5 (May 1965): 116ff.

[37]I am preparing a three-volume work that will show the inconsistencies of evidences and arguments used to support secular humanism.

2

The Relationship of Disciple Building

to Other Goals

The Scriptures indicate that God's ultimate goal on earth is to establish His kingdom among men. It is not to save the present world or nation from social disaster, important as that may be. He is accomplishing this goal of establishing His kingdom in three phases: (1) Types and models of God's rule over men were presented in the Old Testament. These prepared men to understand the meaning of the kingdom. (2) In the ministry of Christ, His apostles, and subsequent disciples, God is working to bring people under His government through the provision of righteousness in Christ and to remake them morally into the image of the second Adam. (3) His ultimate goal will finally be realized after Christ returns in power and glory. Then all evil will be crushed, the will of God will be done on earth as it is in heaven, and believers will receive glorified bodies like that of the Son of God.

In this chapter we will examine the second phase, dealing with the purposes and goals of ministry. All these goals interrelate and each affects the others. The tendency of our sinful nature is to see the particular ministry goal we are working for as all-encompassing and all-important. For example, when I specialized in evangelism, I thought all Christian teaching and ministry should be evangelistic to be valid. While I feel disciple building is the greatest need of the church today, *it is important that we not overdo disciple building to the exclusion of other biblical goals. At the same time, as we see the interrelationship of the goals, we will better appreciate the need for more emphasis on the goal of disciple building.*

If God's government is to be established in the lives of people, sinful persons must be transformed into godly persons. This cannot be achieved by a random or chance program. It is to be attained by a well-devised plan — God's plan — with well-defined goals — God's goals.

SCRIPTURE REVEALS GOD MANAGES HIS AFFAIRS TO ACHIEVE GOALS

In biblical thought, the idea of "fulfillment" is very important. Fulfillment refers not only to the realization of prophecies (cf. Gen. 15:13,14; Exod. 12:40,41; Mark 1:15; Gal. 4:4, et al.), but also to the achieving of divine goals. God moves all things in order to accomplish His purposes. He is the best manager of His work.

God's stewards must be like Him. Poor management wastes time and energy. It also leads to confusion and frustration. Every Christian ought to have the purposes of God clearly in view, so that he may energetically pursue God's goals.

God has given Christian workers five primary ministry goals: (1) to evangelize the world, (2) to form edifying churches, (3) to build individual disciples, (4) to build disciples and churches into Christlikeness, (5) to bring glory to God as the end of all effort. Each succeeding goal is built on the preceding ones. The ultimate goal of bringing glory to God is realized in the fulfillment of the law of love (Mark 12:30,31), which, of course, is the same as being Christlike. The following is a graph of these goals:

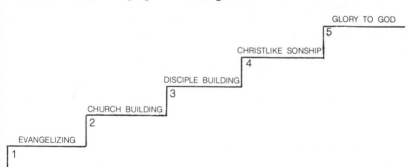

These goals may be illustrated by what I used to do in growing a tomato garden. I would go to a greenhouse, purchase the tomato plants, and plant them together in my garden. Then I would tend the garden — fertilizing, watering, weeding, and tying up the plants on poles. Every day I would inspect the plants to see if they were growing toward producing fully ripe tomatoes and to do what was necessary to encourage their growth. When the tomatoes had grown to be large and fully mature, I would eat and enjoy the fruit.

The purchasing and transplanting of the young plants may be compared to the job of evangelism, whereby men are removed from the house of Satan and planted in God's kingdom. The planting of them in the garden together is the task of forming a church. The tending of the garden is the job of building disciples. The mature fully-grown tomato is like the mature Christian, who is being conformed to the image of Christ. This is the ideal in quality toward which we aim. We daily inspect the plant to see what progress is made in that direction. The enjoyment of the fully ripe fruit symbolizes the glory God receives from a fruitful and Christlike life.

THE SCOPE OF THE FIVE GOALS IS WORLDWIDE

There are five main goals involved in establishing the kingdom of God. The Scriptures reveal that Christ envisioned His kingdom to be worldwide in scope, so that each of these five goals has worldwide implications. The intent that the kingdom of Christ would be established worldwide is both implicit and explicit.

The worldwide extension of the kingdom is implied by the biblical teaching about God Himself. He created the world and all men in it. In Adam and Eve, man's first ancestors, all men departed from God's purpose for them to rule the world for Him. God judged the world of sinful men through the Flood and later at the tower of Babel. The Old Testament prophets spoke to all the nations of their times and warned them that God would judge them for their disobedience to His moral law and for their mistreatment of Israel, His people, to whom He had given that law. It is not surprising that the redemption of lost sinners to be children of God is offered to all.[1]

The following is an evaluation of each of the five goals as presented in Scripture. Since the goal of disciple building is the main theme of the book, this will be dealt with only briefly in this chapter.

1. EVANGELIZING

The word *evangelism* does not occur as such in the New Testament. It comes from the word *evangel,* which means "good news." An evangelist was one who told good news or good tidings; he preached the gospel (cf. 1 Cor. 15:1ff.). Evangelism describes the task of calling men to repent and be reconciled to God because He has provided for the forgiveness of their sins and offers them new life in Christ. This is basically what takes place in the first step of discipleship, which has been named "Repentance and Faith." This goal is that of bringing others to turn from walking according to the course of the world under the power of Satan, and to submit to God's government. Through evangelism they accept deliverance from the domain of darkness and are transferred to the kingdom of God's Son (Col. 1:13; cf. Eph. 2:1-5).

Scripture indicates that this God-given goal aims at all men, as noted above. At Christ's birth the angel appeared to the shepherds and proclaimed, ''I bring you good news of great joy that will be for all the people'' (Luke 2:10). The divine phenomenon of the miraculous guiding star that brought wise men from the East to worship Christ soon after His birth shows God's concern for people from distant nations to join His people.

Jesus told Nicodemus, ''God so loved the world that he gave his one and only Son, that whoever believes in him shall not perish, but have everlasting life. For God did not send his Son into the world to condemn the world, but to save the world through him'' (John 3:16,17). Peter says the Lord is ''not wanting anyone to perish, but everyone to come to repentance'' (2 Peter 3:9). Paul states the same truth in 1 Timothy 2:3-6:

> This is good, and pleases God our Savior, who wants all men to be saved and to come to a knowledge of the truth. For there is one God and one mediator between God and men, the man Christ Jesus, who gave himself as a ransom for all men — the testimony given in its proper time.

John insists that Christ ''is the atoning sacrifice for our sins, and not only for ours but also for the sins of the whole world'' (1 John 2:2). Peter says that Jesus even paid the redemption price for false teachers destined for destruction (2 Peter 2:1). The task of evangelism extends to making the gospel known even to false teachers.

Expanding Outreach. The principle of evangelistic expansion is found explicitly in this concept of God's concern for all men. The fact that Christ went to the Samaritans even in the early part of His ministry is therefore not surprising. Also, after having begun His popular ministry in Capernaum, Jesus came from a time of prayer and announced to His disciples that they were to leave Capernaum to tour other cities: ''Because that is why I was sent'' (Luke 4:43). He broke away from the people who would constrain Him, leaving the crowds who sought His ministry, and reached out to others throughout Galilee. When Jesus left this established work to move into new areas, He was declaring for the first time the principle of expanding outreach that is implicit in the concept of God's love for all men.

That principle was enunciated by Christ in Acts 1:8 when He said, ''You will receive power when the Holy Spirit comes on you; and you will be my witnesses in Jerusalem, and in all Judea and

Samaria, and to the ends of the earth.''

In Romans 15:18ff. Paul seemed to have been consciously carrying out Christ's command in Acts 1:8: "From Jerusalem all the way around to Illyricum, I have fully proclaimed the gospel of Christ. It has always been my ambition to preach the gospel where Christ was not known, so that I would not be building on someone else's foundation" (Rom. 15:19,20). Paul preached from Jerusalem to Judea, Samaria, Syria, Galatia, Asia Minor, Macedonia and Greece, and Illyricum. He then mentioned that he would come to the Christians in Rome (the next place in a westward movement), but that he was not planning to stay. He planned to go on to Spain. The Scriptures clearly command us to be continually carrying the gospel to new people. Evangelism must continue even though discipleship is also in demand.

At the end of His earthly ministry, Jesus commanded His disciples to proclaim the gospel to all nations and every person (Matt. 28:18-20; Mark 16:15; Luke 24:46,47). This command extends until the end of time.

Unfortunately, most of church history reflects the tendency of God's people to lose their vision of outreach. Very often, the command to expand is ignored. But anyone who is willing to be honest with the biblical data must admit that one of the goals of Christian ministry is to evangelize the world.

2. CHURCH BUILDING

Jesus generally worked with His followers in groups. While disciples do at times need individual attention, they can best and most efficiently be taught in a group. In fact, the word *church* is defined as "a group of people who are gathered or called together." (The Greek verb related to the noun *ekklēsia* means "to call out of [their houses]" or "to assemble together.")

Jesus disclosed the fact that the gathering of the body of believers was one of His objectives when He said, "I will build My church" (Matt. 16:18). After the resurrection, Christ's people first assembled in Jerusalem (Acts 2:1ff.,47). Soon afterwards they began to gather throughout Judea and Galilee (Acts 9:31), and the first Gentile church was assembled at Antioch in Syria (Acts 13:1).

The apostle Paul (with Barnabas) was the first missionary whose objective was establishing churches (Acts 14:23,27; 15:3,4,41; 16:5). When Paul established a church, his main concern was that the people be taught and edified (Acts 20:28).

When he wrote to the Ephesians, he explained that spiritual gifts were given to edify the church, the body of Christ (Eph. 4:11,12).

Unless these gifts were being used to help build up the church, they were not accomplishing their ends. To the Corinthians Paul wrote, "Since you are eager to have spiritual gifts, try to excel in gifts that build up the church" (1 Cor. 14:12). Later in the same letter he exhorted them, "All of these must be done for the strengthening of the church" (1 Cor. 14:26; cf. vv. 3,4,5,17). The author of Hebrews emphasized the importance of Christians' assembling as churches (Heb. 10:25). Both Paul and Peter were concerned about the leadership and pastoral oversight of the churches (1 Thess. 5:12,13; 1 Tim. 3; Heb. 13:7; 1 Peter 5:2-4). Therefore, it is evident that the planting and building of churches was a primary objective of Jesus Christ and His followers.

3. DISCIPLE BUILDING

Jesus commanded His followers to make disciples of all nations, teaching them to observe *all things* He had commanded (Matt. 28:19). The Greek word for disciple is *mathētēs,* which means "a learner." Thus, a disciple is one who is taught — one who learns. The word *disciple* occurs 232 times in the Gospels and 27 times in the book of Acts — a total of 259 times. But it does not occur once in the New Testament Epistles. There it seems to be replaced by the word *saint* from the Greek word *hagios,* meaning "one set apart" or "a holy person." This word occurs 57 times in the Epistles and Revelation. The word *saint* is clearly used of those to be taught (cf. Rom. 15:25; Eph. 4:12, et al.) but it has the broader connotation of any believer set apart to God. The abrupt cessation of the use of the word *disciple* probably occurred because in the Greek world it had a more distinctive meaning associating a person as a learner of worldly wisdom from the philosophers and rhetoricians.

Although Jesus commanded His followers to teach all that He taught, Christians generally have not done so. We have typically viewed this as an impossible task. "How can we begin to teach all that Jesus taught?" The fact is, we can — if we follow the pattern Jesus set. In three years men can be trained to teach "all things" that Jesus commanded. When men are trained as Jesus intended, a multiplication process of disciple building is set in motion.

Paul instructed Timothy, "The things you have heard me say . . . entrust to reliable men who will also be qualified to teach others" (2 Tim. 2:2). Four spiritual generations are mentioned here: Paul, Timothy, Timothy's disciples, and their disciples. Teaching people to teach what they have learned is the principle of multiplication. It is *not just teaching them to evangelize.*

Two contrasting strategies of fulfilling the Great Commission will illustate the wisdom of Paul's instruction of Timothy. Suppose Timothy, exercising considerable evangelistic ability, won to Christ an average of three people per day — slightly more than 1000 in a year. At the end of fifteen years of this fruitful activity, he could have been pastoring an enormous congregation of more than 15,000 people, all of whom would be looking to him to teach and lead them.

On the other hand, suppose he won only twelve men to Christ and then discipled them for a period of three years. At the end of three years each of them would be capable of discipling twelve new converts. Following this plan for fifteen years would give Timothy 371,292 well-trained disciples — a veritable army ready to entrust the scriptural truths to another generation of more than 3½ million.

Obviously, we cannot rationally expect such mathematical precision when dealing with people who are maturing in Christ. Yet the lesson is clear: spiritual multiplication is far more effective in winning the world than is singular concentration on winning people. *The effectiveness is not only in numerical growth but in quality of life in disciples and effectiveness of leadership.* Therefore, disciple building is very important.

4. CHRISTLIKE SONSHIP

The objective of evangelism is to win people and bring them to a point of public identification in baptism so they can be placed into churches to be taught and cared for. But what is the objective of building disciples? The answer is to help them develop into the full image of Christ, as individuals and as a group. Jesus said, "A student (disciple) is not above his teacher, but everyone who is fully trained will be like his teacher" (Luke 6:40).

In Romans 8:28,29 Paul said, "We know that in all things God works for the good of those who love him, who have been called according to his purpose. For those God foreknew he also predestined to *be conformed to the likeness of his Son,* that he might be the firstborn among many brothers."

In other words, God's plan is for His sons to become like Jesus Christ by conforming to His image. In Ephesians 4:10-13 Paul emphasizes that Christ's gift of leaders to the church is to equip the body to minister. He says in verse 13:

> . . . until we all reach unity in the faith and in the knowledge of the Son of God and become mature, attaining *the full measure of perfection* found in Christ.

In Colossians 1:28,29 Paul declares this as his own ministry objective:

We proclaim him, counseling and teaching everyone with all wisdom, so that we may present everyone *perfect* in Christ. To this end I labor, struggling with all the energy he so powerfully works in me.

In the beginning, when God created man, He created him in His own image. The Scriptures imply that when Adam walked in the Garden of Eden, he was morally like God and radiated the very glory that Jesus displayed on the Mount of Transfiguration and that Paul saw on the road to Damascus (Luke 9; Acts 9). God's objective is to restore Christians to the glory that Adam had and that now is seen in the exalted Christ.

Hebrews 2 discusses the glory and authority that God gave Adam when He created him (Gen. 1:26-28; Ps. 8). Man no longer bears that glory because he has "fallen short of the glory of God" (Rom. 3:23). No longer are all things under man's subjection. Jesus, however, is the leader of a new race. He is crowned with glory, and all things are subjected to Him. He suffered and experienced death in order to bring "many sons to glory" (Heb. 2:9,10).

Presently, through the disciple-building process, God is restoring the inward moral image that Adam had. God is now renewing our minds in knowledge in the image of Christ (Col. 3:10). By obedience to knowledge He renews our moral character. At the future resurrection He will also restore the external glory (Rom. 8:21-23).

Salvation promises other benefits also. Because of his personal relationship with God, the Christian escapes the corruption that is in the world through lust and finds a more abundant life (John 10:10; Acts 2:40; 2 Peter 1:4). He also escapes hell and eternal separation from God (Matt. 25:41; 1 Thess. 1:7-10). However, the main objective is that of transforming the saved person into God's image.

5. GLORY TO GOD

When the first four goals are met, the fifth and highest goal — that of glorifying God — will also be accomplished. Evangelization, church building, and disciple building have as their end the building of persons into the image of Christ, and those who bear the image and character of Christ glorify Him. Paul said that the Holy Spirit "is a deposit guaranteeing our inheritance until the redemption of those who are God's possession — to the praise of his glory" (Eph. 1:14; cf. Rom. 11:36; 16:27; 1 Cor. 10:31; 2 Cor. 1:20; 4:15, et al.).

All the goals of the Christian's life are subordinate to the ultimate goal of glorifying God. The Christian should desire through all of his efforts to glorify God. The consummation of all moral action is to bring glory to God.

The world seeks to glorify man rather than God. The Christian's goal is completely opposite to that of the world, for man's will is at cross purposes with God's will. When God's will is fulfilled, He will be glorified and man will be blessed. When man's will is fulfilled, the result will be self-destruction.

Importance of All the Goals

Christians often do not keep God's ascending purposes in perspective. For instance, the Christian may focus on the goal of preaching the gospel to every person, losing sight of the other objectives. The worker will then become obsessed with numbers and will reach people only in a very superficial way. Possibly in the eyes of those working with him and surely in his own eyes, his esteem will be determined by the number of people he reaches. As has been said in chapter 1, if discipleship and church building are minimized, evangelism will become so superficial that it will lose its momentum and strength. The workers will become frustrated as a result of the increased pressure to evangelize. Because fewer converts will show evidence of changed lives, the goal of evangelism will become meaningless.

While numbers are recorded at times in the book of Acts, the Holy Spirit obviously intends to glorify God by recording the numerical growth of the churches (cf. Acts 2:41; 4:4; 5:14; 6:1,7; 8:6,12; 9:42; 11:21, et al.). The numbers are not an end in themselves, for exact numbers are seldom recorded and the intent is not to exalt the evangelists. But when the approval of men is sought (as it often is today), numbers will become more important than they should be.

Another perversion is evident when men seek to build churches in a competitive way for the sake of prestige or numbers. How sad it is when a pastor has a large staff and a big budget, but homes are breaking up, church members are not growing, and the church groups do not reflect Christ's character of love or bring glory to Him. A leader's pride in the size of a church or a denomination only indicates that he is seeking the praise of men more than the glory of God. When churches are properly built, Christ, and not the leader, will be the topic of conversation.

The goal of building disciples can also be perverted. Those who teach can so emphasize their teaching programs that they lose sight of those being taught. On the other hand, they can so focus on the individual that they do not establish him in groups with proper government and discipline. Also, sometimes leaders become so obsessed with their programs of teaching that they neglect the discipling of their own families.

Evangelism, church building, and disciple building must be

seen in relation to each other. If a proper perspective and balance is attained, there will be greater evangelism, more opportunities to build disciples, and more growing churches established. The purpose of these first three goals is to build Christians who are like Christ in their love. When this aim is achieved, God the Father will be glorified. Even though the latter is a result of the first four, we should consciously be aware of the end goal — bringing glory to God.

The modern church often errs by making the blessing of men its chief aim, rather than the glorification of God. Unfortunately, in ecumenical efforts, social reform is emphasized almost to the exclusion of faith and obedience to Christ.[2] In the New Testament, social concern was always a product of the apostolic preaching (Acts 2:42-45; 4:31-35). It was not the main goal but resulted when the main goals were kept uppermost. It was considered a secondary priority (Acts 6:2). Likewise, political loyalties and activities were not considered goals in themselves but played supporting roles to the main goals. Their purpose was to support the government so that evil would be restrained and God's commands obeyed (Rom. 13:1-10; 1 Peter 2:11-17). The aim of political involvement is to promote obedience and bring glory to God (not to make the material benefits of this world available to men), for the outcome of obedience is love.

As men consider the attributes of God the Father and become obedient to His will, their ministries will be guided and motivated by these truths. While the last two goals are entirely qualitative, the first three can be measured both quantitatively and qualitatively. Hence, it is easier to misuse any of the first three in order to receive the praise of men. Disciple building links the functional goals to the ideal ones.

EVALUATION OF TODAY'S NEEDS IN REGARD TO GOALS

In evangelism and church building, the twentieth-century church is doing well, but it is weak in disciple building. Far too often, the objective of teaching is to "follow up" evangelism or to ground the new believer in a few "basics" of the faith. The goal of Christ-likeness is lost sight of and far too much teaching never rises above a humanistic level because the leaders are no longer consciously seeking to bring glory to God the Father. And because of this, great social inequities appear among members. All the goals must be kept in proper perspective if New Testament disciple building is to be given its proper place.

Notes

[1] The question of the limited or unlimited atonement cannot be extensively argued here. The position of this author is that God accomplishes a limited atonement by offering an unlimited one. The atonement is thus seen as sufficient for all but efficient only for the elect. The Scripture given under the goal of *Worldwide Evangelism* seems to state clearly that God desires all men to be saved (pp. 53-59). On the other hand, God is sovereign and His sovereign purposes will be carried out. This apparent contradiction can only be resolved in the greater mind of God (Isa. 55:8). The conflict of human responsibility and divine sovereignty cannot be resolved on earth. One may deny human responsibility at the point of responding to the gospel. But one meets the problem again at the point of man's original sin. If man is not freely responsible there, then God is made the author of sin. From the human perspective, if Adam was free to sin, then God's sovereignty is lost. Yet it must be remembered that it was God who gave man freedom.

[2] This trend was begun at New Delhi (W. A. Visser't Hooft, *New Delhi Speaks* [New York: Reflection Book, 1962], pp. 42, 43), and became dominant at Bangkok. There was a slight reversal of emphasis on evangelism at Nairobi, Africa, 1975, and that was encouraging.

3

The Biblical Approach to Disciple Building

MODERN DAY EFFORTS TO BUILD DISCIPLES

Many good efforts are being made to train people to build disciples. Most churches are seeking to build their people through various forms of Christian education, not only through regular preaching and worship services but usually through the Sunday school and youth groups. Almost every evangelistic organization has some plan to train people to "follow-up" and teach new converts to some extent, even though they later turn these converts over to the churches. Some organizations specialize in training people to build disciples. Some organizations and some churches are focusing on one or two aspects of building disciples.

The church needs to reevaluate what is being done and seek to find a philosophy of disciple building that agrees with sound logic, that is applicable to our modern world, that people can be trained to do so that it can be multiplied, and, most important of all, that is biblical.

A SOUND APPROACH TO DISCIPLE BUILDING

What is a sound logical approach to building disciples in which others can be easily trained? This can best be seen by looking at two extremes. Some people advocate a detailed program for building disciples that is planned under the Spirit's guidance for the whole Christian life and that is rigidly followed. Others say there should be no planned program but that a leader should rely entirely on the Holy Spirit to teach the disciple as circumstances and the need of the disciple dictates.

Those advocating leading disciples undeviatingly down a long-range rigid plan would know what they would teach next week, next year, and the next ten years, and the individual would be expected to fit in and achieve the designed goals. The other extreme of responding spontaneously to each disciple's needs in each situation would mean the leader would wait on, and watch for, each disciple to manifest his needs and then he would proceed to meet the needs. Thus, the leader could make little preparation for what he would teach; he would need to know all things and be ready at all times to teach anything. Since every person is different, a group ministry would have little value. It would obviously be very difficult to train leaders how to minister this way.

The approach of using a rigid plan seems to fail to see the disciple as an individual with special needs in changeable circumstances that require flexibility to apply appropriate truth. The spontaneous approach, on the other hand, fails to acknowledge that there is a normal logical progression to spiritual growth as there is in physical growth, and that plans can be made to help a person develop logically. Moreover, it fails to see that an individual needs to learn to be a part of a family group and that there are basic truths that all Christians need to be taught and that apply to them as a group, as well as truths that need to be applied individually. It also ignores the fact that the Holy Spirit can later apply truth taught earlier in a group situation. The spontaneous individual discipleship theory fails to recognize that it is very inefficient for a leader to teach *only* individuals and only as each individual's needs arise. More good can be accomplished by teaching several persons at once and there can be better teaching by adequate preparation when there is a plan.

When an analogy is made to child development, the absurdity of either of these positions alone is obvious. A parent who insists that a baby eat (every four hours), sleep (all night), urinate (infrequently), et al., on a precise schedule is due for a surprise and will have a frustrated baby. Moreover, a parent cannot exactly schedule the time when his child will walk, talk, read, etc. If a parent tries to require precise conformity to a plan in all details through high school, college, and on into adult life, a neurotic person is sure to result.

But if a child is left to do what he feels like doing when he feels like it, and the parent is always waiting to meet his needs, it will also create an insecure and frustrated person. Also the parent and other members of the family will be frustrated and worn out. The family has got to eat together, sleep approximately at the same hours, travel together, and the like, for efficiency's sake. Moreover, a child thus reared would become exceedingly selfish, uncooperative, and very dependent. This latter view is related to the old John Dewey philosophy of education, which tends toward a relativism in ethics and anarchy in life style. Dewey rejected planned controlled development. But there is a normal general pattern of development in children, and planned development can aid a healthy growth process, provided attention is also paid to the individuality of each child.

I believe the New Testament view of disciple building recognizes the important things in both of these views. There is a normal, logical, general pattern of spiritual growth, there are truths that help promote different aspects of that growth, and there should therefore be a plan for teaching that truth chronologically. But the teacher should be alert to teach truth at the time when it is most relevant to the disciples according to the circumstances that arise. Yet, the disciples need to be taught in a group to become a part of a group. Also, there should be a time when individuals reach a point of spiritual training when they take on adult spiritual responsibilities and controlled training ceases.

INADEQUATE VIEWS POPULAR TODAY

The term "follow-up" conveys a beneficial but inadequate concept of discipleship. Evangelistic groups deplore leaving a new-born spiritual baby unattended, so they have initial correspondence Bible studies, follow-up appointments, initial basic study workbooks, and the like. These help new converts get started in Christian growth, with the hope that the church will carry on from there.

While these efforts have been essential for evangelistic work, they have given some people an *inadequate* concept of disciple building. *After doing basic follow-up with a new Christian, most Christian workers don't know what else to do!* Rather than leave him a spiritual baby, they teach him how to eat and walk and then leave him a spiritual toddler. While follow-up to evangelism needs to be encouraged, this inadequate concept of disciple building must be corrected.

On the other hand, a disciple-building program can extend indefinitely over many years. If it is carried on by one teacher, dependence can be greatly prolonged. There are far too many adults going to Sunday school year after year, often bored to death, when they ought to be out involved in a ministry themselves. The result is that we are still spoon-feeding grandmother and telling her what to do. While most Christians need to be involved in regular preaching, pastoral, and fellowship aspects of a church, an indefinite nurture program for disciples is not healthy, resulting in unnecessary dependence or boredom.

Some years ago a staff man working under me and ministering to high school students came to me with a problem. He had won a boy to Christ, met with him for a few weeks taking him through a brief "follow-up" program we had outlined. His question was, "I have gotten him started in the Christian life, but where do I take him from here?" I knew the general approach I would have with a new convert, but was there a way I could train him to build men?

This experience sent me searching the Scriptures to discover the New Testament approach to disciple building. Feeling that God had given me some biblical insights in this area, I wrote a brief manual on *Dynamic Discipleship* which was used to train those in the advanced classes of Explo '72, an international youth conference attended by 85,000 students in Dallas. We planned to train 15,000 with this manual but printed 40,000 copies. Within a few months all 40,000 were gone. The need to help people in this area was evident, and my approach had helped more than a few. That initial study (although now considerably refined) became the basis for this book.

NEW TESTAMENT APPROACH TO DISCIPLE BUILDING

It is my conviction that *Jesus and His apostles had a program for about three and a half years that formed the foundation for future growth to maturity and for the basic skills for carrying out a ministry.* After that they were ready to have a ministry of their own under the guidance and power of the Holy Spirit. Just as a public school education is given to students to give them a foundation for future life, so these three years were basic training for growth and ministry. Since this covered only a three-year period, a transferable training could be developed and communicated by repeated demonstration.

The New Testament record tells of a rapid spreading of the gospel in the first century as well as a complementary emphasis on training people how to build new converts. But can it be demonstrated that the New Testament Christians had a specific approach to training believers how to build disciples? If they did, can it be recovered from the Scriptures?

Obviously, the Epistles present no *overall,* all-inclusive description of how to build disciples. The Epistles were written to meet *specific* needs. Therefore, they deal only with certain principles of disciple building. If one is to discover a pattern for building disciples, his source must be the Gospels, for they primarily record the ministry of Jesus Christ and the method He used to build His men.

REPRODUCIBLE PATTERN

If Jesus' method of building men can be recovered from the gospel record, can this model be reproduced? Indeed, did Jesus intend it to be reproduced as a pattern?

There is only one way to discover if Jesus intended His method of building men to be repeated, and that is if He himself repeated it! If Jesus taught the Seventy (who had been appointed later in His ministry) the same things He had taught the original Twelve, He would seem to be following a pattern.

The appointment of the Twelve is recorded in Matthew 5:1; 10:2-4; Mark 3:13-19; and Luke 6:12-16. Taking these passages as a point of departure and studying the events that unfold chronologically in Mark and Luke, one can discover both what Jesus taught the Twelve and the order in which His truths were presented. The appointment of the Seventy is recorded in Luke 10:1-16.

If there were parallels in the training of the Twelve and the training of the Seventy, they could be seen in a comparison between what Jesus taught the Twelve and what He taught the Seventy in the chapters following Luke 10:1-16. While the whole ministry of the Seventy is briefly described in those first sixteen verses, it is obvious that it extended over a much longer period of time. The subsequent chapters of Luke record Jesus' teaching of the Seventy. These teachings were a review for the Twelve and included some new material probably mostly for the Twelve.

The following two parallel columns present data showing that Jesus taught the same truths to both the Twelve and the Seventy. The order in which He taught these truths is almost identical. But because Jesus always taught His truths when they were most relevant, variations do occur in the chronology. Also, at times the teaching differs according to emphasis and subject, but the principles are the same. One may observe the Scripture references as listed below and see the points where chronology is shifted slightly. It is clear that Jesus was teaching the same basic truths at about the same time after He appointed the Seventy as after He appointed the Twelve. (For a more careful study of your own to see this, read A. T. Robertson, *A Harmony of the Gospels for Students of the Life of Christ* [New York: Harper and Row, 1950]; see section 53, pages 47ff. for data following appointment of the Twelve, and section 102, pages 120ff. for that following the appointment of the Seventy.)

TRUTHS TAUGHT TO THE TWELVE AND THE SEVENTY

Twelve Apostles Appointed Matthew 5:1a; 10:2-4; Mark 3:13-19a; Luke 6:12-16	Seventy Apostles Appointed Luke 10:1-16
Attacked prejudice against foreigners — healed centurion's servant (Matt. 8:5-13; Luke 7:1-10)	Attacked prejudice against foreigners — love for neighbor by story of Good Samaritan (Luke 10:25-37)
Showed acceptance of women — received a sinful woman (Luke 7:36-50)	Showed acceptance of women — allowed Mary of Bethany to take the place of study with male disciples (Luke 10:38-42)
Taught principles of prayer and Christian piety (Matt. 6)	Taught principles of prayer and Christian piety (Luke 11:1-13)
Demonstrated the conflict of the kingdom of Satan and the kingdom of God by exorcism of demons (Matt. 12:22-33; Mark 3:22-30; Luke 11:14-26)	Demonstrated conflict of kingdom of Satan and the kingdom of God by exorcism of demons (Luke 11:14-26)
Warned against appearing good outwardly while being evil within — or with Pharisees and scribes "an evil tree" (Matt. 12:33-45)	Warning against the hypocrisy of the Pharisees (Luke 12:1-2)
Parables of the secrets of the kingdom of heaven demonstrating growth and influence of the kingdom until a coming final judgment (Matt. 13:1ff; cf. 13:30, 47-49)	Depiction of the Lord's return and warning to settle now with the judge and to become fruitful unto God (Luke 12:35–13:9) Parables of the Kingdom (Luke 13:18-21)
Miracles demonstrating Christ's deity (Matt. 8:18; Mark 4:35 Luke 8:22)	Miracle demonstrating His deity (Luke 13:10-17)
Twelve apostles instructed and sent (Matt. 10:2-23; Mark 6:7-13; Luke 9:1-6)	Seventy instructed and sent. The account shows them "appointed and sent" at the same time but the probability is that the sending occurred at this time since He promised to follow them to their assigned cities and goes to many cities at this time (Luke 13:22ff, cf. Luke 10:1ff)
Warning not to fear men (Matt. 10:26-31)	Warning not to fear men (Luke 12:4-12)
Admonition that He will divide men, bringing a sword, not peace (Matt. 10:34-36)	Admonition that He will divide men, bringing a sword, not peace (Luke 12:49-53)

Crisis with Jews over Jesus' divine heavenly origin and authority (John 6:22-71) Plot to kill.	Crisis over claims of being sent from God and messianic claims. Attempt to arrest and kill. (John 10:31-39)
Conflict with Pharisees over tradition and warning against leaven of Pharisaic hypocrisy (Matt. 15:1-20; 16:1-12)	Conflict with Pharisees over vain legal interpretations, desire for honor, and hypocrisy (Luke 14:1-11; 15:1-32)
Offer of keys to the kingdom, announcement of His coming and a call to take up cross and give up life for His sake (Matt. 16:13-28; Mark 8:27–9:1)	Call to take up the cross and give up life to be a disciple (Luke 14:25-35)
Warning to avoid causes of sin and admonition to restore the sinner (Matt. 18:21-35)	Warning to avoid causes of sin and admonition to restore one in sin (Luke 17:1-10)

There are other teachings not included in the parallel columns that actually were interspersed with those listed. However, one is still struck by the distinct parallels in the instruction of both groups. It is evident that Jesus taught certain truths in a general chronological order so that it would be relevant to the progressive growth of each of the two groups. While the parallels may not be as exact as they appear to be in this chart, the evidence does indicate a definite, planned pattern in His teaching and His communication of basic principles. From this analysis we can assume that Jesus had an overall plan for building His men from His first association with them until He left them.

Outline of Seven Steps in a Harmony of the Gospels

In order to determine Jesus' strategy for building disciples, I have studied the harmony of the Gospels in depth. There are apparently seven steps through which Jesus sought to lead His disciples, each being a step of greater commitment and trust in Him. A survey of the basic ideas in each step follows.

During the first step, John the Baptist and Jesus sought to lead people to *Repentance and Faith.* They called them to change their minds about their past life of sin and accept a new life with God. They warned of the coming judgment and talked about the meaning of sin. But they also taught their listeners about God's love and His forgiveness of the sinner. Many were converted, being persuaded to turn from their selfish, sinful lives and to trust God.

During the second step, *Enlightenment and Guidance,* Jesus helped His followers understand who He was so that they would trust Him as their leader. He taught them that He was the Messiah and

He showed them His power — that of the glorious Son of God. They were led to understand that there was continued acceptance and forgiveness through Him. They learned to follow Him obediently.

In the third step, *Ministry Training and Appreciation of Benefits,* Jesus called men to commit themselves publicly to minister with Him, trusting God to draw men to Himself and help them grow. Jesus called these men, saying, "Come, follow me . . . and I will make you fishers of men" (Mark 1:17). He taught them the principles of evangelism. He showed them His love for the sinner and His power to forgive sin and give new life. He demonstrated His power over physical evil. He taught them that He was the Lawgiver who brought freedom from the curse of the Law to all who followed Him and that He had the authority to judge all men at the resurrection and to justify the believer.

The fourth step is *Leadership Development and Government Under God.* In this step Jesus organized His kingdom and gave men responsible leadership roles, instructing them and giving them authority. The theme of His teaching was the kingdom. He proclaimed its blessings and talked about the new law of inner righteousness. He contrasted the kingdom of heaven with Satan's, and He used parables to teach them how God's kingdom would grow.

The purpose of the fifth step, *Reevaluation and Separation,* is to bring a person to trust God for the eternal things of life above the temporal. At this time, Jesus challenged the status quo. He offered His followers heavenly bread instead of earthly bread, divine authority over human authority, and assurance of eternal life and future glory rather than eternal damnation. This led to a hostile separation by the world.

During the sixth step, *Participation and Delegation,* Jesus brought His disciples to the point of trusting Him both to work in other members of the body and to cope with those outside of and suspicious of the body of Christ. Jesus reviewed with the seventy new apostles what He had already taught the Twelve, who now observed how Jesus delegated to the Seventy. In addition, He taught them how to relate to others and what the priorities of the Christian life are. He also warned them about evils that would harm the Christian life. During this time of "Body Life," Jesus taught them how to relate to those who demanded legal obedience, those who wanted to work independently rather than as a unit, those who rejected them, false teachers, a brother who sinned, and others.

In the seventh step, *Exchanged Life and Worldwide Challenge,* a person learns how to rest in the sufficiency of the risen Christ through the Holy Spirit. The disciples, who had become profession-als in the Christian ministry and who were confident in themselves, discovered through the crucifixion and the resurrection that the flesh is inadequate. They learned of God's sovereignty, the crucifixion of the flesh, and sufficiency of Christ in and through His Holy Spirit who is in the world. They learned that His kingdom is not to be confined to Israel, but to be worldwide.

Through the book I will hereafter use the first part of the title of each step as a shorter form for convenience' sake — e.g., Repent-ance, Enlightenment. The shorter title focuses on the main emphasis of training for the original disciples as contrasted to that of disciples who joined Christ later.

The chart on page 66 is a brief synopsis of the Seven Steps, including the truths Jesus taught at each step in order to bring the disciples to the faith commitment He desired.

After the step of Ministry Training Jesus focused on teaching a more and more select group of leaders as well as on the large group who followed Him. He skillfully united the teachings of both, to-gether with special emphasis in application.

The seven steps were developed by studying two harmonies of the four Gospels (see footnote 1 at the end of this chapter) with a view to discovering the discipleship objectives of Jesus. A detailed outline of the materials was formed and the book was written based on that. A copy of that detailed outline may be obtained from the Worldwide Discipleship Association, Inc., 1001 Virginia Avenue, Atlanta, Ga. 30354. Or the reader may keep open A. T. Robertson's *Harmony of the Gospels* as he reads through chapters 4 to 10. He can then follow the gospel material as it is chronologically discussed. For conve-nience in doing this, the sections and page numbers of Robertson's harmony are listed below the name of the steps of column one. Only by comparing Robertson's harmony with my detailed outline, or by following it through this book can the reader see that the seven steps are derived from the biblical data and are not arbitrarily con-trived.[1]

A MULTIPLIED MINISTRY RESULTED FROM JESUS' DISCIPLESHIP PLAN

Jesus' approach to disciple building resulted in training an in-creasing number of men who were reproducing His ministry. This meant that as the work grew, there was a constant flow of new leadership to assume responsibility. This in turn promoted additional growth in the movement. Today the modern church operates so the work load continually increases on the pastor, and his load becomes heavier, which limits the church's ministry and harms the pastor.

OUTLINE OF THE SEVEN STEPS OF DISCIPLESHIP

Step	Trust Objective	Theme of Truth
1. Repentance and faith (sections 20-26)	Conversion — trust God to forgive sin and give new life.	Sin, judgment, love, forgiveness.
2. Enlightenment and Guidance (sections 27-39)	Understand who Jesus is and trust Him as leader.	Deity, power, glory of Christ, continued forgiveness by the Lamb of God.
3. Ministry Training and Appreciation of Benefits (sections 40-52)	Trust God in public identification to win people to Jesus	Nature of Christ's kingdom; ministry of forgiveness, new life, healing and freedom from law through the Son; divine guidance.
4. Leadership Development and Government Under God (sections 53-72a; Mark 6:30; Luke 9:10)	Trust Christ in assuming a responsible place of leadership in family or movement and trust Him to govern our lives.	The blessings and new righteousness of the kingdom; contrast of two kingdoms, Christ's and Satan's; growth; instructions and authority of leaders.
5. Reevaluation and Separation (sections 72; Mark 6:31; Luke 9:11-88)	Trust God for the eternal above all temporal matters, and separation to Christ from the world.	Greater value of eternal over temporal; challenge to the status quo; heavenly bread over earthly; divine authority over man's; this life for eternal life and glory; separation to Christ and from the world.
6. Participation and Delegation (sections 89-124)	Trust Christ to work in other members of the Body.	Review of basic truths, teach relationships to others, priorities, warnings. "Body Life." How to relate to those demanding legal obedience, those wanting to work independently, those who reject you, false teachers, a brother who sins, et al.
7. Exchanged Life and Worldwide Challenge (sections 125-184)	Rest in sufficiency of the risen Christ and begin to trust Him to use you to reach the world.	God's sovereignty, crucifixion of the flesh, the sufficiency of Christ through the Holy Spirit; resting in truth about the Holy Spirit learned earlier but not fully appreciated; challenge of worldwide outreach.

The diagram on this page helps clarify this. In the diagram on the left the pyramid is upside down. The weight is resting on the shoulders of one man — the pastor of the church. The pastor (with perhaps one or two others he has hired) is trying to hold up and balance the pyramid. If the church has any outreach and growth through evangelism, the pastor's burden gets heavier. He must then take management courses, employ new staff, etc., in order to support the pyramid.

The diagram on the right shows the way Jesus worked. The leader is at the top of the pyramid, which develops beneath him. Jesus began by associating with a group of men from whom He selected the Twelve. He gave these twelve the responsibility to do the same thing He was doing. As the crowds continued to grow, He selected and trained seventy more. Finally on the day of Pentecost, there were 120. By training others to assist Him, Jesus built the pyramid right side up. All looked to Him as the true leader and the ultimate source of truth, but He did not do all the work. He trained others to become like Him. Thus, Jesus established the biblical method of building the church through the building of disciples. But also important is the fact that Jesus did not build the disciples merely to use them to do His work, but because He cared about them and wanted them to grow to personal fulfillment.

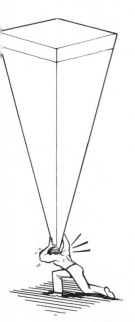
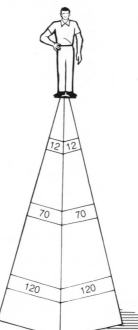

HOW TO CHANGE THE PYRAMID

IMPORTANCE OF MIDDLE LEADERSHIP

Because Jesus continued to produce a progressively larger middle leadership who could teach all things He had commanded, His ministry had growing momentum and power.

In a certain sense, what I am talking about here is like creating the middle management in a factory for instructing, motivating, and supervising the men who actually do the work at the machines. I once worked in a factory that produced aircraft parts. My job was to operate a lathe that cut metal parts to the right size. When I started work, I had never seen a lathe before. A foreman took me in and showed me step by step what to do. He came back from time to time to see how I was doing and help me after I got in trouble. He continued to inspect my work to see if it was right.

Suppose I had reported to work the first day with a group of new workers and the manager had addressed us by saying, "This factory operates only when every man in it does his job. *All of us,* not just the management, are supposed to work to meet our production schedules. All of you are the key to successful productivity. Now, go to it, men, and do your job well." But suppose no one showed any of us how to operate the machines and what to do. How much would get done? Nothing! We would have sat there excited at the thought that we were so important to the company. Or we might try to run the machinery and produce chaos.

I have heard pastors speaking on Ephesians 4:12, telling the people that the Bible teaches that *all the members* are supposed to do the *work of the ministry.* "The preacher alone cannot do it all," they say; the people are all supposed to evangelize, teach, and give aid to those in need. The pastor wonders why the people do not follow through and do anything. But he has not trained any foremen to associate with the people and show them what to do, to encourage them, help them in problems, and supervise.

Jesus was constantly building more and more middle management to give leadership to His growing movement. There were first the Twelve, then the Seventy, and so on. In Ephesians Paul shows that Christ was seeking to continue to produce the middle leadership by giving gifts that would enable the people to know how to do the work of the ministry.

EARLY TEACHING OF DISCIPLESHIP THROUGH MODELS

Was this pattern of teaching transferable and was it followed by Christ's disciples when they assumed the leadership roles in the church? There is no evidence that Jesus ever taught an outline for a seven-step program of developing disciples. However, people learn basically by models.

Jesus spent more than three years building His followers. In those three years He taught the original twelve disciples all He wanted them to know and began repeating these teachings over again several times to other new groups of followers. The disciples would have intuitively used the same approach in building their own disciples as Jesus used with them and with the Seventy. Having seen this process at least twice and partially a third time, they would have followed it subconsciously. (For an evaluation of arguments for a four-year ministry in the life of Christ, see Addendum 3, p. 310.)

PAUL'S METHOD

Did Paul, who was one of the principal builders of churches and disciplers of men, use such a program of disciple building?[2]

It appears that Paul spent approximately three years in the cities that were his centers for teaching. He then left, apparently having taught all he thought the believers needed to know. In Acts 20:31 Paul specifically states that he had been in Ephesus teaching for three years and that he had declared the whole counsel of God to the Ephesian church (cf. v. 27). He seemed to be saying that he had obeyed Christ's command to teach His disciples to observe all things whatsoever He commanded.

Paul probably stayed in Corinth, Antioch, and elsewhere approximately three years. Barnabas, Paul's early leader, was probably one of the Seventy and certainly a member of the apostolic community. Paul learned from Barnabas' model at Antioch and elsewhere. He was also probably familiar with Jesus' early ministry. (See Addendum 4 for consideration of Paul's exposure to and use of this three-year discipleship program.)

Although not all second-generation disciples went through the models of the seven steps of Christian growth under apostolic leadership, many did. And many went through the models led by those who did.

THE IMPLICATIONS OF THE SEVEN STEPS

After the disciples had been through these seven steps, they were equipped to continue growing to maturity. Growing to maturity is a lifelong process. The apostle Paul said that he had not attained maturity but that he was pressing on toward the goal of the prize of the upward call of God in Christ (Phil. 3:14). In the seven steps a person learns the basic truths that will help him continue that growth process.

Through the steps one receives basic training for an independent ministry under the guidance of the Holy Spirit. After their completion of these seven steps, the twelve apostles became the leaders who motivated the Christian church. In these three years of training, Jesus had equipped them to multiply by training others.

These *seven steps* relate *the usual pattern* of development of a disciple. There are some exceptions, such as John the Baptist, who was filled with the Holy Spirit from his mother's womb. But most will go through this logical sequence of steps.

A person must become a Christian (that is, he must trust Jesus as his Savior) before he can trust Jesus as his leader. He must fully understand who Jesus Christ is and trust Him as his leader before he can begin a public ministry in which he will encounter opposition and difficulties. Many new converts are taken out witnessing before they really understand the true meaning of Christianity, and ordinarily they do not continue to witness.

People cannot become leaders until they have learned how to minister and how to carry out their ministry. If a person is challenged to change his temporal values for the eternal values of the kingdom of God before he has come to a point of responsible involvement, he will not be likely to continue. To challenge him to live for eternal values immediately after conversion demands too much for his immature faith. It is like asking a toddler to lift a hundred-pound weight. Although a new convert may need to be challenged to count the cost of total obedience (Luke 14:26-33), the weight of demand put on him must grow as the power of his faith grows (2 Cor. 10:15; 2 Thess. 1:3). Giving too great a challenge too soon will often lead to the disciple's drawing back from following the Lord. Also, only after he has begun to work with others in a large group is it relevant to teach the disciple how to participate with and delegate to others as a part of the Body of Christ.

Thus, the order of these steps is logical. If the presentation of the truths is reversed, they will not be applicable to the individual life.

We Christians make many mistakes in helping disciples grow. Far too often we try to put spiritual diapers on adults and full suits of clothes on little babies. Often we share with others the things that inspire us and meet our true needs rather than ministering to them at the level of their own maturity.

These steps of growth are not new. The Holy Spirit has not left the church in darkness all these years, now suddenly to reveal these steps. Because they are logical steps, most Christian groups follow at least the first ones. Three groups with which I am familiar use materials that start with the basic teaching on repentance and salvation, and go secondly to a study of who Jesus Christ is. In this book I seek to define all of the steps of Christian growth, as presented in the Bible, in a way that has to my knowledge not been done before.

Because the inadequate view of discipleship called "follow-up" has dominated disciple building in recent years, the church has found it had become stronger in things taught in the earlier steps (1-4) and is suffering a deficiency of knowledge concerning what is taught in the latter steps (5-7). Today the church is wrestling with the consequences and seeking to solve the problems in regard to values (Step 5), body life and church discipline (Step 6), relying on fleshly means to promote growth (Step 7) and others.

While one may question my outline of my seven steps from the Harmony (e.g., p. 66), question whether Jesus repeated the same process of discipleship (pp. 62-63), and question the divisions I have made in grouping the data of the Gospels, he still is bound by the lordship of Christ to teach men "to observe *all things*" that He commanded (Matt. 28:19). Hence, as a minister of Christ he must find some way in his teaching to cover all the things Jesus taught. Since I have shown that this order is logical, follows reasonably close to the order in which Jesus gave His teachings, and seeks to include all His teachings, I believe this outline for building disciples can be useful to most ministers, whether or not they accept all the details of my book.

PRINCIPLES INVOLVED IN DISCIPLE BUILDING

In leading a disciple through these seven steps of Christian growth, the teacher must understand the development of certain principles as they unfold from step one through step seven. The teacher's relationship to his disciples changes at each successive step and he must understand how it changes as he leads them step by step. He must know how to build a warm fellowship that produces openness and loyalty.

With each step, a disciple's involvement in the ministry grows. He assumes greater and greater responsibility, with the kind of responsibility varying at each step.

Knowing how to motivate the disciples is essential, for if they are properly motivated, the momentum of the movement will grow. The proper timing of evangelistic outreaches throughout the seven steps is vital to motivation and growth.

Another important principle of gaining and developing disciples in Jesus' ministry was prayer. Nothing was more important than God's supernatural working in the lives of His disciples. The things for which Jesus prayed differed with each step of growth. All of these principles produce obedience to God and result in growth. The last section of this book deals more fully with these principles.

One will not, of course, use only what Jesus taught His men or only the harmony of the Gospels when discipling others. The rest of the Scriptures, notably Acts and the Epistles, complement and amplify the truths Jesus taught in the Seven Steps.[2] For example, when teaching who Jesus is in the step of Enlightenment, one will add the teachings from the rest of the Scriptures that communicate the same ideas Jesus taught. One would teach His eternal preexistence, the virgin birth, the incarnation, the evidences for the resurrection and other doctrines. Each step must be expanded to include other relevant biblical teachings.

SUMMARY AND CLARIFICATION OF PART I

One of the main reasons the church is not being salt to stop corruption and light to drive back the darkness in America is the loss of its capability to disciple its people. Proper discipleship must effectively teach God's people to observe all things that Jesus commanded so they manifest sacrificial love and display the image of Christ to the glory of God. It should result in concern for and outreach to new people in evangelism. The key to the church's ability to build men into the image of Christ and reach out to others lies in the discipleship program also producing the quality middle leadership (e.g., foremen) that increases in number and is capable of training and teaching the new people.

The church in the United States lost its ability to produce capable middle leadership and its ability to teach and apply God's Word when it lost the colleges and universities to secular humanism and when secular trends forced the church to operate in such a way as to lose its ability to apply truth to people's lives by personal involvement and association. The pastor was forced into a role of lecturer and administrator, and teaching in general became impersonal and not specific in application and discipline. Therefore, a return to Jesus' approach to discipling men is needed.

A study of a harmony of the Gospels seems to indicate that Jesus led His men through seven steps of growth. These steps unfold in a logical sequence that cannot easily be changed or transposed. By personal association with His men, He applied the respective truth to their lives that if obeyed would move them toward the faith objectives in each successive step. As His ministry expanded, His program of disciple building was producing an increasing number of middle leadership through which He could continue to teach the growing number of people involved.

The seven steps we have outlined are not a rigid formula that

Jesus mechanically applied. They are rather an outline of the normal development that most of His men were led through. As He developed His men, He dealt with them as a group with this as a plan as to what He wanted to accomplish, but He accomplished it by dealing with them as individuals. He deviated within the pattern to meet their felt needs, which became obvious in various circumstances, but He continued to apply His teaching to carry through His planned steps of growth for meeting their needs even though sometimes the needs were not seen and felt. Sometimes He created the circumstances to make various needs felt and to make the teaching relevant.

The outline of the seven steps should not, therefore, be used as a neat formula into which we press all individuals. Rather, the steps offer a logical and biblical plan whereby the church can train its leadership to be organized to teach in a meaningfully successive presentation. The discipleship leaders can then be equipped to guide the growth of the disciples. By being trained to communicate all Christ's teachings in a logical unfolding, the teacher will have greater freedom to deviate to meet specific felt needs as the Holy Spirit indicates. The mother who has received instruction about the normal development of a baby and has been taught how to meet the various problems as they would ordinarily occur is the mother who is also best equipped to meet those needs if they spontaneously occur when they are not expected. The public school teacher who has worked out her lesson plans for her entire course is the one who can relax and let the class ask questions that may go to other materials that would arise in a later lesson than that scheduled. Also, understanding the normal pattern of development for a disciple prevents a teacher from dumping materials and ideas on his students that the student is not mature enough to assimilate.

Jesus' program of disciple building gave momentum and direction to His whole movement. But it did not constitute all that He was doing, nor was His teaching of His disciples all of the Christian education they were getting. The men Jesus discipled apparently became more interested in going to the synagogue to read Scripture and being taught and became more excited about the meaning of worship at the temple. No doubt, the disciples also talked at home with their wives and children with greater excitement and diligence about what the Scriptures taught.

In like manner, *a program in a church aimed at building disciples should become the catalyst to spark greater interest in the church school and in the worship services.* Moreover, *it should be the nucleus to guide the understanding and direction of thought and activities of the entire church.* The three years of training will not end growth in maturity even for those being discipled but become the foundation for growth to maturity and effectiveness of ministry for many years to come.

To be the catalyst and nucleus of education in the church, the discipleship program must be built around those who enter the program *voluntarily* and not because it is traditionally required or expected. Hence, it will not aim at beginning with everyone, but at those who desire to grow. The program will begin small and expand to include more and more people and will permeate the whole congregation. Those who enter the program voluntarily and continue to respond to responsibility will move to a closer association and a deeper commitment.

The discipleship program will produce an increasing number of people involved in evangelism and ministry so that the size of the congregation continues to grow. The involvement of the original disciples in evangelism will develop, moving from those being evangelized, to those helping evangelize, to those training others to evangelize. A discipleship program that does not involve continuous outreach of evangelism is not the program Jesus had.

The program should also produce more and more middle leadership who can teach all that Jesus commanded. Jesus seems to have begun a new discipleship group each year and this in turn successively produced the 12, the 70, and the 120. This prevented putting people together who were at different levels of growth. A group will gravitate to the lowest growth level.

While we in the church of today cannot reproduce the ministry and circumstances of the life of Jesus, we can follow the general plan for developing disciples that He demonstrated.

The second part of this book, which follows, is an effort to trace the materials through the harmony of the Gospels with a view of discovering what Jesus was seeking to accomplish *in the life of the original disciples who became the Twelve,* while also seeing how the total ministry of Jesus to others might relate to the Twelve. In order to interpret what Jesus was doing with the Twelve, I have tried to see the training He was offering at any one point in the light of the total context of what He had taught them before and what He would teach them soon after, as well as in the light of the broader context of His overall ministry. Those who follow the material through the harmony of the Gospels can see how closely this is tied to the objective historical record.

In Part Two, I discuss some points in greater detail than others when it is helpful to see how they fit into the emphasis of that particular step, and when the meaning has not been generally clear.

For example, the cleansing of the temple of John 2:13-23 has not been commonly recognized as a clear messianic claim, so I have given a detailed analysis to show this is true, since it is important in seeing that at that period of His ministry Jesus was demonstrating that He was the Messiah. Other points where the meaning has been generally agreed upon, I have passed over with brief mention, although they were equally important teachings.

Notes

[1] The study was originally based on the harmony of Albert Cassell Wieand, *Gospel Records of the Message and Mission of Jesus Christ,* 3435 Van Buren St., Chicago 24, Ill., 1946. A. T. Robertson's *A Harmony of the Gospels for Students of the Life of Christ* (New York: Harper and Row, 1922) is almost identical in chronology and more useful because it is more readily available.

[2] There has been considerable controversy as to how much the apostles built their writings on the teachings of Jesus. Many deny especially that there is any connection between Paul and Jesus. R. Bultmann has said, "The teaching of the historical Jesus plays no role, or practically none, in Paul" *(Theology of the New Testament* [New York: Charles Scribner's Sons, 1951], 1:35). But Bultmann based this on the presupposition of Hellenistic influence on Paul as on all the New Testament writings. His views were formed before the discovery of the Dead Sea Scrolls, which demonstrate evidence for Palestinian origin of much of the New Testament. Some scholars who do hold that Paul had some familiarity with the teachings of Jesus are Heinrich Panet, W. D. Davies, Arnold Resch, Alfred Seeberg, G. Matheson, J. Weiss, E. Vischer, A. Deissmann, Anton Fridrichsen, Eberhard Jüngell, W. Schmithals, W. G. Kümmel, and David L. Dungon. Some hold that Paul knew oral traditions that were passed on from those who heard Jesus; some hold he heard teachings that Jesus required the Twelve to memorize; and others see him as using New Testament writings with Jesus' sayings. Much of these views are speculative and some deny a belief in the supernatural. See Addendum 4.

II

The Seven Steps Presented

4

Repentance and Faith

REPENTANCE — WHAT DOES IT MEAN?

The process that leads to conversion is called repentance. The word *repent* is translated from the Greek word *metanoeō*, which means "to change one's mind." In the Christian context, repentance means that a person changes his mind about his past life of sin. He turns away from sin, trusting God for forgiveness and new life. The actual "act of turning" (which occurs when the process of changing the mind is complete) is called *conversion*. During the step of Repentance, people are prepared to become disciples.

A non-Christian trusts in himself and chooses to do what he wills. But when a person is converted, he turns from seeking his own will and begins to trust God, seeking His will. Jesus said, "Whoever *does the will* of my Father in heaven is my brother and sister and mother" (Matt. 12:50).

The call to self-denial in Scripture is a call to yield one's will to God. He who denies himself is crucified to the affections and desires of the flesh and begins to follow Christ under the control and in the power of the Holy Spirit (Gal. 5:24,25).

BY GRACE THROUGH FAITH THE WILL IS CHANGED

God in His wisdom gives the gift of forgiveness and salvation only to those who trust Him. As long as a person still has confidence in his ability to make himself acceptable to God, he will continue trusting in himself. He will not yield his will to God. But when he admits that there is nothing he can do but trust God to give him forgiveness in Christ, he has come to the point of yielding his will. That is why anyone who is a child of God will want to do God's will. That is why the process of repentance leads to a person's giving up the chief idols of his life. As long as his affections are set on his selfish idols, he is not teachable. He cannot grow as a disciple. Growth occurs by faith.

THE BACKDROP FOR JOHN THE BAPTIST

In the first century A.D., pagan practices permeated the nation of Israel. Greco-Roman thought had penetrated deeply into Jewish culture during the intertestamental period. From the time of the high priest Jason, c. 175 B.C., sensualism and materialism had prevailed.

The crass immorality of the Greeks and the Romans penetrated even into the temple precincts. Intertestamental literature refers both openly and in veiled form to the sexual sins that took place there.

The Jewish people were obsessed with their desires for material wealth, status, and power. First under Greek and then Roman domination the Jewish priesthood had become chiefly a political office open to the highest bidder.

The land of Palestine was spiritually dry, and the Holy Spirit's working had not been evident for several hundred years. When the temple was retaken and purified during the time of Judas Maccabeus (c. 165 B.C.), the people tore down the defiled altar. Then they had to decide what to do with the stones. In futility they determined to put them aside and wait until a prophet appeared again (1 Macc. 4:46[1]). Not until John the Baptist was there a man who was considered a prophet. And John's call for repentance was urgently needed.

FIRST THINGS FIRST

Generally, the role of repentance in disciple building is not adequately emphasized, even in some of the most significant books on the subject.[2] While these books do correctly assert that the close teacher-disciple relationship begins after repentance and conversion, they do not stress the fact that repentance involves the acceptance of certain teachings preparing a person to be a teachable disciple. Thus, discipleship begins with repentance. John the Baptist, Jesus, and His disciples dealt with the idols in men's lives as the first step of discipleship.

This first step differs from the succeeding steps, however, because it prepares the disciple to enter into a personal or small-group relationship with his teacher. Subsequent acts of repentance may be required of a Christian (as with Peter in Luke 22:32), but it is the initial act of repentance and conversion that is definitive in that it leads to the new birth and adoption into God's family. Jesus said, "Unless you change and become like little children, you will never enter the kingdom of heaven" (Matt. 18:3). True repentance produces faith and conversion (Mark 1:15; Acts 3:19; 26:20).

THE CHALLENGE OF THE OLD TESTAMENT

The Old Testament refers often to repentance and conversion (Ps. 80:3,7,19; Jer. 25:5; 31:21, et al.). David prayed:

> Create in me a clean heart, O God,
> And renew a steadfast spirit within me.
> Then I will teach transgressors thy ways,
> And *sinners will be converted* to Thee (Ps. 51:10,13).

Jesus also quoted Isaiah's prophecy that tells how people become dull so they could not "understand with their hearts and *turn*" (Matt. 13:15; Isa. 6:10).

PREPARE YE THE WAY

John the Baptist called men to turn to God from their sins. Before his birth an angel of the Lord prophesied:

> Many of the people of Israel will he *bring back* to the Lord their God. And he will go on before the Lord, in the spirit and power of Elijah, to *turn the hearts* of the fathers to their children and the disobedient to the wisdom of the righteous — to make ready a people prepared for the Lord (Luke 1:16,17).

Repeatedly the idea of turning occurs; a change from the past pattern of life to a new life with God is implied.

John's father, being filled with the Holy Spirit, also prophesied of his son. He foretold the content of John's *message, which* would *prompt people to turn back* to the Lord (Luke 1:76-79).

John was to proclaim "salvation by forgiveness" for men's sins through God's mercy, which would guide to the way of reconciliation or peace. Later, after he had begun his preaching, some priests and Levites came to him asking who he was. John replied, "I am a voice of one calling in the desert, 'Make straight the way for the Lord' " (John 1:23).

Although the Pharisees and John's disciples (as well as some modern scholars) tried to make a distinction between the message of John and Jesus (Mark 2:18), the gospel record indicates that Jesus and His disciples preached the same message as John (cf. Matt. 3:2 with 4:17). Both John and Jesus prepared men to be baptized (John 4:1).

However, their ministries did differ. The prophetic order of the Old Testament, whose purpose was to prepare the way for the Messiah, ended with John, for he introduced the Christ (Matt. 11:13; Luke 16:16). John and Jesus in some ways emphasized different aspects of the kingdom. John *primarily* motivated men to turn from their sin by urging them to consider the coming judgment. After John's imprisonment, Jesus shifted the emphasis of His message. He began to stress the benefits of the kingdom — forgiveness, healing, deliverance, and blessing. Whereas John's life style was austere, Jesus' expressed the joy of the kingdom. John did no miracles but came fasting, dressing like Elijah in camel's hair with a leather girdle, and eating wild honey; Jesus came eating and drinking, and He healed men of their diseases.

The Scriptures do not indicate a discontinuity between John and Jesus but rather a phasing from one emphasis to the other — the one preparing for and leading to the other.

When Paul rebaptized some of John's disciples in Acts 19:1-7, he did not indicate that John's baptism was invalid; rather, it was incomplete. It did not lead men to trust in Jesus as the One who gives the Spirit. But because their hearts had been prepared when Paul introduced Him to them, they recognized Jesus as the Messiah and received Him readily as the giver of the Spirit.

Putting a Finger on Sin

Jesus. In both His public preaching and personal interviews, Jesus forced men to confront the major idols in their lives. Then He called them to repentance.

Nicodemus, a teacher of repute (literally, John 3:10 in Greek reads *"the* teacher of Israel"), came to Jesus with a spiritual need. And Jesus' words puzzled him. He spoke of an experience that could not be explained by reason. Jesus said, "Unless a man is born again, he cannot see the kingdom of God." Nicodemus then asked, "How can a man be born when he is old? Surely he cannot enter a second time into his mother's womb to be born!"

Jesus explained that a man enters the kingdom not through any physical means but through a spiritual one. The spiritual rebirth cannot be understood, nor is it seen. One can only see its effects, much like the blowing wind (John 3:3,4,8).

Nicodemus was esteemed for his knowledge and his position of leadership as a rabbinical teacher. Yet Jesus presented him with a truth he could not understand. He unveiled the idol in Nicodemus' life — his intellectual pride.

"Go, call your husband," said Jesus to the Samaritan woman

He had met at Jacob's well. But she said, ''I have no husband.'' He replied, ''You are right when you say you have no husband. The fact is, you have had five husbands, and the man you now have is not your husband'' (John 4:16-18). He confronted her with her immorality.

The rich young ruler was seeking eternal life. Although he had kept many of the commandments, sin dominated one area of his life. In His love for the young man Jesus said to him. ''One thing you lack. Go, sell everything you have and give to the poor, and you will have treasure in heaven'' (Mark 10:21). But this man's idol was his wealth, and he went away grieved because he had many possessions.

To the religious legal authority whose sin was self-justification, Jesus told the story of the good Samaritan who loved his neighbor (Luke 10:25-37). He commanded the lawyer, ''Go and do likewise'' (v. 37). But the proud scribe hated the Samaritans, and his sin was exposed. In a similar manner Jesus dealt with idols of many others.

John the Baptist. In calling men to repentance, John hit at the heart of the sin of his time — materialism. He admonished his followers to bring forth fruits in keeping with their repentance (Luke 3:8). To the materialistic multitude he said, ''The man with two tunics should share with him who has none, and the one who has food should do the same.'' He instructed the tax gatherers, ''Don't collect any more than you are required to.'' To the soldiers he said, ''Don't extort money and don't accuse people falsely — be content with your pay'' (Luke 3:10-18). John cut the very nerve of materialism.

Paul. When Paul preached on Mars Hill, he addressed himself to the Athenian's idolatry (Acts 17:29), urging them to repent before the future judgment. In Ephesus the call to turn from idols was so effective that idolatry throughout Asia was threatened (Acts 19:26).

When Paul appeared before the Roman governor Felix, it was the judge who felt guilty:

> As Paul discoursed on righteousness, self-control and the judgment to come, Felix was afraid and said, ''That's enough for now! You may leave. When I find it convenient, I will send for you'' (Acts 24:25).

At the meetings of the early church, nonbelievers were confronted with their sin. God's people called them to account for their deeds and led them to repentance:

> But if an unbeliever or someone who does not understand comes in while everybody is prophesying, he will be convinced by all that he is a sinner and will be judged by all, and the secrets of his heart will be laid bare. So he will fall down and worship God, exclaiming, ''God is really among you!'' (1 Cor. 14:24,25).

On many occasions Paul called people to turn to God from idols, warned them of the future judgment, and encouraged them to confess their sin publicly (Acts 17:23-31; 19:18-20; 1 Thess. 1:9), as did Peter and the other apostles (Acts 2:23,36-41; 3:19-26).

THE THEME OF JUDGMENT PROMOTES REPENTANCE

Judgment is an essential part of the call to repentance. John the Baptist, Jesus, and Paul warned people that unless they repented, they would be judged and found wanting.

John the Baptist's arrival, in fact, heralded the One who would come in judgment. In Luke 3:4-6 John quoted Isaiah 40:3-5, a passage that reveals his identity as the forerunner. It is from a passage that stresses the need for God's people to be prepared for His coming in judgment. Malachi 3:1-3 also deals with the theme of judgment, telling of a messenger who would come to prepare the way for the Lord, who, when He had come, would cleanse the worship, judge the priesthood, and bring judgment on His people.

Jesus frequently spoke of judgment. From the beginning of His public ministry, He preached, "Repent, for the kingdom of God is near" (Matt. 4:17). Even toward the end He said, "Unless you repent, you too will all perish" (Luke 13:3,5). Again near the end of His life He warned that some would be cast into the eternal fire that has been prepared for the devil and his angels (Matt. 25:41).

Paul was motivated to call men to repentance by his knowledge of the future judgment of God. He said in 2 Corinthians 5:11, "Since, then, we know what it is to fear the Lord, we try to persuade men." In 2 Thessalonians 1:7b-9 he said:

> This will happen when the Lord Jesus is revealed from heaven in blazing fire with his powerful angels. He will punish those who do not know God and do not obey the gospel of our Lord Jesus. They will be punished with everlasting destruction and shut out from the presence of the Lord and from the majesty of his power. . . .

Judgment must be preached as a part of the message of repentance. But we must not have a vindictive or a sadistic spirit, for we need to express God's love and concern for the lost (Luke 15:1ff.; 19:10).

POSITIVE ASPECTS OF REPENTANCE

There are also positive aspects of the message of repentance that need to be emphasized. Forgiveness is available to those who confess their sin and their need for God. John the Baptist pointed people to the source of that forgiveness, saying, "Look, the Lamb of God who takes away the sin of the world!" (John 1:29). Here Jesus is described as the fulfillment of the Old Testament sacrifice, and is therefore the

One who removes from the people their sin against God.

In addition to granting forgiveness, Jesus is the One who gives new life through the Holy Spirit. John said, "I baptize you with water for repentance. But after me will come one who is more powerful than I, whose sandals I am not fit to carry. He will baptize you with the Holy Spirit and with fire" (Matt. 3:11). The eternal life of God, His Spirit, will indwell the believer, guiding and strengthening him. Later, in talking with Nicodemus, Jesus described this as the new birth (John 3:3-16).

REPENTANCE AND NEW LIFE FROM A POST-RESURRECTION PERSPECTIVE

From our post-resurrection perspective, forgiveness is seen in broader terms. It centers in the cross of Christ where God judged people's sin (their rejection of Him), for through Christ's death, God provided a way for them to be forgiven.

Paul emphasized the importance of the cross in 1 Corinthians 1:17,18, where he said that Christ did not send him to baptize, but to preach the gospel, and that the word of the cross is to those who are perishing foolishness, but to those who are being saved it is the power of God. Elsewhere he said:

> I resolved to know nothing while I was with you except Jesus Christ and him crucified . . . not with wise and persuasive words, but with a demonstration of the Spirit's power, so that your faith might not rest on men's wisdom, but on God's power (1 Cor. 2:2-5).

In Romans 10:1-17 Paul explained why the Jews had failed to obtain salvation. They had tried to establish their righteousness through works, that is, through obedience to the law. But Paul asserted that salvation had a different source: "If you confess with your mouth, 'Jesus is Lord,' and believe in your heart that God raised him from the dead, you will be saved" (v. 9). Again, in 1 Corinthians 15:1ff. Paul declared that forgiveness comes through Christ's death for our sins. He taught that knowledge of God's kindness leads people to repent (Rom. 2:4).

This *emphasis on faith in Christ as the way of salvation is the key* to New Testament thinking (Acts 16:32; Eph. 2:8,9). Jesus had emphasized faith as the way of salvation to Nicodemus and others (John 3:16).

The promise of new life to the one who repents and finds forgiveness also takes on expanded meaning in light of the resurrection of Christ. Following His resurrection and enthronement in heaven, Christ sent the Holy Spirit to impart new life.

In 1 Corinthians 15:45,47 Christ is presented as the One who has the power to inbreathe man and give him new life. Paul explained that

Christ redeemed us from the curse of the law in order that the promise of Abraham might come to all people through the life-giving Spirit (Gen. 12:3; Gal. 3:8,13,14). The theme of Romans 3:9–6:23 is also that of forgiveness of sin through Jesus and the receiving of new life through the indwelling of the Holy Spirit.

Several New Testament passages deal with judgment, forgiveness, and new life. For instance, in 2 Corinthians 5:9–6:4 Paul discusses the coming judgment of God, Christ's death for man's sins, the living and risen Christ, and the urgency of receiving Christ. He warned men to repent and to be reconciled to God through Christ. Paul repeatedly gave this message in Acts and in his Epistles, and it is Peter's basic message also (Acts 2:14-41; 3:12-26; 4:8-12; 10:24-46; 1 Peter 1:10-21).

As the step of Repentance was consummated in baptism by John and Jesus, so today everyone becoming a Christian should be encouraged to be baptized as a public declaration that God has cleansed the heart and given new life by the Spirit. It is a symbol of dying with Christ and of sharing in His resurrected life.

SUMMARY

The first step in the process of disciple building is *Repentance and Faith* — changing one's mind about one's past self-life of sin and turning to God for forgiveness and new life. The seriousness of sin, the future judgment, the forgiveness that God offers through Jesus Christ, and new life through the Holy Spirit all must be preached. These elementary teachings are summarized in Hebrews 6:1-2:

> Therefore leaving the elementary teaching about the Christ, let us press on to maturity [go on to the other six steps], not laying again a foundation [1] of repentance from dead works and of faith toward God [that is, faith leading to salvation through Christ's substitutionary death], [2] of instruction about washing, and laying on of hands [that is, the cleansing work of the Holy Spirit and the giving of gifts to serve Him], [3] and the resurrection of the dead [that is, new life through the power of the Holy Spirit who is imparted by the risen Christ], and [4] eternal judgment.[3]

THE RELATIONSHIP OF REPENTANCE TO OTHER STEPS OF GROWTH

There was a continuing emphasis on repentance throughout Jesus' ministry. His original group of disciples had repented during the time of John the Baptist's ministry or immediately following it. In the successive stages of disciple building, they helped Jesus preach the gospel in different areas and promote the step of repentance in other men. (See chapter 15 on Evangelism and Disciple Building.)

As a result of their evangelistic efforts, more people began to follow Jesus and became His disciples. These in turn also began to preach the gospel to others and call them to repentance. Thus, momentum grew in Jesus' movement as His disciples began to evangelize.

With each step of growth Jesus broadened the twelve disciples' understanding of the scope and meaning of repentance. He especially concentrated on this during the period of Ministry Training. When He healed the paralyzed man (Mark 2:1-12), He demonstrated His power to forgive sins and save sinners. He thereby reinforced His claims and the disciples' understanding.

HOW TO PROCLAIM REPENTANCE

But how should you proclaim repentance? John the Baptist spoke to people in personal conversations, in small groups (Luke 3:10-18), and in mass meetings. Jesus also talked with people both personally and in groups (John 4). Likewise, the apostle Paul said that he preached publicly and from house to house (Acts 20:20). Following these examples, the New Testament church proclaimed repentance both through personal encounter and by public proclamation.

If others are to turn back to God we must not only actively proclaim repentance, but we must also pray. Prayer is essential, for it is the Holy Spirit who convicts people of sin and convinces them to repent (John 16:7-11).

Although the New Testament does present repentance as being man's responsibility (as in Peter's message in Acts 2:37,38; 3:19), it also presents it as being from God. Paul said in 2 Timothy 2:24-26:

> And the Lord's servant must not quarrel; instead, he must be kind to everyone, able to teach, not resentful. Those who oppose him he must gently instruct, in the hope that *God will give* them a change of heart [repentance] leading them to a knowledge of the truth, and that they will come to their senses and escape from the trap of the devil, who has taken them captive to do his will. (italics mine)

If people are to repent, the Holy Spirit must draw them. Therefore, one should pray for the Holy Spirit to work in and through him as he witnesses. He should also pray that God will work in the lives of those to whom he witnesses, convicting them of their sin and bringing them to the point of repentance.

But we must not stop there. We should ask God to open doors for us to preach the gospel, for the ability to make the gospel clear, and for boldness to make it known (cf. 2 Cor. 5:20; 6:2; Eph. 6:18-20; 1 Thess. 1:5).

CONCLUSION

The step of Repentance and Faith is important to disciple building. Unless a person truly sees his sin and sees himself the way God does, he will want God only for what He can give him, instead of loving God for who He is. As he accepts and yields to God in Christ, he will be willing and desirous to go on to maturity. Therefore, we as Christians should proclaim the message as Paul did: "We implore you on Christ's behalf: Be reconciled to God. . . . I tell you, now is the time of God's favor" (2 Cor. 5:20; 6:2).

Notes

[1]Maccabees is an apocryphal book. Protestants do not consider it part of the canon.

[2]A. B. Bruce, *The Training of the Twelve* (New York: A. C. Armstrong and Son, 1906), pp. 1-10; Robert E. Coleman, *The Master Plan of Evangelism* (Westwood, N.J.: Revell, 1968), p. 21; et al.

[3]The New American Standard Bible (La Habra, Calif.: The Lockman Foundation, 1971).

5

Enlightenment and Guidance

During the period of Enlightenment Jesus drew a few men into a close relationship with Himself.

To become disciples, they first had to understand who their Leader was and how to follow Him. Jesus therefore began to reveal His identity to them. He taught them that He was the Son of God — that He had become a man in order to redeem men and that when His mission was completed, He would return to heaven to resume His position of power and glory. Later He would come back to earth to set up His eternal kingdom.

He taught them who He was in light of the Old Testament, explaining that He was the One who had been anticipated, the One who had come to fulfill and give meaning to the Old Testament revelation (Luke 24:27,44). He was the promised Messiah.

Jesus also demonstrated through His miracles that His claims were true, proven by the power He manifested. Miracles provided the evidence for His claims.

It was important for the disciples to understand at this time that Jesus was the Messiah. He would be leading them to maturity and equipping them to minister for the kingdom of God. Without complete confidence in Him, however, they would not have grown.

If He had not revealed that He was the Christ from the beginning, they would have placed more importance on performing works (natural man's tendency) than on worshiping Him. But as they understood that He was the Messiah, they could focus on Him as God and worship Him. Then the power to serve and to minister would come out of their personal relationship to Him.

It was also important that Jesus' disciples understand His deity because only as they knew who He was would they be able to tell others about Him. They, of course, did not then understand the full implications of His claims.

Modern disciples need to understand who Jesus Christ is. Far too often a new convert busily starts working for Christ before he grasps the significance of the Person of Christ and how to follow Him. In such cases, the new convert usually will not mature properly. He then fails in his zeal and does not complete his task.

First the disciple must be fully committed to his Leader. He must understand the greatness of Christ before attempting to testify on His behalf. Therefore, for a new convert to grow as a disciple, he must grow in his understanding and in his faith in Jesus.

Just as he has trusted Jesus Christ for forgiveness, turning from his old way of life to God, so he must trust Jesus for the power and guidance to live if he is to grow. Thus, it is important for a disciple to come to understand the deity and authority of Christ so that he may trust Him as the leader of his life on a daily basis.

ENLIGHTENMENT INVOLVES GATHERING ONLY A FEW
IN AN OBSCURE MINISTRY

The step of Enlightenment took four to six months, partly overlapping the step of Repentance. It began with Jesus' public disclosure — His baptism by John the Baptist. After His baptism He went into the wilderness for forty days while John continued to call people to repentance. The actual gathering of the disciples did not begin, therefore, until Jesus returned from the wilderness and John the Baptist began to direct disciples to Him. Even then, as Jesus began to draw the small group of men to Himself, He continued to call people to repentance (especially during His stay in Aenon). The period of Enlightenment ended with His move to Capernaum after His rejection at Nazareth.

At this time Jesus' aim was not to reach the masses but to focus on the small group of people who were to become His intimate disciples. This is evident from the geographical locations in which He operated. Only once — when He went to Jerusalem — did He go to a large metropolitan city. Otherwise, He stayed in the area of the wilderness around the Jordan River and in the smaller towns of Galilee (such as Cana and Nazareth).

Because He was trying to convince only a few men of His deity during this period, He did not perform numerous miracles in order to impress the masses. Those He did perform, though, were directed specifically towards revealing His identity to His intimate followers.

The question of whether or not Jesus was fully human never seems to have been raised by those who knew Him or who wrote about Him in the New Testament. The question asked was whether or not He was truly God incarnate. But by the time the apostle John wrote his first Epistle, His humanity may have been questioned (1 John 4:2; 2 John 7). We do know that a later Gnostic sect denied that the body of Jesus was real flesh and blood (cf. Hippolytus and Epiphanius). Jesus was recognized in the gospel records as having normal human qualities. He became tired, hungry, thirsty, angry, sorrowful, and the like. The apostles recognized that He was human — made of flesh and blood like other men (Romans 1:3; 8:3; 1 Timothy 3:16; Hebrews 2:14-18, et al.) — and they concentrated on presenting His deity.

EARLY TEACHING TO ENLIGHTEN THE DISCIPLES CONCERNING HIS DEITY

Many have taught that Jesus did not clearly claim to be the Messiah until later in His ministry. Some, for instance, point to the declaration of Peter in Matthew 16 as the first time His disciples really understood who He was.[1] While it was important that Peter and the disciples affirm the messiahship and deity of Jesus at that particular moment when influential opposition was denouncing and maligning Him, the disciples had long before understood Jesus' claims.

John the Baptist's witness. As early as the baptism by John, Jesus' identity was revealed. His baptism was a dramatic, public declaration of Christ's identity by God:

> At that moment heaven was opened, and he saw the Spirit of God descending on him like a dove. And a voice from heaven said, ''This is my Son, whom I love; with him I am well pleased'' (Matt. 3:16,17).

John the Baptist had taught the multitudes that Jesus' identity was disclosed by this event. He was the Messiah, for the Spirit had descended on Him (John 1:30-34). John had declared, ''I have seen and I testify that this is the Son of God.'' The early Christians also interpreted the baptism of Jesus to be a public declaration that He was the Messiah (cf. Heb. 5:5,6,10).

Jesus' witness to His first disciples. As evidenced in the record of His teachings and in the words of His earliest followers, Jesus taught that He was the Messiah (cf. John 1:35-51). The Jewish people expected the Messiah to be both a perfect human king from the lineage of David[2] and the very person of God who had come to rule His people.[3]

Andrew said to Simon Peter, "We have found the Messiah" (John 1:41). Andrew had formerly been one of John's disciples and had been directed to Jesus by John. He would have understood John's role in fulfilling the prophecy in Isaiah 40:1ff. This passage claimed that God Himself would come to take over the rule of His people and that someone would precede Him to prepare His way. Thus, Andrew recognized that John was the forerunner. He was preparing the way for the Messiah — that is, for this man Jesus.

Philip also declared to Nathanael that Jesus was the Messiah. He stated, "We have found the one Moses wrote about in the Law, and about whom the prophets also wrote, Jesus of Nazareth" (John 1:45). God had promised Moses in Deuteronomy that He would send a prophet to lead God's people — a prophet who would be like Moses[4] — and the people awaited such a prophet:

> I will raise up for them a prophet like you from among their brethren; and I will put my words in his mouth, and he shall speak to them all that I command him. And whoever will not *give heed to my words which he shall speak* in my name, I myself will require it of him (Deut. 18:18,19).

Therefore, when Philip approached Nathanael, he was apparently claiming that Jesus was the messianic Prophet of the order of Moses.

In disclosing to Nathanael that He was the Messiah, Jesus demonstrated His omniscience. He shocked Nathanael by declaring that He understood his basic nature (John 1:47). He also told Nathanael that He had seen him sitting under a fig tree before Philip had found him. Being impressed by this miracle, Nathanael responded by confirming the report that Jesus was the Son of God:

> "Rabbi, you are the son of God; you are the King of Israel." Jesus said, "You believe because I told you I saw you under the fig tree. You shall see greater things than that." He then added, "I tell you the truth, you shall all see heaven open, and the angels of God ascending and descending on the Son of Man" (John 1:49-51).

Jesus was referring to two Old Testament ideas. When the Lord appeared to Jacob in a vision as the glorious Lord in heaven, Jacob saw angels ascending and descending the stairs to heaven. This was the time Abraham's covenant was renewed with Jacob (Gen. 28:12,13). When He used the title "Son of Man," He was referring to one of Daniel's visions. In this vision a multitude of angels was attending the throne of God where one like the Son of Man was given the power to establish God's eternal kingdom (Dan. 7:10,13,14; cf.

Matt. 26:63,64). Thus, the name "Son of Man" is a messianic title, and Jesus used it to affirm Nathanael's declaration.[5]

A MIRACULOUS DEMONSTRATION OF HIS DEITY

Jesus, knowing that He was the Messiah,[6] told others who He was. If He had not known that He was the Messiah, He would not have demanded that men worship and follow Him. It was not enough for Jesus to make these claims; He had to give evidence of their truth. Thus, He began to demonstrate publicly the reality of those claims. He first did so at a wedding feast in Cana of Galilee, where He appeared publicly for the first time with a group of His followers. Here He changed water into wine. John explained the purpose of this miracle in John 2:11: "This, the first of his miraculous signs, Jesus performed in Cana of Galilee. He thus revealed his glory, and *His disciples put their faith in Him."* The meaning is clear: the disciples now accepted Jesus' claim as fact.

This wedding and the miracle Jesus performed here are symbols of great significance. As a bride commits herself to her husband, trusting him for the claims he makes and the promises he gives, so the disciples committed themselves to Jesus at this time. They were, in a sense, wedded to Him, and to celebrate their union with their leader, Jesus provided the wine that symbolized the joy of marriage.

From that point on, Jesus' relationship to His disciples was interpreted as being analogous to that of a bridegroom and his bride (Matt. 9:15; Mark 2:19; Luke 5:34; John 3:28-30; Eph. 5:25).

ADDITIONAL CLAIMS OF MESSIAHSHIP AND DEITY

The claim of the temple cleansing. John the Baptist's mission was to prepare the way for the Messiah (Mark 1:2,3). Malachi 3:1-5a specifically says that he would precede *the Lord,* the One who would cleanse the temple:

> "Behold, I am going to send My messenger, and he will clear the way before Me. And *the Lord,* whom you seek, will suddenly come to His temple; and the messenger of the covenant, in whom you delight, behold, he is coming," says the Lord of hosts. "But who can endure the day of His coming? And who can stand when He appears? For He is like a refiner's *fire* and like fullers' soap. And He will sit as a smelter and purifier of silver, and *He will purify the sons of Levi* and refine them like gold and silver, so that they may present to the Lord offerings in righteousness. Then the offering of Judah and Jerusalem will be pleasing to the Lord, as in the days of old and as in former years. Then I will draw near to you for judgment" (NASB).

When Jesus cleansed the temple during the Feast of the Passover

(John 2:13-25), He was publicly declaring Himself to be the Messiah.

John the Baptist said, "I baptize you with water for repentance. But after me will come one who is more powerful than I, whose sandals I am not fit to carry. He will baptize you with the Holy Spirit and *with fire*" (Matt. 3:11). John the Baptist was no doubt referring to this passage in Malachi. It states that the Lord will go to the temple and in anger purify the worship, bringing judgment on the priests who were responsible for the corruption of the worship.

John's claim to be the messenger who was preparing the way for the Lord had probably made the public conscious of this particular prophecy. When Jesus went into the temple and cleansed it, they understood that He was declaring Himself to be the Lord, the Messiah, the King of Israel, who had come to cleanse the worship of His people. Their awareness is indicated by the fact that they immediately demanded a sign to authenticate His messianic authority (John 2:18). But Jesus refused to give them any signs. Instead, He pointed to the future resurrection when He would truly transform the temple worship from fleshly pursuit to worship of God through the Spirit. And He claimed that if the temple were destroyed, He would raise it up again in three days (John 2:19-22). He was referring, of course, to His body.

This act had a twofold effect. First, it called the public's attention to Christ's messianic claim. Second, it offended the leaders of the people in Jerusalem (cf. John 2:17).

Claims to Nicodemus. Understanding the significance of this event, Nicodemus came to Jesus, inquiring how he could enter the kingdom of God. In the presence of His disciples, Jesus set forth His claims to be the Messiah more directly. He told Nicodemus that if he would believe in Him, he would be born of the Holy Spirit and he would gain new life in the kingdom of God (John 3:3-8). He called Himself both "the Son of Man," the One who had descended from heaven (John 3:12,13), and "the Son of God." As God's Son, He explained that the Father had sent Him into the world to give eternal life to those who believe in Him (John 3:15,16). Jesus even claimed that a person's belief in Him or rejection of Him would determine his judgment before God (John 3:17,18).

Immediately following these events in Jerusalem, John the Baptist confirmed Christ's messianic claims both to his own disciples and to the crowds. He clearly told them that Jesus was of heavenly origin, that He was the Christ, and that He had the supreme authority both to give life to people and to judge them:

> The one who comes from above is above all; the one who is from the earth belongs to the earth, and speaks as one from the earth. The one

who comes from heaven is above all. . . . The Father loves the Son and
has placed everything in his hands. Whoever puts his faith in the Son
has eternal life, but whoever rejects the Son will not see that life, for
God's wrath remains on him (John 3:31,35,36).

As a result of John's confirmation, the crowds left him and began to
follow Jesus.

The claim to the woman at the well. Leaving the Jordan area,
Jesus passed through Samaria on His way to Galilee. In Samaria He
met a woman at Jacob's well. Presumably Jesus recounted His
interview to His disciples, for John records it. Jesus told this woman
that He would give her the water of eternal life. Because He disclosed
His knowledge of her sins, she believed that He was a prophet. Then
she recalled that the future Messiah would also have great prophetic
powers, so Jesus revealed His identity to her, declaring, "I who
speak to you am he [the Messiah]" (John 4:13,14,16-18,25,26).

The claim of Jubilee fulfillment. From Samaria Jesus took His
disciples to Nazareth. As was their custom, they worshiped in the
synagogue on the Sabbath (Luke 4:16-30). On this occasion, Jesus
read from Isaiah 61:1,2a:

> The Spirit of the Lord God is upon me,
> Because the Lord has anointed me
> To bring good news to the afflicted;
> He has sent me to bind up the brokenhearted,
> To proclaim liberty to captives,
> And freedom to prisoners;
> To proclaim the favorable year of the Lord. . . .

When He had finished reading, He said, "Today this scripture is
fulfilled in your hearing" (Luke 4:21). In other words, He claimed to
be the One who was to fulfill the prophecy.

The Jews had a law requiring that the land lie fallow every
seventh year. This seventh year was called a Sabbath year. After
celebrating seven Sabbath years, the Jews would celebrate the year of
the Jubilee (the fiftieth year) as a Sabbath (Lev. 25:8-10). In this year
all slaves were set free, and any property that had been bought was
restored to its original owner. The year of Jubilee was a time of
liberation and rejoicing.

Isaiah pictures the final, great Jubilee as the time when God's
people will be released from all things that bind and restrict them. The
Book of Jubilees, written in the intertestamental period, reinforces
Isaiah's picture. It implies that God's ultimate reign will be a time of
jubilees. When Jesus stated that He had come in fulfillment of
Isaiah's prophecy, He was claiming to be the Messiah, the One who
would usher in God's eternal kingdom.

Second demonstration of messiahship. The number of people who followed Jesus had undoubtedly grown by the time He arrived in Nazareth. He left Nazareth where He had been unfavorably received and went back to Cana where He apparently had relatives. In this small village Jesus performed His second great miracle, demonstrating the reality of His claims to His new disciples.

A nobleman from Capernaum came to Jesus, pleading for Him to heal his sick child. Jesus said to him, "Your son will live." As the nobleman traveled home, his slave met him and told him that his son (in Capernaum) had been healed at the seventh hour (one o'clock) — the very hour in which Jesus (in Cana) had told him that his son lived. As a result of this miracle, both the nobleman and his household believed (John 4:46-54). John noted that this miracle was "the second sign" that Jesus performed after He had come to Galilee from Judea.

By this time a solid group of men were following Jesus. They understood that He was the Messiah. They were convinced of the truth of His claims by the supernatural evidence of His power to perform miracles.

SUMMARY REVIEW

A summary of the claims Jesus made about Himself is shown below. It gives a complete overview of His messianic ministry.

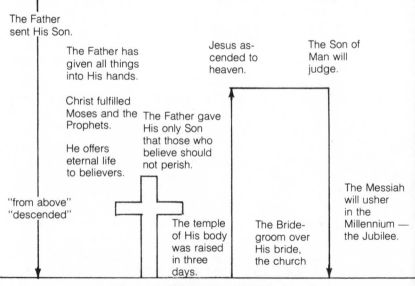

OVERVIEW OF CHRIST'S MESSIANIC MINISTRY

As the apostles looked back on Jesus' life, His teachings, and His ministry, they could more easily see the evidence of His messiahship. To communicate the evidence that He was eternal and supernatural, they taught the doctrines of His virgin birth, His incarnation, and His resurrection and they emphasized His credentials — the heavenly voices giving approval and the miracles He performed. They also taught believers to hope in His return in glory.

POST-RESURRECTION CHANGES IN THE STEP OF ENLIGHTENMENT

Continual forgiveness through Christ's sacrifice. After John the Baptist pointed some of his disciples to Jesus, calling Him the Lamb of God who takes away the sin of the world (John 1:29,36), Jesus began to draw these men (along with others) to Himself as disciples. Calling Jesus the Lamb of God meant to the Jew that Jesus Christ took the place of the Old Testament sacrifices that daily symbolized their being cleansed from their sins and trespasses, allowing them to continue in fellowship with God as His people. Doubtless, the first disciples did not grasp the significance of this until after the cross. Yet they accepted Jesus as God incarnate and followed Him daily without fear.

After His resurrection and ascension, when Jesus was no longer bodily present and could not be seen (1 Peter 1:8), Christians were faced with the question of whether the unseen Christ continued to accept them after they had sinned.

The Jews believed that through the blood of the Passover lamb God had delivered them from Egypt and made them His people. Later the sacrificial system of the temple was designed to assure the Jew daily of his continual acceptance by God. On the basis of the burnt offering (which preceded and followed all the offerings), the priests burned incense and interceded for the people daily, asking God to forgive their sin and cleanse them so they could continue in fellowship with Him.

Jesus Christ offered His own blood once for all on the cross, and no daily sacrifice for sin is now needed. But just as the *shekinah* light of God revealed to the priest the sin of the people, today the light of the Holy Spirit convicts God's child of wrong committed. As the disciple agrees with God, the blood of Christ cleanses his conscience from dead works so that he might serve the true God in Christ. And he is relieved of guilt and fear (cf. 1 John 1:1-10). As a modern disciple begins the Enlightenment phase, he must understand that Christ's death is adequate for his daily acceptance by God, so he can continue to follow Christ without fear (cf. also Romans 5:10; 6:10-13, et al.).

Following the leading of Christ through the Holy Spirit. Of supreme importance after the day of Pentecost was the teaching that Jesus had been raised from the dead, was enthroned at God's right hand, and had sent the Holy Spirit into the world to indwell, give guidance, and inward power to the Christians (Acts 2:30-36; Gal. 3:2,3,5,8,9,14; Eph. 1:13,14; 3:16; Rom. 8:3-17). Jesus had emphasized that following His ascent to the Father He would send the Holy Spirit to be with them. The Spirit would guide them into all truth.

Jesus enlightened His first disciples to believe in His deity so that they would follow Him *personally*. Today a vital part of Enlightenment is to show new disciples Jesus' power to lead and direct their lives *through His Holy Spirit*. Just as Christ directed His first disciples' lives while He was here in the flesh, the Holy Spirit now directs Christians while the exalted Christ reigns in heaven. Christ's divine guidance and power is just as much available today as it was during His earthly sojourn. This truth of the indwelling and filling power of the Holy Spirit is essential for this second step. The new convert must be taught how to be filled with and led by the Holy Spirit.

For many years the church did not adequately emphasize the importance of the Holy Spirit except as the Giver of the new birth — as the initiator of the new life. But it is only through the Holy Spirit's power and teaching that the Christian can discern Christ's leading through the Scriptures and in other ways today. The charismatic movement has forced the church to face this great doctrine the world around. So have other movements, such as Campus Crusade for Christ, but each in a different way. The presence of the Holy Spirit is the crowning evidence of the deity of Christ. He is the One who makes Christ's presence vitally known today.

Praying in Christ's Name for God to give credence to our claims about Christ. Christians today must trust God to answer prayer and do the miraculous in order to validate the deity of Jesus Christ. We can no more expect people to follow Jesus Christ today without some evidence of His power being manifest than Jesus could expect His first disciples to believe on Him had He not turned water to wine or healed the nobleman's son.

The New Testament records that the Holy Spirit gave *unique* divine confirmation to the apostles' preaching (Mark 16:20; Heb. 2:3,4).[7] While there is a difference between the apostolic ministry and the life of a Christian today, the Holy Spirit is still the One who must work in the disciple's life, disclosing the teachings of Christ to him and demonstrating Christ's power to change lives. In other words, the Holy Spirit must confirm our teaching. It is still the Holy

Spirit's mission to bear witness to the deity of Jesus Christ (1 Cor. 2:4-16; 1 Thess. 1:5).

Jesus seemed to indicate that anyone in subsequent generations could expect Him to work miracles (in answer to believing prayer) to convince others that His messianic claims were true. In John 14:12,13 Jesus said:

> Any one who has faith in me will do what I have been doing. He will do even greater things than these, because I am going to the Father. And I will do whatever you ask in my name, so that the Son may bring glory to the Father.

Anyone seeking to enlighten new disciples, teaching them who Jesus Christ is, can believe that God will do the supernatural in order to confirm Christ's deity.

Notes

[1]K. A. Hase (1829) first taught that Jesus was not recognized as the Messiah until Matthew 16 and he divided Jesus' life into two parts on this basis. He was followed by H. J. Holtzmann, T. Keim, and others, until Johannes Weiss.

[2]Ps. 89; Isa. 9:6,7; Jer. 23:5; 33:15-22; Amos 9:11,12; Mic. 5:2-5, et al.

[3]Pss. 82:1,8; 83:15-18; 94:1-3,13; 96; 97:3-6; 98; 99:1; 102:15-17; Isa. 33:10-24; 40:10; 43:15; 44:6; 49:7; 60:2,3,10,11,16; Jer. 10:7,10; Hos. 13:10; Zech. 14:9,16,17; Mal. 1:14, et al.; cf. noncanonical 1 Enoch 46:2; 48:2,3; 51:3; 62:1; 69:27; 105:2; [4]Ezra 7:28,29; 13:32-38,52; 14:9.

[4]The voice of God from heaven that was heard on the Mount of Transfiguration when Jesus appeared with Moses and Elijah seems to refer to this passage: "This is my Son whom I have chosen; listen to Him" (Luke 9:35).

[5]There was much effort to deny the messianic meaning of the phrase "Son of Man" by H. Lietzmann on linguistic and other grounds. G. Dalman showed this invalid. Anyone reading Daniel 7:13,14 and Matthew 26:64 and other uses by Jesus without a bias cannot doubt the identity of the two. When one also compares the references in 1 Enoch in note 3 of this chapter, he can see there is also extracanonical evidence to support this.

[6]Geerhardus Vos has pointed out the importance of Jesus' self-awareness in his book *The Self-Disclosure of Jesus* (Grand Rapids: Eerdmans, 1954): "Jesus' self-consciousness is the focal point in which all rays of religious contemplations of Jesus and communion with Jesus meet and whence they derive their reflection" (p. 14).

[7]The first apostles hold a unique place in the church, in that theirs is the only authoritative witness as to what Jesus did and taught. Their teaching is the basis of the Christian faith for all future believers. Through them the Holy Spirit performed signs and wonders that will not be repeated by other Christians (John 14:26; 15:27; 17:8,20; 2 Cor. 12:12).

6

Ministry Training and Appreciation of Benefits

During the months of Enlightenment, Jesus stayed in rural regions and confined His teachings to a few men. But as the period of Ministry Training began, he moved to Capernaum. Here He addressed the masses, attracting their attention through miracles.

Jesus had prepared for this shift in His ministry. Shortly before, while in Cana, He had miraculously healed the son of a nobleman from Capernaum (John 4:46-54). No doubt it was this nobleman who helped Jesus establish a residence in that city. Because of this miracle, the people of Capernaum were expectant. They hoped in Jesus as the Messiah. Their great sense of expectancy undoubtedly accounted for the great numbers who immediately began to flock to Him.

Throughout this period of His ministry, Jesus continued to perform miracles — perhaps as many as in any other period of His ministry. These continued to attract the attention and interest of the multitudes and gave Him many opportunities to teach and heal. If His ministry were to continue and to expand, Jesus needed assistance in dealing with the great crowds of people. Therefore, soon after launching His popular ministry, He began to challenge men to become involved in His ministry, saying, "Come, follow me . . . and I will make you fishers of men" (Matt. 4:19).

If certain disciples were to be involved in Christ's ministry and explain it to others, it was necessary for them to understand the benefits Jesus offered. At the same time, those who did not become

58235

involved in a full-time ministry but continued to follow and contribute in other ways also needed to appreciate the benefits.

The continued growth of the disciples required some form of ministry involvement. As the physical body requires eating and *exercise,* the new disciples who had been taking in spiritual food were beginning to need spiritual exercise in ministry. Good stewardship demands that a disciple share what he has learned. The Scriptures say, "From the one who has been entrusted with much, much more will be asked" (Luke 12:48). Elsewhere, Jesus indicated that if one were faithful in a little, he would receive a much greater reward and greater responsibility (Matt. 25:21,23; Luke 19:17). God expects people to invest wisely what He has given them, including knowledge and understanding.

INVOLVEMENT

The step of Ministry Training is critical to the expansion of the movement. At this point most organizations and local churches reach their peak. If they do not train believers other than the pastor to evangelize and build disciples, their expansion stops. Their maximum potential is reached without a continuing growth and a broadening impact. True multiplication occurs only when disciples are trained in evangelism and disciple building. No matter how dynamic the pastor, no matter how financially stable and well organized the church, expansion will not continue if people are not trained to minister.

This principle of ministry is recognized by the communists as crucial to their development and growth. Douglas Hyde, in his book *Dedication and Leadership,* emphasizes the importance of this particular step for personal growth in communism. He points out that after a person commits himself to the communist ideology, he must become publicly involved in promoting the communist movement. Even though he may have a Ph.D. degree or be a great dignitary, he is required to promote his new beliefs actively and publicly. He may simply stand on the corner to sell *The Daily Worker,* but this act of involvement gives him a sense of vision and a sense of being important to the movement. In so training its members, the Communist party is actually borrowing a principle from Christianity. Jesus practiced this principle of involvement in His own ministry during the period of Ministry Training.

DIFFICULTIES IN MINISTRY TRAINING

Scripture, reason, and experience indicate five reasons why training a disciple to minister is difficult. The first group of disciples is especially hard to train, but after they have begun to have a ministry of their own, it is easier to train others.

1. The disciple will be *tempted to fear people* because he knows the world is hostile to the things of God. The natural man follows the prince of the power of the air and lives according to the desires of the flesh — not according to the will of God (Eph. 2:1ff.). The Bible teaches that "the sinful mind is hostile to God. It does not submit to God's law, nor can it do so" (Rom. 8:7). When a Christian begins to minister for Jesus Christ publicly, he is intuitively aware of the world's antagonism to his ministry. He is committing himself to basic objectives and desires that are in opposition to those of the world system. As a result, the fear of men may cause a disciple to hesitate beginning a public ministry for Christ. Peter, James, and John had to deal with this, as do we.

All people want to be accepted by others. Young people in high school and college especially rely on the approval of their peer group. Satan uses the pressure of friends, family, and other influential people to keep a disciple from becoming involved in a public ministry. Almost inevitably a Christian is labeled a fanatic when he begins to share his faith, talking to others about Christ and seeking to teach others the Christian faith. People think that he takes his religion too seriously. Because some fear disapproval, they do not easily respond to the challenge of learning how to evangelize and build disciples for Christ. This fear of men is a great hindrance to Ministry Training.

The Bible continually emphasizes that the godly should not fear men. Isaiah 51:7b says, "Fear not the reproach of men. . . ." Jeremiah also commented on the problem of the fear of men:

> Cursed is the man who trusts in mankind
> And makes flesh his strength,
> And whose heart turns away from the Lord. . . .
> Blessed is the man who trusts in the Lord
> And whose trust is the Lord.

As Jesus later sent His disciples out to minister, He spoke directly about this kind of fear:

> So do not be afraid of them. There is nothing concealed that will not be disclosed, or hidden that will not be made known. . . . Do not be afraid of those who kill the body but cannot kill the soul. Rather, be afraid of the one who can destroy both soul and body in hell (Matt. 10:26, 28).

2. *People resist change.* Jesus said, "No one after drinking old wine wants the new, for he says, 'The old is better' " (Luke 5:39). Most people become comfortable with their lives and have no desire

to adjust to changes. Also, change may imply failure. In such cases, pride becomes involved.

To take a public stand of ministering in the name of Jesus Christ involves a tremendous change in a disciple's relationship to the world and to others. Human nature tends to resist this.

3. *Inertia and laziness* are also factors that inhibit training for a ministry. Most people want to be spectators and not participants. As at a football game where thousands of fans desperately in need of exercise sit in the stands, while twenty-two men desperately in need of rest play on the field, so it is with the church. The body of Christ needs participants, not spectators.

During the period of Ministry Training, Jesus drew a group of men from among His followers and challenged them to become involved in the "game" itself. As He tried to motivate them to become active participants, He dealt with their laziness and inertia. When they were in Samaria, He challenged them with an important task — the evangelization of the world:

> Do you not say, "Four months more and then the harvest"? I tell you, open your eyes and look at the fields! They are ripe for harvest (John 4:35).

4. *Ignorance* is another obstacle to Ministry Training. The first disciples did not know how to minister. They were fishermen and tax collectors — untrained laymen. But Jesus promised them, "Come, follow me . . . and *I will make you* fishers of men" (Matt. 4:19).

Today we often challenge believers (sometimes even scold them) to accept the responsibilities of a ministry before they are ready. So often we do not even show them how to minister. Jesus did not make this mistake. He dealt with the ignorance of His followers. He recognized their need to be taught and promised to help them develop.

5. The disciples also had *conflicting priorities*. Each had committed himself to a specific vocation. Peter, James, and John were fishermen. Matthew was a tax collector, and the other disciples followed various vocations. They had developed professional skills, and these were the sources of their incomes.

Jesus motivated His men to place higher priority on having a ministry than on earning money or being successful in their vocations. The Gospels record that the fishermen left their nets and the others left their vocations to follow Him (Matt. 4:18-22; 9:9; Mark 1:17-20; 2:14; Luke 5:10,11,27,28; John 1:43-51).

HELPING PEOPLE OVERCOME THE DIFFICULTIES OF HAVING A MINISTRY

Under the Father's direction, Jesus encouraged His disciples to overcome obstacles that might have kept them from having a ministry. He challenged them to become involved in *the most important undertaking of all time*.

Jesus announced that *the kingdom of heaven* was near (Matt. 4:17). Throughout the centuries men had anticipated the coming of God's kingdom with great hope and excitement. Now, as He challenged men to become involved in His ministry, He told them that He was the One who would establish this kingdom. He charged them to become involved in something big, something important, something enduring.

Jesus emphasized the *urgency* of the task in which He was engaged. He said that the time was fulfilled, the kingdom of God was *near*. History had reached a climax, and the establishment of the kingdom was imminent. By pressing the urgent, He was able to get His disciples involved immediately.

Jesus impressed His disciples with the fact that *His work was more important* than their vocations. He made His supremacy known to them by demonstrating His greatness. He even showed them that He knew more about their jobs than they did. Through a miracle He humbled the fishermen in the area of their highest priority. After they had fished unsuccessfully all night, He directed them to a place where they were able to catch many fish. In fact, the catch was so huge that the nets of two boats almost broke with the weight of the fish. Luke recorded Peter's reaction and Jesus' response to him:

> When Simon Peter saw this, he fell at Jesus' knees and said, "Go away from me, Lord; I am a sinful man!" . . . Then Jesus said to Simon, "Don't be afraid; from now on you will catch men" (Luke 5:8,10).

In essence, Jesus had shown them that He could direct them into a much more important ministry, for men are far more important than fish.

Appealing to natural affinities, Jesus could better encourage these men to become involved in His ministry. A person is more prone to accept the challenge of trying something new if he can do it with someone he knows intimately. So Jesus called these men in groups of twos and threes: Peter and Andrew, James and John. He called a friend with a friend and a brother with brother. Ecclesiastes 4:9,10 points out the advantage of two working together over one working alone: two can sustain each other. By calling men to work together with those they knew and liked, Jesus appealed to their natural affinity.

When engaging the first group of men in the ministry, Jesus *chose* a *place* where there would be a *good response* and the *least resistance.* Jerusalem, Judea, or Samaria would have been difficult places, so He began His public ministry in Galilee of the Gentiles, a land that had long been in darkness (Isaiah 9:1-7). He went specifically to Capernaum, a city that was prepared to receive Him because He had previously healed a boy (the nobleman's son) from that city. He had an advantage there, for the influential people of the community and government were likely to be favorably disposed to His ministry. It was an opportune place to launch His public ministry and call His men to help Him.

Jesus also encouraged His disciples by *personally teaching and showing them how* to have a ministry. He did not send them out in their ignorant state.

D. James Kennedy has been very successful in training laymen to witness. In his book *The Evangelism Explosion,* he says:

> Finally it struck me like a bolt of lightning. I had taken classes for three years and had not learned how to witness. It was not until someone who knew how had taken me out into people's houses that I finally got the confidence to do it myself. Thus, I began the program in my church which has continued for the past eight years. It began by taking out one individual until he had confidence to witness to others, and then another and then another.[1]

By taking individuals with him to witness, Dr. Kennedy simply followed the pattern Jesus Himself had established with His own disciples.

During the period of Ministry Training, Jesus performed many miracles. Through these He demonstrated His power to the multitudes and persuaded His disciples that His *power was adequate* for the job.

Jesus gave His disciples *an example* to follow. He constructed an effective model of His work, demonstrating both how to draw men to Himself and how to carry out various aspects of the ministry.

Jesus earnestly prayed for His disciples, rising long before daybreak to pray alone, apparently doing so every morning (Mark 1:35, Luke 4:42; cf. John 17:6-19). As a result, the Spirit of God moved in their hearts. They boldly followed Him, and He trained them to minister with Him. By His example Jesus impressed upon them that the power to minister comes only through the power of the Holy Spirit and not from the flesh.

TRAINING MEN TO MINISTER

During this period Jesus also trained His men in ministry skills. He trained them in *personal evangelism,* showing them how to share the truth of God with individuals (Mark 2:14 et al.). They had seen

Him deal with Nicodemus in Jerusalem (John 3:1ff.), and He undoubtedly had recounted His witnessing experience with the Samaritan woman to them (John 4:1ff.). During this period they were fishing for men by dealing with individuals in this way.

As He drew the crowds to Himself, Jesus also demonstrated the "how to's" of *mass evangelism* — how to attract the crowds, how to handle them, and how to teach them. He even showed them how to deal creatively with the problem of obtaining a good vantage point from which to preach. Once He had stood in a boat to preach while people gathered along the shore to listen.

At this time Jesus began to hold *small-group evangelistic meetings*. Frequently, new converts invited their friends to supper so that He might talk to them, thereby establishing a precedent (cf. Matt. 9:9,10; 11:19; Luke 5:27-29; 19:5-7).

When taking His disciples on evangelistic tours of the rural areas, Jesus communicated many principles of missionary expansion. He set an important example by leaving the big crowds in Capernaum and moving on to the villages and other cities of Galilee, even though there was still a demand for His ministry in Capernaum (cf. Matt. 10:1ff.; Mark 1:35-39; Luke 4:42, 43; 10:1ff.; Acts 1:8; Rom. 15:20-24).

A NEW COVENANT

During this time of training, the tone and meaning of Jesus' message changed. He no longer talked about the old legal requirements of Moses and the prophets but proclaimed a new covenant. Jesus said, "The Law and the Prophets were proclaimed until John. Since that time, the good news of the kingdom of God is being preached" (Luke 16:16). (Cf. pp. 234-243 for a comparison of the old and new covenants.)

At the time that Jesus began His popular ministry and began to train men to help Him, John the Baptist was imprisoned by Herod. Many of John's followers then followed Jesus. This event marked the shift in emphasis from the old to the new covenant (Matt. 4:12-17; Mark 1:14,15).

The providential removal of John turned the full attention of the multitudes to Jesus. As the crowds grew, He used this opportunity to train His disciples to win and teach others.

TEACHINGS NECESSARY FOR THE MINISTRY

As Christ trained His disciples to witness, it was necessary for Him to teach that God was establishing a new covenant through Him. He also demonstrated His power over disease and demons, His authority to forgive sin, and His authority over the Sabbath (Christian liberty). These teachings, demonstrations of power, and demonstrations of authority provided meaning and evidence to support the gospel that the Twelve began to share. They helped all the disciples to appreciate and understand the wonderful blessings Christ came to give.

REDEMPTION DEMONSTRATED

Power over physical disease. Jesus taught His disciples that He had authority to deliver men from infirmities and diseases caused by Satan and sin. He healed Peter's mother-in-law of fever (Matt. 8:14,15) and He exorcised demons (Matt. 8:16,17; Mark 1:21-28,32-34; Luke 4:31-37,40,41).

The Jew understood sickness and death to be the result of sin in general, which had begun through the satanic deception of Adam and Eve (Gen. 3:1ff.). Jesus clearly taught and demonstrated that He had come to remove these physical infirmities and the diseases that produced death, fulfilling what was spoken by the prophet Isaiah (Isa. 53:4), "Surely he has borne our griefs [lit., sicknesses] and carried our sorrows [lit., pains]" (cf. Matt. 8:17).

After Jesus' resurrection there is a shift in emphasis. The New Testament perspective includes the idea of complete healing through the bodily resurrection of believers (cf. Rom. 8:23; 1 Cor. 15:4-58) and these healings of specific illnesses pointed toward that. But at that stage of Jesus' ministry, healing miracles were important so that people would understand that the physical consequences of sin were overcome under the power and authority of Jesus Christ.

As a result of His message and miracles, Jesus' fame spread throughout all Syria (Matt. 4:24). Mark and Luke also called attention to His growing fame: "Jesus could no longer enter a town openly, but stayed outside in lonely places. Yet the people still came to Him from everywhere" (Mark 1:45; cf. Luke 5:15).

Power to forgive sin. Jesus emphasized that He not only had the power to heal people of their diseases but that He also had the authority to forgive sin. Before a crowd that included many Pharisees and teachers of the Law, Jesus healed a paralytic by offering him forgiveness of sin. This miracle, He claimed, would demonstrate that He had the authority to forgive (Matt. 9:2-8; Mark 2:3-12; Luke 5:18-26).

Jesus not only demonstrated His power to forgive sin, but He also publicly demonstrated his love for sinners. He called Matthew (Levi), a tax collector, to join Him as a disciple. Because Matthew collected taxes from his own people both for the Roman government and for his own profit, he was scorned as a sinner. Thus, when Jesus dined at Matthew's home with some of his old friends, teachers of the law and the Pharisees reacted. They did not approve of His open association with sinners and his concern for them. But Jesus told them that His purpose was to call sinners to repentance (Matt. 9:9-13; Mark 2:14-17; Luke 5:27-32).

Through these two events Jesus communicated to His disciples that He had the authority to forgive sinners and that His mission was to call sinners to Himself.

After Jesus' death and resurrection, the apostles explained the basis of Jesus' power to forgive sins as being His substitutionary death on the cross. They explained that this forgiveness was received by grace through faith alone and not from any merit of the sinner. Justification of the sinner by God's grace through faith became the central message of the apostolic church (cf. Rom. 3:21–5:21; Gal. 2:15–3:14; 1 Peter 1:18-21; 3:18; et al.). They also continued to point to the miraculous working of the Holy Spirit as the evidence of Christ's forgiving power (Acts 2:16-21,38; 3:16,19).

Freedom from legalism. Jesus taught that through a personal relationship with Himself a person could be freed from the bondage of legalism and could experience liberty as a child of God. John the Baptist and his disciples had come with a tone of severity, but Jesus had come eating and drinking and demonstrating liberty and joy in God (Luke 7:31-35). Jesus' ministry was an example of the joy of the Lord as opposed to the somberness of John the Baptist's ministry and the legalism of the Pharisees (Matt. 9:14,15; Mark 2:18-20; Luke 5:33-35). Just as new wine should be put in new wineskins and a new patch should be put on new cloth, so should the new message which Jesus brought be put in a new form (Matt. 9:16,17; Mark 2:21,22; Luke 5:36-38).

The subsequent events in Jesus' life were filled with the turbulent hostility of those who were clinging to the old and unwilling to accept the new. Jesus focused His attack against the old legalism on the laws concerning the Sabbath day. In Palestine if a person kept the Sabbath outwardly, he was considered a good Jew. But Jesus went to the heart of the matter. He showed that resting *in God* was the true meaning of the Sabbath and that God made the Sabbath for man's benefit.

This principle was first demonstrated by the healing of a paralytic at the pool of Bethesda. Following this healing, Jesus claimed as the Son of God to have authority to judge all men, living and dead (John 5:2-30). In other words, people were responsible to Him for their actions. He is "Lord of the Sabbath." Jesus caused agitation among the Jews by two other acts done on the Sabbath. The second concerned the threshing of wheat (Matt. 12:1-8; Mark 2:23-28; Luke 6:1-5), and the third the healing of a man with a withered hand (Matt. 12:9-14; Mark 3:1-6; Luke 6:6-11).

Jesus condemned the Jews for putting legal practice over human compassion. He pointed out that even they would pull a sheep out of a pit if he fell into it on the Sabbath. How much greater was the need to minister to human beings! In this context He emphasized God's desire for mercy and not sacrifice. Jesus was stressing that commitment to a sacrificial, ceremonial ritual could in no way make up for a heart of love and concern for others. He wanted people to understand that God is merciful. God wants His children to come to Him, accepting His love and His forgiveness and not trying to keep the letter of the Law to please religious men.

The removal of legal restrictions opened Jesus' ministry to the Gentiles. His fame spread to Syria, to the Decapolis (the ten Gentile cities), and to Tyre and Sidon. A great number of foreigners came to listen to Him, fulfilling the prophecy of Isaiah 42:1-4 (Matt. 12:15-21). Isaiah promised that Christ would proclaim justice to the nations, quietly and gently bringing right to firm existence and giving hope to the Gentiles.[2] Thus, the disciples learned to avoid a crass legalism and to obey Jesus and God the Father instead. This teaching of Christ prepared the way for His new moral righteousness that would involve *heart obedience* to God's law. This teaching Christ gives in the next step in the Sermon on the Mount.

After the resurrection the conflict over the Jewish legal code became an even sharper issue. Paul had to deal with a similar legalism. He ministered in areas outside of Palestine where the test of a true Jew was considered to be circumcision. But Paul clearly expressed that the important issue was the circumcision of the heart (Rom. 2:28,29; Gal. 5:6,11; 6:15; Phil. 3:3; Col. 2:11, et al.). He was merely applying the principle that Jesus Christ had taught during this time of Ministry Training — those who followed Him and became children of God were no longer under rabbinical Law but were free to follow God's leading as expressed through Christ so that they kept the law in their heart (Rom. 8:4).

Paul expounded more fully on the freedom from the Law that Christ's followers have as sons of God (cf. Rom. 7; Gal. 5, et al.). He explained that through the indwelling of the Holy Spirit believers are brought into a personal relationship with Christ and the Father, and the Spirit writes God's laws on their hearts (cf. Rom. 8:3,4; Heb. 8:8-13; 10:16,17).

CONCLUSION

If lay ministers are not appointed for a rapidly growing Christian work, its growth will soon dwindle. Failure to select and train lay men and women to minister will dam up the life stream at its source so no leadership will develop. In order for the ministry to expand, disciples must break through the obstacles that hinder a person from publicly propagating the Christian faith. This is one step farther in a deeper commitment to their leader Jesus Christ and involvement in His kingdom.

In leading disciples to have a ministry, one must overcome five major obstacles: (1) the disciple's temptation to fear men; (2) resistance to change; (3) laziness and the problem of inertia; (4) ignorance (people need to be taught how to share their faith and how to perform specific tasks peculiar to the ministry); (5) conflicting priorities (a person's highest priorities must be Christ and the kingdom of God).

Those learning to have a ministry today must be taught the same truths Jesus taught His disciples. Although a person has experienced personal salvation and the resurrection power of Christ, he must have these truths explained again from the point of view of equipping him to teach them to others. He must understand that Jesus' death and resurrection were sufficient to save man from the physical consequences of sin, that is, sickness and death. Christ's death is the basis for the removal of man's guilt and the pouring out of God's love to the sinner. Jesus also died in order to free man from the bondage of man-made requirements for salvation and holiness and to give him the freedom that exists in God. During this step of Ministry Training, a disciple begins to understand in his head what God has done in his heart and he is better able to teach the truths of God to others.

Notes

[1]D. James Kennedy, *The Evangelism Explosion* (Wheaton: Tyndale, 1970), p. 94.

[2]Franz Delitzsch, *Commentary on the Prophecies of Isaiah* (Grand Rapids: Eerdmans, 1950) 2:174-176 as it relates to Matthew 12:18-21.

7

Leadership Development and

Government Under God

When Jesus initiated His appeal to the masses in Galilee (at the beginning of the third step of Ministry Training), He created an expectation that He would *institute His kingdom soon.* He preached, "The time has come. . . . The *kingdom of God is near.* Repent and believe the good news" (Mark 1:15). For several months following, there was no action indicating He was beginning His reign.

But at the end of that period He had a definite break with Judaism. The leaders of the Pharisees held a council and determined to destroy Him because He claimed that He, like God, had the power to forgive sin and that He was the Lord of the Sabbath and giver of the law who would judge all men. This led to His withdrawal from Capernaum and to His beginning to organize His kingdom (Matt. 12:14,15; Mark 3:6,7,13; Luke 6:11,12).[1]

In the Old Testament after Joshua had made the initial conquest of the land of Canaan, he led the people to a plain between the Mountains of Ebal and Gerizim. There he instituted the kingdom of Israel as Moses had instructed him to do (Deut. 11:26-29; Josh. 8:30-35). He placed the twelve patriarchal leaders in the midst and the people on both sides on the two mountains. He then pronounced the blessings and the curses that would come from obeying or disobeying the laws of God their King.

After withdrawing from Capernaum, Jesus went up into the mountains nearby and proceeded to copy the scene at Gerizim and

Ebal, showing He was organizing His kingdom. After a night of prayer He came down and stood on a plain between the mountains where He chose twelve leaders and then pronounced the blessings and the woes. Thus He taught them the way they were to conduct themselves under His rule as their King. He soon after demonstrated His kingly power by miracles and claimed to demonstrate that the kingdom of God had come (Matt. 12:28).

This organization of His kingdom involved two things for His disciples. He began to develop them as leaders and to teach all His followers the kind of conduct of life He expected His subjects to have under His government. Thus, the next step for a select few was to learn how to be leaders, and for all, to learn the nature of the kingdom of God and their responsibilities as subjects.

IMPORTANCE OF LEADERSHIP

Whether or not the goals of a movement are achieved depends primarily on adequate and effective leadership. Up to this point in His work Jesus alone had furnished the necessary leadership for His movement. But the movement had grown so large and the opposition had increased so significantly that other leadership was needed. So Jesus' next step was to choose, appoint, and begin to train men to help Him.

God has always considered the focal point of responsibility to rest on the leaders of His people. When the people of God prospered and honored His name, they always had leaders who were strong, wise, and committed — men such as Abraham, Moses, and David. When sin dominated and the nation departed from God, the prophets were always sent to rebuke hireling shepherds who had led the people astray (Isa. 56:11; Jer. 25:34,35; 50:6; Ezek. 34; John 10).

At this point in His ministry, Jesus was seeking men to train to stand with Him and work with Him against the satanic world powers. J. Oswald Sanders has said,

> The overriding need of the church, if it is to discharge its obligation to the rising generation, is for a leadership that is authoritative, spiritual and sacrificial. . . . The Church has always prospered most when it has been blessed with strong and spiritual leaders who expected and experienced the touch of the supernatural in their service. The lack of such men is a symptom of the malaise that has gripped it.[2]

Part of the reason for the lack of spiritual leaders today is that many people have the idea that such leaders are produced only by a mysterious anointing of the Holy Spirit. The anointing by the Holy Spirit is, of course, indispensable and central to good leadership. But ordinarily God has chosen to anoint men like David who already was "a man after God's own heart" who would do his will (1 Sam. 13:14; Acts 13:22). David was a man who loved and studied God's law so he could please Him. Jesus chose men who were dedicated and would follow Him obediently. These He set apart through the Word of God that He taught them (John 17:17). Men are developed into leaders when they are willing to be led and taught by Christ.

CONDITIONS AT THE TIME THE KINGDOM WAS INSTITUTED

By midsummer of A.D. 28 Jesus' popularity had grown. Great crowds came to hear Him at Capernaum. Then He traveled to the cities and villages of Galilee, spreading His fame to greater distances. When He returned to Capernaum He began to center His ministry there, and people came from everywhere to hear Him. Samuel J. Andrews wrote:

> The fame of Jesus seems at this time to have reached every part of the land. Crowds came, not only from Galilee and Judea, but also from Idumea and from beyond Jordan and from the territories of Tyre and Sidon. That so great numbers and from such remote regions should gather at Capernaum shows that he remained at that city for some time after His return from His first circuit.[3]

Jesus envisioned reaching other cities (Mark 1:38), yet He had a large number of people to minister to already, and the men He had trained helped spread His fame.

After Jewish religious leaders had begun plotting to destroy Him, Jesus withdrew from Capernaum and public places (even avoiding Jerusalem). He began to minister by the sea, in the hills, in small towns, and in foreign communities. He returned to Capernaum intermittently but never stayed long. During the following months He sought to keep His miracle-working a secret, frequently ordering people not to make Him known. His ministry continued in this manner for the next two steps — Leadership Development and Reevaluation (Matt. 12:15,16; Mark 3:7,12). The crystallization of opposition must have unsettled many of His followers and presented a need for additional strong leadership and supervision.

The need to organize was evident. Jesus proceeded to meet the needs after a full night of prayer. He now chose and appointed official leaders — men who would constitute the backbone of that kingdom organization. And He focused intently on training those men.

THE STRATEGIC APPROACH OF FOCUSING ON TRAINING LEADERSHIP

Robert Coleman wrote of Jesus' strategic approach:

> When his [Jesus'] plan is reflected upon, the basic philosophy is so different from that of the modern church that its implications are

nothing less than revolutionary. . . . His concern was not with programs to reach the multitudes but with men whom the multitudes would follow. . . . Men were to be His method of winning the world to God. The initial objective of Jesus' plan was to enlist men who could bear witness to His life and carry on His work after He returned to the Father.[4]

Everett Harrison has expressed a similar idea:

At the end of His public ministry Jesus had nothing tangible to leave as a monument of His life work. . . . He had chosen instead to invest himself in a small group of men. . . . Looking back from the vantage point of the apostolic age, it is not difficult to see that the most important work of Christ prior to his death and resurrection was the selection and training of the men who would represent him in the world in the coming days. . . . These disciples were the product of the Lord. They bore His stamp. His summons to them emphasized not only their potential fitness for the task but His own creative activity.[5]

Coleman and Harrison do not mean to overstate the importance of Jesus' concentration on the training of a few leaders. One must be careful to maintain a proper perspective. Jesus did not forsake all other activities to focus on the Twelve. He *continued to proclaim the good news* of His kingdom *to the multitudes* and to invite people to follow Him. He also *broadened His association* with the people who listened to His teaching. From this wider following He later selected the Seventy. However, the selection of the Twelve was undoubtedly the most significant step He had taken thus far. The appointment of the Twelve had long-range effects on the functioning of the early church that were not fully visible at this stage of growth.

THE LOGIC OF LEADERSHIP TRAINING AS THE FOURTH STEP

Appointing and training men for official leadership (Step 4) is a logical consequence of training them to have a ministry (Step 3). In order for His ministry to continue to expand, Jesus had to have men to whom He could give responsibility. Otherwise, the existing ministry would have begun to lose impetus instead of continuing to build momentum. Such is the case with any growing ministry. New leadership must be appointed when the need arises.

Not all who were called to be fishers of men were appointed to be among the Twelve. There were probably many people who helped in the ministry of evangelism and teaching, but only a few of these were appointed as official leaders (Acts 1:21,22).

Previously, Jesus alone had been responsible for the ministry, but now its success or failure would also devolve upon these twelve men. They too would be criticized for the new ministry, but they would also share the credit for its success. In assuming such a position of leadership, they would be accepting an awesome responsibility (as does any modern disciple who assumes a leadership role in a Christian organization). Their stand before the world as Jesus Christ's representatives would put them in a threatening position that required faith in their leader.

The appropriate time to initiate leaders. The appropriate time had arrived to select and appoint some men as leaders, and Jesus proceeded to do so. Unless the step of Leadership Development is made at the right time, disciples will not continue to grow, and the movement will begin to falter.

For many years I was involved in a Christian youth movement. I worked with one director who had a group of young men who were eager to learn about God. They shared their faith and grew in the Lord. But this director enjoyed being the leader, and he failed to give these men responsibility. Soon their interest began to wane. By the time he did try to develop their leadership potential, they did not respond to the challenge of leadership. Their ardor had cooled.

On another occasion a director was so eager for his ministry to grow that he appointed leaders far too soon. The young men were not ready to assume the responsibility. They had not learned to trust him as their leader, nor had they learned how to minister. Timing is important when leaders are being appointed. We must look to the Holy Spirit to guide us in this area.

THE CHOOSING OF TWELVE MEN AS LEADERS

Reasons for selection. The Twelve were not randomly or carelessly selected from the general multitude. They were men who had been intimately associated with Jesus and who had responded to His teaching, had followed His leadership, and had been trained by Him. Yet it was the Father who led Jesus in His choice of men. Luke tells us that Jesus spent the entire night in prayer seeking the Father's will before choosing the Twelve the next day: "When morning came, he called his disciples to him and chose twelve of them" (Luke 6:12-16; cf. Matthew 5:1; 10:2-4; Mark 3:13-19). He felt that He could do nothing of Himself unless it was something He saw the Father doing (John 5:19). Later in His ministry Jesus communicated to His disciples that they had been selected entirely by His choice under God's leading. He said, "You did not choose Me, but I chose you" (John 15:16).

The disciples were men who through long association understood Christ intimately. They knew how to carry on His ministry. At the end of His ministry He said to them, "You also must testify, *for you have been with me from the beginning''* (John 15:27). The requirement of long acquaintance is emphasized in Acts 1:21,22, when the early apostles decided to replace Judas. They chose a man who had been associated with Jesus from the time of His baptism until His ascension and one who had been chosen to follow Him and become a fisher of men.

These twelve were men who had the qualities of a good leader. They had a hunger for the truth of God. Their motives were pure, and they were humble. They were responsible people who had stuck with Jesus and had done what He had asked them to do. They were persistent in their participation in His work and no doubt they were fruitful in winning men through their witness. In a certain sense, the attributes expressed in the Beatitudes were characteristic of these men. Christ's purposes for appointing the Twelve are summarized in Mark 3:14,15: "He appointed twelve . . . that they might be with him and that he might send them out to preach and to have authority to drive out demons."

Why the choice of twelve men? Jesus specifically selected twelve men because the number twelve symbolizes the patriarchs — the leaders of the twelve families or tribes of Israel. Later He promised the Twelve they would sit on twelve thrones, judging the twelve tribes of Israel. Thus, the Twelve *symbolized* the *total leadership* of the people of God.

The Twelve also symbolized the twelve *fathers* of the original families of Israel. The leaders of Israel's tribes were the fathers of those families. Paul viewed the relationship between leadership in the home and leadership of the church in terms of his traditional Hebraic training; he saw leadership of the family as basic to the leadership of the church (1 Tim. 3:4,5). Every male needs to be trained to lead his family, and wives need to be trained to lead and teach both their children and other women (Titus 2:3-5).

Perhaps the greatest cause of failure in American churches is the failure of men to be true spiritual leaders in their homes. Jesus said that a great Christian leader is not one who lords it over his followers but one who seeks to be a servant (Mark 10:42). The husband and father should lead by demonstrating the sacrificial spirit of Christ who loved the church and gave Himself for it (Eph. 5:25). Many Christian men leave the spiritual teaching, the discipline of children, and financial and other decisions to their wives. They are not furnishing the moral backbone to the home. Neither are they in touch with the needs and desires of their wives and children. The church needs to develop home leadership.

Several years ago, as national director of a large youth ministry,

I became concerned about young people who had accepted Christ returning to broken or troubled homes. I began a seminar training program for parents called Family Enrichment Institutes. It was held in a number of cities across the nation. Many husbands and wives caught a vision of the ideal Christian home and had the joy of straightening out many problems in their lives. Unfortunately, many of these couples drifted back into their old way of life and the same problems recurred. They needed more than a seminar to give them the ideals of a Christian family. They needed to be discipled and built into mature Christians who could live up to these ideals. The father especially needed to be trained to lead and build the rest of his family into mature people. When Christian ideals are taught to families that have not developed the maturity to realize them, greater frustrations may result.

RESPONSIBILITIES AND LIMITATIONS OF LEADERS

The Twelve called "apostles." Jesus named these men "apostles," a title derived from the Greek word *apostolos,* "one who is sent." This title bespeaks the mission of the Twelve — that of outreach. The apostles would give a horizontal dimension to the church, establishing new local churches (the vertical dimension) and influencing old ones. They were to continue the ministry that Jesus Himself had begun. In Luke 19:10 Jesus said, "The Son of Man came to seek and to save what was lost." Later, the resurrected Christ said to them, "As the Father has sent me, I am sending you" (John 20:21). They began with responsibilities over the immediate congregation and later they were to have responsibility over remote ones (so also with Paul, Acts 12:24,25; 13:1ff.).

Women as leaders. Scripture indicates that a group of women traveled with Jesus and His men. The names of several of them are listed in Luke 8:1-3; 24:10. These women were active in a *leadership* capacity. Although they never received official leadership status, they greatly helped Jesus in His ministry. And in the early church a number of women were also of great help to Paul in his ministry. Lydia of Thyatira, Phoebe, and Priscilla were among these (Acts 16:13-15; Rom. 16:1-3). In Titus 2:3-5 Paul teaches that women should fulfill a leadership role in the teaching of younger women.

Leaders of leaders. There are indications that later Jesus increasingly focused upon Peter, James, and John as the three who would lead the Twelve. They were with Him at the healing of Jairus' daughter (Mark 5:37), at the Mount of Transfiguration (Matt. 17:1; Luke 9:28), in the Garden of Gethsemane (Matt. 26:36,37), and at other times (Mark 13:3). Mary Magdalene, Joanna, and perhaps the other Mary were similarly selected to give leadership to the women disciples.

It seems that eventually Jesus gave a prominent position to Peter among the male apostles and to Mary Magdalene among the female disciples. The fact that after His resurrection Jesus appeared alone first to Mary Magdalene and then to Peter emphasizes the prominence He gave them. He appeared to Peter probably also because of his special need after his blatant denial of Jesus.

When Jesus appointed the Seventy, sending them out two by two just as He had sent the Twelve and with much the same instruction, He obviously gave them leadership positions in close association with Himself and the Twelve (cf. Luke 10:1-24; 24:13-15; Rom. 16:7). Thus, there was both a widening and a development of leadership in Jesus' program of evangelism.

Team leadership. Although Peter had been given a prominent position, no one leader stood out as dictatorial to or independent of the others. Some years later when the council of the total church met in Jerusalem to determine whether the Gentiles must keep the law of Moses in order to become Christians, both Peter and Paul (with Barnabas) shared how they had handled this matter, and James helped them reach a conclusion (Acts 15:2-29).

The twelve apostles worked together as a unified team. They stood together, helping and encouraging each other as they conducted and governed the work of the early church (cf. Acts 4:33,35; 5:12,18-42). In so doing, they helped to form the great impetus of the early church. Peter did not stand alone to preach on the day of Pentecost: "Then Peter stood up *with the Eleven,* raised his voice and addressed the crowd. . . ." (Acts 2:14). Acts 2:42 records, "They [the disciples] devoted themselves to the *apostles'* teaching . . ." — not just to Peter's teaching. In the early church Peter led the Twelve, but his leadership was modified and backed by the others. He was also kept in certain bounds by Paul (Gal. 2:11-21). While some exercised leadership over others, they were subject to the criticism of the people and of their fellow apostles (Acts 17:11). The leader was one among equals.

The apostle Paul always acted in accordance with a group of men as well. In Acts 13:1-3 a group of prophets and teachers gathered at Antioch: "While they were worshiping the Lord and fasting, the Holy Spirit said, 'Set apart for me Barnabas and Saul for the work to which I have called them.'" Paul and Barnabas did not lead the church in Antioch by themselves but worked with a group of six or seven men. Acts 14:23; 15:2; 20:17 also refer to Paul's traveling and working with a team of men. Usually in the history of the church God has used teams of leaders.[6]

Public presentation and charge of the leaders. While Jesus selected His disciples in the quiet seclusion of prayer, He publicly presented them as leaders, giving an example of how to transfer power. When a new leader is presented publicly, everyone knows where his authority comes from, and he is forced to continue being loyal to the one who has appointed him. The crowd knew that the Twelve must continue to answer to Jesus.

This public presentation also enabled Christ to set the limits of their power and to designate their responsibilities. It was an opportunity for the people to know that these men had the responsibility of being light and salt to them as well as of being concerned for them.

Leadership in the early church. Jesus Christ's practice of appointing leaders over the people was continued in the early church. Paul and Barnabas went through Galatia visiting the cities where they had had a ministry:

> [They returned,] strengthening the disciples and encouraging them to remain true to the faith. "We must go through many hardships to enter the kingdom of God," they said. Paul and Barnabas *appointed elders for them in each church* and, with prayer and fasting, committed them to the Lord in whom they had put their trust (Acts 14:22,23).

Paul instructed Timothy and Titus, his young disciples, how to appoint leaders in every church (1 Tim. 3:1ff.; Titus 1:5-9).

TEACHING FOR LEADERS AND ALL PEOPLE
WHO WERE HIS SUBJECTS

After selecting the Twelve, Jesus brought them down to a plain where a large number of people were waiting. Here He displayed His power and authority in an unusual manner: "And the people all tried to touch Him, because power was coming from him and healing them all" (Luke 6:19). Then He gave His disciples their ordination sermon. What Jesus had to say in the Sermon on the Mount was not directed only to the Twelve, but the message was specifically applicable to them. In this sermon Jesus set forth the government and the nature of His kingdom.

During the time of Ministry Training Jesus taught a small group how to minister with Him while He continued to teach a large group of interested followers. Now He chose to be leaders, some of those who had learned to minister, and this resulted in three levels of followers. This will be discussed in detail in the chapter on Association (pp. 171-183, especially graphs on pp. 176, 182). However, it is important to observe here that as the Twelve move on to the step of

Leadership, the many followers were trained in the principles of God's government over their lives through Jesus Christ.

In like manner today, a pastor or leader of an effort to disciple people must come to a point of selection and development of leaders, at which point he will also have to continue to teach the whole church these principles of God's government. But he must especially train the leaders to set the example and to teach others these principles of government.

THE PRINCIPLES OF THE KINGDOM

The principles of the kingdom of Christ differ from those of the Old Testament in that they emphasize obeying God from the heart rather than obeying the letter of the Law before men. Therefore they fulfill the Law (Matt. 5:17). God blesses His people when they possess the attitudes He desires them to have. On the other hand, He warned them against accepting the world's motives and objectives, which oppose those of the kingdom (cf. beatitudes and woes, Luke 6:20-26). Jesus reminded the disciples how important their influence on the world was because they were a part of His kingdom. They were the salt that gives taste for new life and keeps the world from corruption. And they were the light that drives back the darkness (Matthew 5:13-16).

Jesus told His disciples that to be a part of His kingdom they must have an inward righteousness — a righteousness that transcends that of the teachers of the Law and the Pharisees. The teachers of the Law and the Pharisees strictly upheld various commandments in their outward conduct, but Jesus emphasized the spirit of the Law. He applied these commandments to the intentions of a person's heart (Matt. 5:18-48). Anger and hatred were now considered to be the sin of murder in the heart. Lust was now equivalent to adultery. Jesus demanded that a person be obedient in his heart, because the subjects of God's kingdom are to please God, who sees the heart.

Jesus taught the disciples to have a new attitude of suffering love toward the world. He taught them to take abuses without seeking vengeance, and to leave vengeance to God. His people were to have a new kind of piety. Instead of trying to impress men with their righteousness by offering alms, fasting, or praying so men would see, His people would have an inward desire to please God in all these things.

Jesus set forth a new attitude toward the material world: building the kingdom of God is more important than material gain. His people should not seek material wealth but trust God to supply all their needs. They should have a new attitude toward the weaknesses in others. Whereas the Pharisees were especially critical of others, His people should first deal with their own faults before trying to change the lives of others.

Jesus exalted a new attitude of faith in prayer and He set forth the Golden Rule as the central concept for governing life. He warned those who would be His subjects to avoid going the way of the crowd, to avoid those who profess to know and follow Him but really do not, and to avoid the false teaching of those who would appeal to the flesh. He emphasized that obeying Him was more important than fully understanding His message and storing up knowledge.

When Jesus finished speaking, the crowds were struck by His kingly authority (Matt. 7:28,29).

PRINCIPLES OF THE KINGDOM IN APOSTOLIC TEACHING

Throughout the New Testament the apostles taught the same truths. The themes of humility and righteousness, purity and holiness are common in the writings of Paul, Peter, and others.

The new inner righteousness (as opposed to an outward legal righteousness) dominated the thinking of the New Testament writers. The new covenant prophesied by Jeremiah (Jer. 31:31-34) was seen as fulfilled in the new covenant in Hebrews 8 and 10. In Romans 7 Paul showed how God established the Law but went on in Romans 8 to show that only through the power of the Holy Spirit can a person keep the Law. He pointed out in 2 Corinthians 10:5 that the objective of the Christian faith is to bring every thought into captivity to the obedience of Jesus Christ. After Pentecost, the New Testament writers emphasized dying to self and walking in the Spirit as the way to manifest a righteousness that exceeds that of the teachers of the Law and the Pharisees.

The Sermon on the Mount became the backbone of the whole New Testament ethic. In the early church Christians adopted a new attitude toward material wealth. At first they did not store material goods but sold their possessions and gave all the proceeds to the church and later continued sharing (e.g., Acts 4:34-37; 1 Cor. 16:1-4; 2 Cor. 8:9-15). The death of Ananias and Sapphira emphasized the fact that God wants His people to seek to please Him rather than to please men by an outward show. Ananias and Sapphira had tried to impress men with their almsgiving, but in reality they lied to God.

The New Testament concepts of the kingdom of God also were founded on the Sermon on the Mount. The New Testament writers warned Christians to be aware of false teachings (Matt. 7:15-20; 2 Peter; Jude). They encouraged them to be obedient doers of the Word and not merely hearers of it (Matt. 7:21-27; James 1:22-25). Paul taught the Christians the principle of examining one's own heart and dealing with the sin found there before judging others (Rom. 14). He also taught that people should not seek to avenge themselves but should express an attitude of suffering love, trusting God and the civil rulers to avenge them (Rom. 12:17–13:7).

THE MEMBERSHIP OF THE KINGDOM

After concluding the Sermon on the Mount, Jesus continued His public ministry in different cities. During this period He accepted and praised those who were not accepted by the Jewish people. The unwanted and the belittled could also be part of His kingdom. He praised a centurion, a representative of the hated and oppressive Roman government, for having faith that exceeded that of any of the Jews themselves.

In His time widows were commonly abused and taken advantage of if they had no one to protect and care for them. But Jesus showed great compassion for a widow whose son had died and raised him to life. He praised the sinful woman who anointed His feet with her tears, dried them with her hair, and poured perfume upon them. Her love exceeded that of Simon (the Pharisee) who had given Him no water to wash His feet, no towel to dry them, and no oil for anointing them. She appreciated Him more than Simon did because He had forgiven her more (Matt. 8:5-13; Mark 14:3-9; Luke 7:1-17,36-50).

DOUBT AND OPPOSITION

While Jesus was showing concern for the oppressed and outcast, many doubted and some opposed Him. Even John the Baptist sent his disciples to ask Jesus, ''Are you the one who was to come, or should we expect someone else?'' Jesus answered, ''Go back and report to John what you hear and see'' (Matt. 11:2-5; Luke 7:18-22). His friends began saying that He had lost His senses because such tremendous crowds followed Him that He did not even have time to eat (Mark 3:20,21). The teachers of the Law and the Pharisees accused Jesus of operating in the power of Beelzebub (Matt. 12:24; Mark 3:22; Luke 11:15). Even His mother and brothers sought to hinder His ministry. But Jesus pointed out that those who really have a significant relationship with Him are those who *do* the will of God. They are His true mother and His true brothers and sisters (Matt. 12:46-50; Mark 3:31-35; Luke 8:19-21). All these events of doubt and opposition prepared His disciples to face similar resistance as leaders in the movement (Acts 4–7).

During this time of doubt and opposition, Jesus taught the

Twelve that children of God are not necessarily descended physically from Abraham. Rather, true children of God are born by the obedience of faith. The Twelve, the men who would have the authority to teach about the kingdom in the future, needed to grasp this concept. Later it became prominent in apostolic writings (cf. John 3:16ff.; Rom. 4:11; Gal. 2:15,16; 3:6-9, et al.).

Two Conflicting Kingdoms

When the Pharisees accused Jesus of casting out a demon by Beelzebub's (Satan's) power, Jesus used the incident to point out the conflict between the kingdom of God and the kingdom of evil (Matt. 12:22-45; Mark 3:22-30; Luke 11:14-26). His power had two possible sources — Satan or God. Jesus debated that either Satan had used Him to cast out demons, and was therefore at war with himself, or the Holy Spirit had enabled Him to cast out the demons. In the first case Satan would ultimately fall because his house was divided. In the latter Satan was bound by Christ who had the power to spoil his house. When Jesus asserted that He had been empowered by the Spirit of God to cast out the demon, He was saying, in essence, that the kingdom of God had come among them. (Jesus took this opportunity to warn the Pharisees about their critical attitudes and their blasphemy of the Holy Spirit.)

Through His death on the cross, Jesus Christ conquered Satan. Hebrews 2:14 says, "Since the children have flesh and blood, he too shared in their humanity so that by his death he might destroy him who holds the power of death — that is, the devil."

The conflict between the two kingdoms is also discussed elsewhere in the post-resurrection New Testament writings of the apostles. To the Ephesians Paul explained how Jesus gained power over Satan (1:20ff.). God the Father raised Christ from the dead, seated Him at His right hand above every principality and power, and put all things in subjection under Him. Paul prayed that the Ephesians would be strengthened by the Holy Spirit within (3:16), and discussed how Christians can resist the power of Satan (6:10-12):

> Be strong in the Lord and in his mighty power. Put on the full armor of God so that you can take your stand against the devil's schemes. For our struggle is not against flesh and blood, but against the rulers, against the authorities, against the powers of this dark world and against the spiritual forces of evil in the heavenly realms.

The conflict between Satan and God goes back to Genesis 3:15 when God said to the serpent:

> And I will put enmity between you and the woman,

and between your seed and her seed;
he shall bruise your head,
and you shall bruise him on the heel.

The drama of the seed of the woman reaches its climax in Revelation 12:5,7-12. Here a male child, born of a woman, is caught up to the throne of God and given all authority. Then Satan with all of his angels is cast out of heaven onto the earth, and God's dominion is established.

Parables of the Kingdom

Jesus continued to illustrate Satan's destructive work. In the parable of the sower and the seed, Jesus explained that the seed (the Word of God) that fell on the hard path was stolen by Satan. Thus, it did not grow in the hearts of the hearers. In another parable Jesus talked about the growing seed. He told how Satan sows tares that will grow among the wheat until the judgment. Then the two will be separated, and the tares Satan has sown will be burned (Matt. 13:1-30,36-43; Mark 4:1-20; Luke 8:4-15).

Through other parables, Jesus encouraged the Twelve, the future leaders of the kingdom. He told them that in the beginning the kingdom would be as small as a mustard seed but eventually it would grow to be as large as a tree in which birds could nest. He taught them that the kingdom would grow like leaven: a little in the midst of the loaf would spread throughout the whole loaf. He compared the kingdom to a treasure hidden in a field. It would be so important to a man that he would sell everything just to buy it. Again, it was comparable to a priceless pearl that a merchant would buy even if he had to sell everything he owned. The last parable refers to the last judgment: when the drag-net of God is cast, the bad fish will be gathered and thrown away, and the good fish will be saved (Matt. 13:31-35,44-50; Mark 4:30-32; Luke 13:18-21).

Truth of Parables Seen in the Early Church

The progressive growth of the kingdom, as depicted in the parables, began unfolding in the book of Acts. Jesus said in Acts 1:8, "But you will receive power when the Holy Spirit comes on you; and you will be my witnesses in Jerusalem, and in all Judea and Samaria, and to the ends of the earth." The continual extension of the boundaries of the church through the missionary work of the apostle Paul and others was a further manifestation of this progressive growth.

When Jesus insisted that He should move out from Capernaum to preach the good news of the kingdom to other regions (Mark 1:35-39; cf. Luke 4:42,43; this is the step of Ministry Training), He established a pattern for the expansion of the kingdom. This pattern culminates in the book of Revelation, which foretells the total development of the church to include people of every tribe and nation (Rev. 5:9; 14:6), ending with the return of Christ when Satan and his forces will be destroyed (Rev. 20:10).

THE POWER OF THE NEW KING

After Jesus illustrated the truths of the kingdom through His parables, He demonstrated His power as King by performing some of His greatest miracles. These miracles lent credence to His claim of being the Messiah; they were His credentials from God. Through them Jesus asserted His authority over different areas of life: over *nature* in that He stilled the storm, over *demons* in that He cast out the demons from the man called Legion, over *death* in that He raised the daughter of Jairus from the dead, over *sight* in that He healed two blind men, and over *speech* in that he healed a dumb demoniac (Mark 4:35ff.; 5:1ff.; Matt. 9:18-26; 9:27-31; 9:32-34, respectively). The Twelve believed; they were convinced of Christ's power. On the day of Pentecost Peter said that Jesus was ". . . a man, accredited by God to you by miracles, wonders and signs, which God did among you through him . . ." (Acts 2:22).

Christ's credentials were later passed on to the apostles. Hebrews 2:3,4 says:

> How shall we escape if we ignore such a great salvation? This salvation, which was first announced by the Lord, was confirmed to us by *those who heard him. God also testified to it* by signs, wonders and various miracles, and gifts of the Holy Spirit distributed according to his will.

In 2 Corinthians 12:12 Paul claimed that the signs he performed were evidence that he was an apostle like the Twelve.

LEADERSHIP TRAINING PRIOR TO DELEGATION

When the new leaders were ready to be sent out on their own, Jesus took them on a "demonstration" missionary tour (Matt. 9:35-38). Then He gave them instructions and assigned them to go out two by two to different villages (Matt. 10:1; Mark 6:7; Luke 9:6), giving them the power to perform miracles.

Through the power of the Holy Spirit, Jesus endowed these leaders with the gifts they needed in order to minister. In Ephesians 4:11,12 Paul listed various offices and gifts of the Spirit that build up the church. In his first letter to the Corinthians, he pointed out that the Spirit gives each member certain gifts for the common good of the fellowship (1 Cor. 12:7,11,18). Peter urged each Christian to exercise his spiritual gifts faithfully in order to glorify God in the ministry (1 Peter 4:9-11). Both Paul and Peter agreed that love should motivate Christians in using these gifts to minister (1 Cor. 13; 1 Peter 4:8). It was not until the period of Participation and Delegation, however, that Jesus warned the disciples not to abuse the gifts but to use them in relating to the body.

Jesus' instructions to the Twelve contain important principles that most successful missionary movements throughout history have inculcated. He told them what to preach, how to minister to people in need, how to finance their ministry, and how to respond to opposition. They were to preach that the kingdom of God was near. They were given the authority to heal the sick, raise the dead, cleanse the lepers, and drive out demons. They were to take nothing with them but to expect the local ministry to furnish their needs. When they went to a town, they were to stay at only one house. If they were rejected by the people of a town, they were to shake off the dust from their feet as a testimony against them (Matt. 10:1,7-15; cf. Mark 6:7-13; Luke 9:1-5).

Jesus told the Twelve what they should expect from the world. He warned that persecution and hatred would be theirs because of their witness. Describing them as sheep among wolves, He told the Twelve not to worry when they were brought before the authorities, for the Spirit would tell them what to say (Matt. 10:16-20). Jesus explained that there would even be divisions within their own families — brother against brother and children against parents (10:21,22,34-36).

Jesus instructed the apostles to take what He had spoken in darkness and to proclaim openly what had been whispered to them. Fear God rather than man, He exhorted, for God can cast both body and soul into hell, whereas man can only destroy the body. They were reminded that the Father would take care of them. After all, God watched over the sparrows, and were they not of more value than sparrows? Jesus said that if they would acknowledge Him before men, He would acknowledge them before the Father (Matt. 10:27-33).

Jesus told the Twelve that He had not come to bring peace but a sword. Even though their families opposed them, they were to love Him more than father or mother, son or daughter. The ones who endured would enter into the kingdom and receive their reward (Matt. 10:34-42).

Christ stressed the fact that these men were His representatives. When they spoke, it would be as if He were speaking. When people received them, they would actually be receiving Him (Matt. 10:40).

SUPERVISION IN MINISTRY

When the Twelve completed their journeys, they reported back to Jesus and recounted everything that happened (Mark 6:30; Luke 9:10). Jesus planned to follow them into the towns (Matt. 10:23; 11:1), so that He could speak, supervise the work, and evaluate their success.

LEADERSHIP PRINCIPLES APPLIED IN THE CHURCH LATER

These basic principles were followed in later missionary efforts. For instance, the Seventy were sent out two by two, just as the Twelve had been. Paul and Barnabas, then Paul and Silas, and Barnabas and Mark worked together in teams at various times in their ministry. Paul and Barnabas deliberately followed Jesus' instructions to the Twelve in their tactics (cf. Matt. 10:14 with Acts 13:51; 18:6).

Just as Jesus had told the Twelve that they would be persecuted, so the apostles warned believers about persecution. Paul wrote to the Thessalonians that Christians were called to suffer (1 Thess. 3:3). To the Philippians he wrote, "For it has been granted to you on behalf of Christ not only to believe on him, but also to suffer for him" (Phil. 1:29). Peter emphasized that suffering is part of the Christian's life (1 Peter 2:21).

Following Christ's example, the apostles also warned Christians to live godly lives. They instructed Christians not to fear men but to look forward to the coming of Jesus in judgment. In 2 Thessalonians 1:7-10 Paul wrote that God will reward the Christians and punish the wicked when He returns to judge the world.

In His original instructions Jesus told the disciples that they should not go to the Gentiles or to the Samaritans but only to the lost sheep of the house of Israel (Matt. 10:5,6). This command did not mean that Jesus was prejudiced against anyone who was not Jewish. He had already indicated in both His life and His ministry that His redemptive work was for all men (see pp. 49,50).

This step of Leadership Development came at the right time in God's schedule. It was important in the development of His plan. According to God's providence and foreknowledge, John the Baptist was killed at the time Jesus sent out the twelve new leaders. John's ministry had ended, but the momentum he had created was being continued by the Twelve.

All of the followers of John must have joined the ranks of Jesus' ministry, thus swelling the size of the crowd accompanying Jesus.

By appointing leaders and proclaiming His principles of government to all His disciples, Jesus had launched His kingdom. All of

His disciples had made significant personal growth.

Notes

[1]For arguments as to whether there were two sermons or one in Luke 6:17-49 and Matthew 5-7; cf. J. Oswald Sanders, *Real Discipleship* (Grand Rapids: Zondervan, 1972), pp. 9-12.

[2]J. Oswald Sanders, *Spiritual Leadership* (Chicago: Moody, 1967), pp. 16,17.

[3]Samuel J. Andrews, *The Life of Our Lord* (New York: Scribner's, 1894), p. 265.

[4]Robert E. Coleman, *The Master Plan of Evangelism* (Westwood, N.J.: Revell, 1963), pp. 19, 21.

[5]Dr. Everett F. Harrison, *A Short Life of Christ* (Grand Rapids: Eerdmans, 1968), pp. 136, 137.

[6]Schaff has said, ''In great creative epochs of the Church, God associates congenial leaders for mutual help and comfort.'' He then lists those whom God has teamed together. (Philip Schaff, *History of the Christian Church* [Grand Rapids: Eerdmans, n.d.], 7:191, 192.)

8

Reevaluation and Separation

THE STEP OF REEVALUATION

The kingdom of God is heavenly in origin and eternal in nature, and these qualities distinguish it from the kingdoms of men. As Christians, we can begin to participate in God's government now. Then at the return of Christ the realm of the kingdom will be extended in a cataclysmic way to include the earth. It is a kingdom that will not be shaken, for it is not of this world.

The subjects of God's kingdom live daily under the rule of God's revealed Word — not primarily the words or traditions of men. Their kinship transcends races and national boundaries, for they all serve one Father and through the power of the Holy Spirit obey His will. Their values differ from those of non-Christians.

Most false religions stop short of hope in God's eternal kingdom. They teach that God's primary desire is to make His children rich, healthy, and happy *now!* False religious teachers either debunk eternal hopes or ignore them altogether. They scoff at "pie in the sky by and by." Some, like the Marxists, say that such religion is the opiate of the people. Other false teachers present only proposals for escape from suffering and difficulties rather than victory over them.

When men hope only in temporal values, they are left without moral absolutes and without a sense of the fear of God or willingness to yield to His control. Thus godly living is forsaken. Unless a person believes that he will face eternal consequences for his actions, he will claim license to sin. If he believes he will survive death and enjoy an eternal kingdom, he will be willing to give up the temporal and to stand firm for his faith even to the point of death (1 Cor. 15:32).

The step of Reevaluation is crucial for survival of the individual's faith and of the faith of the church in a world of sin and persecution. In these end times, it is especially important for Christians to exchange temporal values for eternal ones because Jesus and the apostles predicted that in the last days the church would suffer increased persecution.

The disciples did not immediately understand and choose eternal values. First (in the step of Enlightenment) they had to trust Christ as the One who had come from heaven. During Ministry Training they began to understand the acceptance and freedom found in following the King Himself. They saw Him demonstrate daily the power of heaven by the working of the Holy Spirit. In the Leadership stage the disciples experienced the Holy Spirit's working through them as they cast out demons, healed, and proclaimed the good news of the kingdom. Now Jesus confronted them with the necessity of choosing the eternal values *over* earthly ones.

THE NEED FOR REEVALUATION IN JESUS' MINISTRY

Stirred by the excitement of Jesus' ministry, the multitudes followed Him, and their numbers continually grew. The reason is obvious. Jesus ministered to the physical needs of the people. John recorded: "And a great crowd of people followed him because they saw the miraculous signs he had performed on the sick" (John 6:2).

Mark wrote that on one occasion when Jesus and His disciples were so busy ministering to the crowds they did not even have time to eat (Mark 6:31ff.). Hoping to find a deserted area where they could relax for awhile, they got into a boat and crossed the lake. But by the time they reached the other shore, the people had run around the lake to meet Him there. As more people came, Jesus continued to minister to them, having compassion on them because they were like sheep without a shepherd.

When He provided food for them in the desert when they were desperately hungry, they wanted Him to be their political leader. What man could make a better king than one who could solve their economic and health problems? But Jesus knew what they thought and He rejected the idea of being made a materialistic king (John 6:15). He knew that He was popular, not because the people desired to hear God's message and to know His will but because they knew He could solve the problems of temporal life.

The disciples heard Jesus say repeatedly that He had come from above to offer eternal life, but they had never caught the vision of the eternal, spiritual kingdom. Jesus therefore began to test them, forcing them to rethink their entire value system. His goal was to have them understand that the eternal should take precedence over the temporal in their decision-making process.

PREPARATION FOR REEVALUATION

Christ's rejection of an earthly kingdom was crucial, for it affected those who would follow Him. It forced the disciples to reevaluate and choose between Christ and the world. Jesus had prepared them for this step of Reevaluation. After feeding the five thousand, He went to the mountain by Himself to pray, sending the disciples ahead of Him across the lake. He prayed, no doubt, for the disciples to remain faithful when God's will was revealed to them.

Then in the early morning Jesus watched them as they rowed in vain to cross the lake. The winds had kept them from making headway, and they were stranded in the middle of the lake in spite of all their efforts and their skill as seamen. As the sea became more turbulent and their efforts more futile, Jesus came to them walking on the water (Matt. 14:22-33; Mark 6:45-51; John 6:15-21).

Jesus had demonstrated that He was the God of the people of the Old Testament. The fishermen recognized His deeds as those of God Himself. God's power in the sea and over the sea is dramatically told in Psalms 77 and 107, and it was clear to the disciples, therefore, that Jesus was Himself God.

Speaking of God, the psalmist says,

Thy way was in the sea,
And Thy paths in the mighty waters,
And Thy footprints may not be known.
(Psalm 77:19 NASB)

Those who go down to the sea in ships,
Who do business on great waters [such as fishermen];
They have seen the works of the Lord,
And His wonders in the deep.
For He spoke and raised up a stormy wind,
Which lifted up the waves of the sea.
They rose up to the heavens, they went down to the depths;
Their soul melted away in their misery.
They reeled and staggered like a drunken man,
And were at their wits' end.

Then they cried to the Lord in their trouble,
And He brought them out of their distresses.
He *caused the storm to be still,*
So that the waves of the sea were hushed.
Then they were glad because they were quiet;
So He guided them to their desired haven.
(Psalm 107:23-32 NASB)

This miracle of walking on the water and stilling the storm came at the right time. Mark said that the disciples "had not understood about the loaves; their minds were closed" (Mark 6:52). The disciples needed to understand more fully who Jesus was if they were to remain with Him when He refused to be an earthly king and the crowds left Him. Through this miracle their faith in Him was strengthened. After performing the works attributed to God in the Psalms, they "worshiped him" as the Son of God (Matt. 14:33).

REFUSING THE EARTHLY KINGDOM

After having prepared His disciples, Jesus met the multitude and confronted them with His refusal to be an earthly king. He rebuked them and called them to recognize their need to be nurtured by Him:

> Do not work for food that spoils, but for food that endures to eternal life, which the Son of Man will give you. On him God the Father has placed his seal of approval. . . . For the bread of God is he who comes down from heaven and gives life to the world. . . . I am the bread of life. He who comes to me will never go hungry, and he who believes in me will never be thirsty. . . . For my Father's will is that everyone who looks to the Son and believes in him shall have eternal life, and I will raise him up at the last day. . . . The Spirit gives life; the flesh counts for nothing. The words I have spoken to you are spirit and they are life (John 6:27,33,35,40,63).

Jesus was saying that a person can do nothing through his own effort to gain eternal life. This can be gained only by participation in the new covenant of His shed blood and by trusting in Jesus as the Bread who gives eternal sustenance. When Jesus encouraged the people to labor not for the food that perishes but for the food that endures to eternal life, He thereby made eternal values supreme and made all temporal values dependent on them.

EXPLANATION BY DIAGRAMS

The diagrams that follow help explain what God was doing through Jesus Christ at this time. These diagrams are given only to illustrate what the thinking of the people was, what Christ was seeking to do, and how the people and the disciples reacted. They are not meant to give a definitive view of the nature of man (i.e., whether dichotomous or trichotomous).

DIAGRAM 1

The man in the diagram is a symbol of depraved sinful man in general, like those in the crowd that followed Jesus. The arrow from the head indicates that the spirit of the *mind* of the natural man is *focused on* satisfying the *fleshly, bodily desires* through the world. He is thus under the control of Satan and is dead to spiritual things (cf. John 8:44; Rom. 8:7; 1 Cor. 2:14; Eph. 2:1-3).

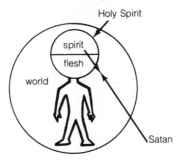

1. Depraved natural man

DIAGRAM 2

In order to get man's attention, God became a man in Jesus Christ and ministered to people in the area of their fleshly needs. He healed their bodies and fed them when they were hungry. He did this in supernatural and miraculous ways. Christ presented these signs as "bait" to catch their attention and show them God's Person and power in Himself.

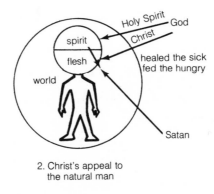

2. Christ's appeal to
the natural man

DIAGRAM 3

The third diagram shows how Christ, having demonstrated the power of the heavenly world, sought to turn the attention of those who responded to His claims back toward spiritual things and to eternal life through the Holy Spirit. But only the twelve disciples (except one) began to turn their attention to the idea of eternal life in an eternal kingdom. Peter said, "You have the words of eternal life. We believe and know that you are the Holy One of God" (John 6:68,69). But they were only *beginning* to get a vision of the eternal.

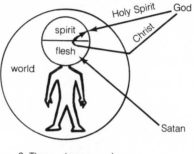

3. Those who respond
to Christ's claims
(spiritually minded, given
life and peace)

DIAGRAM 4

The fourth diagram indicates the response of the multitude. The line in front of the arrow representing Christ's offer indicates their rejection of Jesus' claims and revealed their devotion to living for the flesh when they said, "This is a hard teaching. Who can accept it?" (John 6:60). By their rejection, they considered Jesus Christ a blasphemer and identified Him with the working of Satan.

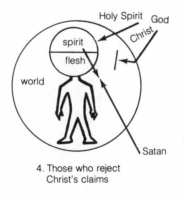

4. Those who reject
Christ's claims

Jesus was aware that God in His sovereignty was choosing those who would follow Him. He said:

> "No one can come to me unless the Father has enabled him. . . . Have I not chosen you, the Twelve? Yet one of you is a devil!" (He meant Judas, the son of Simon Iscariot, who, though one of the Twelve, was later to betray him.) (John 6:65,70,71).

After Jesus challenged them to live for the eternal, telling them that only through Him could they receive eternal life, the multitudes withdrew. Only His intimate disciples stayed with Him, and even among them Judas Iscariot did not believe. Judas was stealing from the common treasury and had his mind on the temporal (John 12:6).

SEPARATION TO CHRIST AND FROM THE WORLD

The shadow of the opposition of the world to Jesus and His movement had been growing larger and more distinct from the outset of His ministry. The early suspicions of the Jerusalem authorities shown in their questions to John the Baptist (John 1:19-28) had reached the point of the Jewish leaders desiring to dispose of Jesus (Matt. 12:14; Mark 3:6; John 5:18). Now the great mass of the crowds joined the Jewish leadership in opposition to Jesus, and this produced a clear separation between Christians and the world. The full image of opposition of unregenerate mankind now stepped from the shadows into clear sight. A separation had occurred. From now on it was understood that to follow Christ meant a break with the world and its temporal values, and persecution by those who were unbelieving.

By the early nineteenth century, temporal values became very important in America and by the end of the century these began to greatly influence the church.[1] One must eventually choose God or mammon (Matt. 6:24). Karl Marx rejected eternal values and made material values absolute. Today there is a desperate need for Christians to be clearly committed to the eternal.

DIVINE AUTHORITY OVER HUMAN AUTHORITY

In the following days Jesus challenged the disciples to put divine authority over all human tradition. He turned the source of their authority upside down — from an earthly authority to a heavenly one. This was the logical implication of giving priority to heavenly values.

For instance, the Pharisees questioned Jesus because His disciples ate without ceremonially washing their hands. They were not observing the rabbinical traditions. These Pharisees said to Jesus, "Why do your disciples break the tradition of the elders?" But Jesus responded by questioning them, "And why do you break the command of God for the sake of your tradition?" He pointed out that the Pharisees followed the law of Corban,[2] and in so doing they put the word of men above the Word of God. They were directly violating God's commandment to honor one's father and mother (Matt. 15:1-9; Mark 7:1-13). Through this incident, He challenged His disciples to put the command and Word of God above all the traditions of men; that is, to put heavenly authority above earthly authority.

While today there are frequently people who inappropriately attack loyalty to religious demoninations and their leaders, it is true that far too often church members allow these loyalties to be above the Word of God. One of the greatest failures in the modern church is the lack of cooperation, denial of fellowship and love, and unethical practice — all resulting from putting the traditions of men above Christ's commands in Scripture.

JEWISH NATIONAL ALLEGIANCE QUESTIONED BY A GENTILE MINISTRY

For a brief period, Jesus put Jewish nationalism aside, practicing an internationalism. The Jews had always felt that they alone were the recipients of God's grace and blessings. They boasted, "We are Abraham's descendants" (John 8:33; cf. Matt. 3:9). They were God's children, and yet as a nation they had not responded to the truth of God as Jesus had presented it. They had turned away from following Him. Therefore, for a short time, Jesus ministered almost entirely to the Gentile people, sharing the blessings of the Holy Spirit with them, performing miracles, and healing them.

Jesus' ministry to the Gentiles began in Tyre when a Syrian Phoenician woman begged Him to heal her daughter. He also went into the ten Greek cities of Decapolis. There He healed many people and miraculously fed four thousand (Matt. 15:21-39; Mark 7:24–8:9).

While Jesus was ministering to the Gentiles, the disciples must have gone through a time of soul searching, for it seemed as though He had forsaken the Jewish people. Their whole earthly heritage seemed threatened.

This experience began to prepare the disciples to put their allegiance to the kingdom of God above any national commitment.

CRUCIFIXION OF FLESH LEADING TO RESURRECTION AND GLORY

Jesus again encouraged His disciples to hope in the eternal by telling them that even death could not conquer His church (Matt.

16:13-28; Mark 8:27-38; Luke 9:18-27). After Peter confessed that Jesus was the Christ, the Son of the living God, Jesus declared, "On this rock [of confession of me as the Son of God] I will build my church [my congregation]; and the gates of Hades will not overcome it" (Matt. 16:18). Many people have interpreted this passage to mean that Satan's power cannot stand in the way of the church. To a certain extent that interpretation can be implied from this passage. However, the phrase "gates of Hades" occurs many times in classical Greek, and in each instance it means the grave or death. Jesus was saying that no matter what happens to His followers, they will have eternal life.

Following this declaration, Jesus told the disciples that He was going to Jerusalem where He would be killed. However, death would not conquer Him, for He would be raised on the third day. Peter's reaction was human. He cried out, "Perish the thought, Lord! This shall never happen to you!" His vision was still fleshly. Jesus said to him:

> "Out of my sight, Satan! You are a stumbling block to me; you do not have in mind the things of God, but the things of men." Then Jesus said to his disciples, "If anyone would come after me, he must deny himself and take up his cross and follow me. For whoever wants to save his life will lose it, but whoever loses his life for me will find it" (Matt. 16:23-25).

Jesus was teaching that man must die to this life and live for the eternal life that comes from God. Christ was trusting the indwelling Holy Spirit to raise Him from the dead. He taught that the flesh profits nothing (Matt. 16:22-25).

PREVIEW OF THE ETERNAL KINGDOM

A week after this prediction of His death, Jesus took Peter, James, and John to a mountain to pray (Luke 9:28). There, as a result of His prayers, He was transfigured. His countenance was changed; He appeared as the glorious Christ in all His brilliance. They saw something of the glory that had been His before He came to earth and that would be His again in the future when He would be seated at the right hand of God. They saw Him as the glorious God of heaven now incarnate. Having predicted the crucifixion of His flesh, He demonstrated His glory. Again, they were encouraged to labor not for that which perishes but for that which endures to eternal life (Matt. 17:1-8; Mark 9:2-8; Luke 9:28-36). They were given an important foregleam of that glory they were to hope for (2 Peter 1:16-18).

EXPERIENCE OF THE WEAKNESS OF THE FLESH

The Transfiguration was followed by another incident that emphasized the disciples' total ineffectiveness because of their fleshly attitude. As Jesus came down from the mountain of Transfiguration, He found that the other nine disciples had been confronted with a demon-possessed boy. They were quite embarrassed, for they were unable to cast the demon out. When the boy's father came to Jesus, He said, " 'Everything is possible for him who believes.' Immediately the boy's father exclaimed, 'I do believe; help me overcome my unbelief.' " Jesus then drove the demon out.

When the disciples came to Jesus later, asking why they could not drive the demon out, He answered, "This kind can come forth by nothing, but by prayer and fasting" (Mark 9:29 KJV). The power of Satan cannot be cast out through the power of the flesh. To cope with this kind of evil, one must turn to the heavenly resources of God through the Holy Spirit by praying and fasting (vv. 14-29). Finally, by again predicting His death and resurrection, Jesus challenged the disciples to reevaluate their lives (vv. 30-32; cf. also Matt. 12:22,23; Luke 9:43-45).

Thus Jesus challenged His disciples to live for things eternal. He challenged them to accept the fact that one must die to the flesh in order to gain new, eternal life through the Holy Spirit. During this period of Reevaluation, Christ helped them exchange their old values for a new set of values.

THE BROADER NEW TESTAMENT PERSPECTIVE ON REEVALUATION

Seen from a postresurrection perspective, the feeding of the five thousand and the sermon on the bread of life both anticipate the Lord's Supper. Just before His death, Jesus celebrated the Passover with His disciples. At this, the Lord's Supper, He instituted the new covenant. He spoke of the wine and the bread as His blood that would be shed and His body that would be broken for us.

In eating the bread and drinking the wine, the disciple is making a statement: he is saying that he believes that he will be sustained not only in this life but also eternally through Jesus Christ. In celebrating the Lord's Supper, he is looking forward to the eternity he will spend with God in His kingdom (Matt. 26:17-29; Mark 14:12-25; Luke 22:7-23).

Throughout the New Testament Christians are taught to live for the eternal. Paul said in Galatians 6:8, "The one who sows to please his sinful nature, from that nature will reap destruction; the one who sows to please the Spirit, from the Spirit will reap eternal life." In other words, the Christian's life should be different from the lives of others. He has been crucified with Christ (Gal. 2:20) and, therefore, should die to the flesh, living through the indwelling Spirit (Rom. 8:5-8). He should allow Jesus, the risen Christ who is seated at the right hand of God (Eph. 1:20), to live in and through him. The Christian need no longer live for the world; instead, he should claim his inheritance as a child of God, waiting for the redemption of the body (Rom. 8:23; see also 2 Cor. 4:14-18; Col. 3:1-4; 1 John 2:15-17). The kingdom of the Christian is eternal and unshakable (2 Peter 3:11-14; Heb. 12:22-29).

The eternal is often presented as the hope of the Christian. Paul said, "Therefore, my dear brothers, stand firm. Let nothing move you. Always give yourselves fully to the work of the Lord, because you know that your labor in the Lord is not in vain" (1 Cor. 15:58). Essentially, Christians must labor for that which does not perish; that is, eternal life, which will be fully attained at the resurrection. Eternal life, in its broadest meaning, is the Christian's great hope. It is that for which we should labor (1 Thess. 4:13ff.).

In the book of Revelation John said he saw the heavenly Jerusalem coming down from above. Those who will participate with Christ in that heavenly kingdom are the ones whose sins are forgiven through the shed blood of the Lamb and who have suffered with Him.

This step of giving priority to the eternal over the temporal is crucial for both the disciple and the church if the disciples are to be bold and strong in a sinful and hostile world. This step will become increasingly difficult as evil increases toward the end times (1 Tim. 4:1ff.; 2 Tim. 3:1ff.).

The Broader New Testament Perspective on Separation

The experience of being separated to Christ from the world is taught throughout the New Testament. Jesus continued to emphasize this (John 14:18-21; 17:14-17). The apostle John continued to emphasize the breach between the Christian and the world (1 John 3:1; 4:4-6; 5:19,20). Paul emphasizes the Christian's separation to Christ from the world (Rom. 12:1,2; 2 Cor. 6:14-18). Peter refers to departing from "the lusts of men" or of "the flesh" and "defilements of the world" and associates these with false teachers and Gentile conduct (1 Peter 4:1-5; 2 Peter 1:4; 2:20).

Today some teach a legalistic doctrine of separation from various activities that are generally unwholesome for a Christian, such as movies, dancing, and the like. The biblical emphasis is on *separation to Christ* to live for Him and eternal things. The result is that the world separates from the Christian. But unless following Christ personally to gain eternal life is the main focus, a new legalism as deadly as that of Judaism can result.

Notes

[1] William Warren Sweet, *The Story of Religion in America* (New York: Harper, 1950), p. 345.

[2] The law of Corban was a rabbinical law by which a man could dedicate money to the temple but still keep it for his own use. Then if his mother or father were in need, the law could not require him to use that money to look after them. While saying that it was dedicated to God, he could still use it for himself.

9

Participation and Delegation

The church is the body of Christ. God works daily in a miraculous way in His church. This commonly known truth should thrill every believer. Every believer is indwelt by the Holy Spirit through whom he is united to all other believers and controlled and empowered by the supernatural presence of the Lord Jesus Christ. "He is the head of the body, the church" (Col. 1:18).

But the control is not entirely mysterious and beyond comprehension. Christ taught the Word of God to His church (John 17:8), including instructions on how members should function in relationship to each other and to those who become involved with the church but are not clearly believers. His directions enable the church to function as an organism and to minister together harmoniously in His name. The step of Participation and Delegation centers primarily around ideas that enable believers to trust God to work in others and in themselves as they relate to others.

The smallest unit of the body of Christ is the home. It is the germ cell for the larger family of all believers who meet together in a community. Most individuals can trust God and believe He can and will work in themselves, but they fail to believe God can correct, empower, and give wisdom to others as the others relate to them. Many men will not trust God to work in their wives or their children. Christian children do not trust God to work in their parents. Christians often do not trust God to work in other members of the church.

141

In this sixth step of Christian growth, Christ taught His disciples how to participate in the body, how to avoid error, how to deal with pressure from outside the body, and how to delegate responsibility to new leaders.

NEEDS REQUIRING INSTRUCTION ON PARTICIPATION AND DELEGATION

By the time Christ had taken His disciples through the fifth step, He had gathered and trained a large number of believers who followed Him consistently. Within this growing group of believers, tensions began to develop. The world's growing hostility to the movement added pressures from without. The members of the body of Christ needed to know how to relate to others in different situations.

Christ's opposition had been strengthened by His refusal to become an earthly king. Until that time Jesus had been supported by the crowds. But now the crowd polarized. Many joined the camp of His enemies. Those who were merely curious and not really committed followers drew back, And the genuine followers were revealed. Judaism and Christianity were now clearly separate.

A similar outburst and manifestation of opposition over Jesus' actions on the Sabbath day occurred just before the appointment of the Twelve. No doubt many superficial followers were purged then. And now before the Seventy were to be chosen, a purging took place. The Seventy were probably chosen from second-generation disciples who had joined the movement as a result of the ministry of the Twelve.

Even though the bread-of-life sermon had caused an initial purging, evidently the crowds quickly returned and in perhaps greater numbers. Even His bitterest enemies followed Him to check on all He was doing and to see if they might trap Him. No doubt the news of bitter criticism brought even more curiosity seekers than before. People follow fame, whether it is favorable or unfavorable.

All of these factors brought out urgent needs. New leadership was needed to minister to the crowds and to lead further evangelistic outreaches. Christians from divergent backgrounds found themselves bonded together against the world. They had to learn to get along with a growing number of people from various walks of life. Relating to those who opposed the message became a primary concern for the disciples, as did keeping the body pure and avoiding false teachers. These same needs seem to repeat themselves with any growing movement or church that is boldly witnessing.

As an adolescent goes through the painful adjustments of growing up physically, mentally, and emotionally, so the body of believers in Christ was experiencing the problems of maturing into a recognized, new, and independent group. Paul, in his first letter to the Corinthians, spoke of the necessity of conducting the affairs of the body of Christ in a way that would glorify God. (He even dealt with such practical matters as eating and drinking.) He said, "Do not cause anyone to stumble, whether Jews, Greeks or the church of God" (1 Cor. 10:32). Here Paul named the three groups to whom the body of believers must relate: the old, stagnant church; the outsiders (unbelievers); and the believers, respectively. For Christians to relate properly to people in each of these groups, faith is necessary.

The Seventy helped meet the needs of the regular followers and control the growing crowds (probably the largest of Jesus' ministry). But their main responsibility was to help evangelize the unreached areas of Judea and Perea. These areas needed to be reached before growing hostility "closed the doors."

When these new leaders were appointed, the Twelve were probably concerned about their positions as leaders. But Jesus continued to recognize their leadership over the Seventy as is evidenced by the fact that "the Twelve" continue to be significantly mentioned. Now the Twelve had the opportunity to see how Jesus delegated authority to the Seventy. This experience was important, for in the future they would be appointing new leaders, and they needed to learn how to exercise authority and delegate responsibility to them.

PLACE, TIME, AND CHRONOLOGY

The period of Participation and Delegation in the body extended from just before the Feast of the Tabernacles (October, A.D. 29) to the Feast of the Passover (April, A.D. 30), covering approximately a six-month period. It began as Christ secretly gathered His disciples in Galilee for private teaching (Matt. 17:22; Mark 9:30,33; cf. Luke 9:44ff.) and ended with His final journey to Jerusalem, just before His triumphal entry.

While the period of time devoted to this step is about equal to other steps, it contains much more material on Christ's teaching. There is a lengthy section that is unique to Luke's Gospel.[1] Luke probably got the material for this section from some of the Seventy who recorded it because they had never heard these teachings before. Since many were repetitious to the Twelve (see chapter 3, pp. 62,63, for parallel showing repetition), they did not record them again. John records Jesus' conflicts in Jerusalem at the Feast of Tabernacles and the Feast of Dedication, which occurred during this period, and they are unique to his Gospel.

The chronology of this period is unclear, especially concerning the appointment and the ministry of the Seventy. It is known that Jesus divided them into thirty-five teams and sent them to specific cities where they were to minister prior to His arrival, but the exact location of their work is unclear. Samuel J. Andrews has discussed the various views in *The Life of Our Lord,*[2] pages 381-384. Most believe that the missionary work done in Perea and in Judea at this period was done by the Seventy.

GUIDELINES FOR INTERPERSONAL RELATIONSHIPS

Many difficult problems arise among members of a church congregation. In addition, people who are not members but who attend and are interested in Christian truth and the possibility of becoming members often raise questions about the meaning of the beliefs and about the functioning of the church. These various situations that arise can lead to the church's splitting into factions. Hard feelings can develop between individuals, and painful conflicts can result. Today many congregations have not been adequately prepared to cope with such matters. When Jesus' followers were meeting such problems, He gave them guidelines to help them determine what to do:

1. Jesus taught His disciples *how to relate to the Jews* who practiced an established, ceremonial, and legalistic religion. When the authorities wanted the temple tax paid, Jesus miraculously provided the money for Peter to pay it by sending him to catch a fish with a coin in its mouth. By this act Jesus demonstrated that although Christians enjoy freedom as sons, they should still comply with the Jewish legal authorities as much as possible in order to avoid offending people of the establishment (Matt. 17:24-27). In other words, to the Jew He became like a Jew.

2. Jesus taught the disciples *how to relate to each other* so that they might become more effective *leaders*. For instance, He urged those who were ambitious to adopt the humility of little children and to seek to be the servant of all (Matt. 18:1-4; Mark 9:33-37; Luke 9:46-48).

3. Jesus' instruction included *how to relate to people who worked independently* of the main body of believers. He told the disciples not to forbid them: "Do not stop him . . . for whoever is not against you is for you" (Luke 9:49,50; cf. Mark 9:38-41).

4. Jesus told the disciples *how to deal with false teachers* within the church who cause the believers to be tempted into sin. His instruction was radical — cut them off by boycott or excommunication like a cancerous member of the body (Matt. 18:6-10;

Mark 9:42-50). Believers must be careful to maintain the savor of the salt.

5. Jesus taught the disciples *how*, with a proper attitude, *to deal with anyone who strays from obedience* to Christ and from Christian fellowship. They should seek his well-being as well as the purity of the Church, seeking diligently to restore the person who is in sin (Matt. 18:12-35).

6. Jesus pointed out that *if a brother offends you* repeatedly, you should forgive him an infinite number of times, even as God has forgiven you.

7. Jesus told *how to relate to those who reject Christians* out of jealousy. When they were not received by the Samaritans, He told them not to respond with vengeance but to move on, ignoring their rejection (Luke 9:51-56).

8. Jesus taught the disciples *how to deal with those who want to become disciples*. Those who are overconfident He would slow down. He would encourage those with wrong priorities to set them aside and move ahead with Him into the work of the kingdom. He told them that to be held back by old affections is not fitting for the kingdom of God (Matt. 8:19-22; Luke 9:57-62).

GUIDELINES BY THE APOSTLES AFTER THE RESURRECTION

After the resurrection the apostles expanded on these basic instructions. Peter and John continued to work in the temple so that they might relate to the Jews (Acts 3:1ff.). In order to show his loyalty to Judaism, Paul took a vow (Acts 21:23-26). He wrote, "To the Jews I became like a Jew, to win the Jews. . . . I have become all things to all men so that by all possible means I might save some" (1 Cor. 9:20,22). When the Gentiles were accepted, they were urged not to offend the Jews (Acts 15:19-21,28,29).

The importance of adopting humility in order to become a leader is emphasized in Philippians 2, James 4, and 1 Peter 5. The idea of boycotting false teachers (those who begin to teach things that do not agree with the basic teachings of Jesus Christ) is brought out elsewhere in the New Testament (Rom. 16:17,18; 2 John 9,10). In Ephesians 4:31–5:2 and Colossians 3:12-14 Paul continues instruction on forgiveness, emphasizing the importance of the unity of the Body. He also instructed Christians about restoring a person who is in sin (1 Cor. 5:1-7; 2 Cor. 7:8-12; Gal. 6:1,2), as did James (5:19,20).

DEALING WITH OPPOSITION

During this time Jesus demonstrated how to deal with opposi-

:ion. He had avoided Jerusalem for a year and a half because of hostilities there (John 7:1; cf. John 5 and 6). Now He went to Jerusalem where He demonstrated how to deal with opposition (John 7:2–10:21). He approached the opposition *openly* and with *honesty.* He claimed again that His authority was from God as evidenced in God's working through Him and by the witness of the Scriptures and He proclaimed confidently that He had come from God. With boldness He warned the Jews not to judge according to the flesh but to assume God's point of view, as He did. He exposed their willful blindness to His deity, for they repeatedly rejected the evidence of the miracles He performed.

During this period Jesus *rested in God's protection,* and God rewarded His trust. Many times He escaped the hands of His enemies. The Scriptures attribute His escape to God's providence ''because His hour had not yet come.'' Again, He offered to satisfy the people with living water, but many did not understand or accept His words. Instead, these claims and encounters with the Jewish leaders led to further division among the Jews and further polarization of the forces of evil and of righteousness. The apostles apparently followed Jesus' example, for later in the book of Acts, men observed their honesty and boldness (Acts 4:13; 5:27-32).

The church in the United States has never been exposed to great persecution and opposition. Most of the churches in the Western world have not experienced great opposition and persecution since the Peace of Westphalia (A.D. 1648). There have been a few outbreaks of bitter religious opposition, such as that against the Methodists in England and that against the church in Germany under Hitler.

As mentioned in chapter 1, the church in the United States and in the Western world is now faced with strong opposition from secular humanism, which has crystallized its forces into an antisupernatural stance. As Dr. Carl Henry has said, ''The two most significant religious developments in the twentieth century have been the collapse of ecumenical Christianity into a theologically incoherent movement of arrested missionary vigor, and the emergence of atheism globally as a mass phenomenon.'' This, he says, ''has now become a mass movement of formidable proportions officially supported by powerful modern nations.''[2] The ideological twin to atheistic communism is religious humanism, which is based on the same philosophical epistemology of logical positivism and equally aims at exalting man. These two are becoming united in the commitment that those who believe in the supernatural are hindrances and a detriment to human progress.

Many prominent scholars, scientists, and leaders of the West signed the Humanist Manifesto II in 1973 to forward and reaffirm Humanist Manifesto I. These documents refer to belief in revelation and to faith in a prayer-answering God who offers eternal salvation as "harmful, diverting people with false hopes of heaven." They are said to "do a disservice to the human species" and to be "obscurantist, impeding the free use of the intellect." The humanists therefore plan that in the future "there will be no uniquely religious emotions and attitudes of the kind hitherto associated with belief in the supernatural."[3]

The new threat is that those who have held this prejudice for years have grown to great strength and influence in the world structure and they are *now willing to use their power against Christians*.

But people are beginning to question man's wisdom. The humanistic intellectuals have made drastic mistakes. And now, just as a threatened animal attacks ferociously, so the humanists will express their hostilities against an outspoken and evangelical Christianity that criticizes the failures of humanism.

Recently, a scientist who is the chairman of his department at a large university angrily said to me, "You Christians who believe in the supernatural are the real menace to society." At another university the staff of Worldwide Discipleship Association recently applied for the privilege of presenting their Christian discipleship program to the incoming freshmen. But the administration had delegated all religious orientation to the antisupernatural Christian leadership on the campus. Our staff as well as those of other evangelical organizations approached the religious leaders, only to be told that they were not eligible to be on the program *because of their views*. These local incidents point to what is beginning to happen in places of higher power.

The false teachings of our modern world are different from those Jesus faced, but there are underlying similarities. They both oppose faith in God's revelation because of man's pride in his own teachings that contradict the truth of God. Modern-day disciples will find that Jesus' method of dealing with opposition and persecution is relevant today.

IMPORTANT CLAIMS OF DEITY

The Seventy were no doubt fearful in the face of such opposition. Before they were sent out to evangelize different areas of the country, they needed to comprehend fully the claims of Jesus' deity and power. During the Feast of the Tabernacles in Jerusalem Jesus made some of His greatest claims. He announced that He was the water of life (in other words, that He could give life through the Holy

Spirit) and that He was the light of the world. Jesus claimed to be the Son of God sent to deliver people from sin, to free them from bondage, and to raise them from the dead. He was the One who could give spiritual sight and He was the Good Shepherd (a messianic concept), whereas others had only been hirelings. This was a clear accusation of the Jewish leaders in Jerusalem as being irresponsible and selfish.

APPOINTMENT, TRAINING, AND GIFTS OF THE SEVENTY

Perhaps before Jesus left Capernaum or while He traveled to the Feast of Tabernacles, He appointed the Seventy, giving them definite assignments and taking them out into the ministry. When training them, Jesus repeated many of His earlier teachings on prayer; the nature of, and the conflict between, the kingdom of Satan and the kingdom of God; and others (cf. Luke 11:1–13:20).

At some point during this period of training (the exact time is hard to determine) the Seventy reported back to Jesus. They shared the amazing successes in exercising the spiritual gifts and the victories of their ministry (Luke 10:17-24). Jesus pointed out to them that such a successful ministry was to be counted insignificant compared to being a part of God's eternal kingdom. This would help keep them from trying to build their own little kingdom on earth through their ministry. It would help them keep their spiritual gifts in the proper perspective.

Later Paul called Christians to have the proper attitude toward spiritual gifts in their ministry of edifying the church (1 Cor. 12–14). Many Christians in the modern church tend to abuse their spiritual gifts and cause divisions in the body of Christ. This step of Participation and Delegation is the proper place for correcting these abuses.

It was also important for the disciples to learn how to deal with prejudice. The parable of the good Samaritan gave them an example of the attitude of love they should adopt when dealing with racial and religious prejudice. Jesus refuted the rabbis' strongly held prejudice against women studying theology. He allowed Mary of Bethany to take her seat at His feet along with His male disciples.

Jesus predicted His return in glory to bring judgment, warning the disciples to be prepared just as the Israelites had been prepared the night of the Exodus from Egypt (Exod. 12:11). He exhorted them to be faithful in carrying out the tasks He had assigned to them.

Jesus also warned the multitudes of coming judgment, rebuking them for seeking signs. He foretold judgment worse than the catastrophies they had recently been experiencing in Palestine. He warned that God would destroy Israel like a farmer destroying a worthless fig tree.

This final appeal and warning angered the Jews. They sought to arrest Him, but He escaped across the Jordan to Aenon. There He warned His disciples against the Jewish legalistic system, which rejected God.

CORRECTION OF RELIGIOUS ERRORS IN PRACTICE AND DOCTRINE

Every body of believing Christians is influenced by the wrong religious practices and teachings in their culture. While the terminology and concepts may differ from age to age, the same errors seem to be repeated. Jesus sought to help His followers maintain correct views.

He warned the disciples not to think they would enter the kingdom by following the broad, easy path with the many. Instead, they should seek the narrow gate of obedient faith that produces righteousness. Many of those going the easy way mistakenly rely on their fleshly heritage through Abraham, not realizing that God will accept men of all nations who come in obedience of faith (Luke 13:23-30; cf. Acts 10:34-36; Rom. 2:26-29; 9:6-8, et al.). Jesus mocked the threat of worldly political power (Herod's) but wept over Jerusalem and the judgment her leaders would receive for crucifying Him.

The Jewish religious world was shaken by Jesus' scathing rebuke of the Pharisees for their misguided practices and views. As He rebuked them, He encouraged the disciples to live righteously. (See Luke 13–17, the Outline of the Harmony of the Gospels.) Jesus exhorted them not to trust in a legal righteousness before others (cf. Rom. 10:3; Gal. 2:16-21; Phil. 3:9, et al.), to seek honor from others, or to try to buy human influence by social entertainment.

This kind of orientation toward others accompanies indifference to God's call in favor of worldly priorities. Moreover, these self-righteous men had failed to see God's deep concern for those who are lost in sin and His desire for their reconciliation. Jesus seems to imply that such fleshly trust leads to idolatry for riches and to sex lust. The selfish accumulation of wealth will lead to neglect of love for a poor neighbor and to condemnation in hell. In contrast to the Pharisees, Jesus encouraged His followers to be humble, to have mercy towards others, and seek eternal rewards from God in the resurrection. He called them to a full commitment to God, love for sinners, and compassion for the poor (cf. the contrasts of the works of the flesh in other New Testament writings, e.g., Gal. 5:19-26; Eph. 4:17-5:20).

Each age of the church is confronted with different forms of error. The errors always center in trusting in the works of the flesh and seeking honor from men. They deny the supernatural and lead to fleshly desires. Current teaching that is erroneous should be exposed at this step.

DEMONSTRATION OF AUTHORITY OVER DEATH

While giving these discourses to His disciples in Aenon, Jesus received word that Lazarus was sick. After a deliberate delay, He traveled to Bethany and there demonstrated His sonship and His authority to judge by miraculously raising Lazarus from the dead. According to the Jewish point of view, if a person is dead three days, his body begins to deteriorate. Lazarus had been in the tomb four days when he was raised. Because of this miracle the multitudes believed in Jesus, but such jealousy and hatred was fermented among the authorities in Jerusalem that they determined to put Jesus to death. They also determined to put Lazarus to death because many were believing on Jesus through him!

PREPARATION FOR WORLD OUTREACH

Jesus escaped assassination attempts in Bethany by going to Ephraim near the desert. As He led His men on one last evangelistic tour, He taught them things that would prepare them for His death and resurrection and for the expansion of His ministry to the Samaritans and the Gentiles. In one case He healed ten lepers. One was a Samaritan and the other nine were Jews. The only one who returned to thank Jesus was the Samaritan. This event prepared the way for a more benevolent attitude toward the Samaritans when the church would evangelize them later.

Jesus spoke against a woman divorcing her husband. Jewish women were not granted the right to divorce their husbands, but this was allowed among the Gentiles. Therefore, Jesus was orienting His followers to deal with domestic problems they would later encounter when the church expanded among Gentiles after the resurrection (Acts 8,10).

Jesus also taught His disciples about the inward and outward nature of the kingdom of God. He explained that in His absence from earth the Holy Spirit would rule in the hearts of believers, and when He returned to earth, He would personally rule in glory. As He instructed them about the second coming, He exhorted them to pray in faith and with humility. After He had left them and was enthroned at the right hand of God, it would be important for them to understand these things about the nature of the kingdom of God.

Jesus' experience with the rich young ruler emphasized that riches are a hindrance to entering the kingdom of God (Mark 10:17-23). The recipients of the kingdom will not be primarily the noble and rich but the poor and humble folk. Others who are looked down on are also to be received. Children are to be welcomed, as are celibates who are dedicated to serving the kingdom. Jesus taught that all people, whoever they may be, who are willing to dedicate themselves fully to Him and to the building of His kingdom will be rewarded.

EXPANSION OF THESE TRUTHS

Paul expanded on many of Jesus' teachings about the church. He dealt with the question of divorce (1 Cor. 7:10-16). He also pointed out that one does not have to be mighty or noble to be called of God — many who are poor and humble are called (1 Cor. 1:27). Paul repeatedly warned that the love of money is a root of all kinds of evil and that Christians should be content with such things as they have (Phil. 4:11; 1 Tim. 6:6-10; Heb. 13:5).

Many of the New Testament writers expanded on the concept of the future judgment at the glorious return of Christ. Paul discussed it in 1 Thessalonians 4:13-15 and 2 Thessalonians 1:9,10. The concluding chapters of the book of Revelation deal almost exclusively with the events that precede the glorious coming of our Lord in judgment. All of these teachings are a warning to the world and should produce faithfulness in the church.

CONCLUSION

Through the teachings and events of this period, Jesus was equipping His people to live together in unity and to face the problems of living in a world that was hostile to them, persecuted them, and did not recognize them as children of God. During this period Jesus appointed the seventy new apostles who assisted in expanding the ministry throughout the world after their dispersion (cf. Acts 11:22; 14:14; Rom. 16:7; 1 Cor. 9:5). The importance of appointing and delegating responsibility to leaders was diligently followed by Peter (1 Peter 5:1-4), Paul (1 Tim. 3; Titus 1:5-9), and others. The book of James is largely devoted to instruction in how to lead a congregation conforming with the principles Jesus gave at this time (e.g., restoring a sinner — 5:19,20; receiving the poor as well as the rich — 2:1-13). Body Life is Paul's chief concern in 1 Corinthians 12–14 and Ephesians 4. Our instruction of disciples today must include teaching them to trust God to work in the lives of others and helping them learn how to relate to people outside the church as a member representing that body.

Notes

[1] Part of the material in this section in Luke could be the same as some listed in an earlier step (cf. Matt. 17 with Luke 15 and 17). I have presented the material here in the order it occurs in most of the harmonies.

[2] Samuel J. Andrews, *The Life of Our Lord* (New York: Scribner's, 1894), pp. 381-384.

[3] Dr. Carl F. H. Henry, *New Strides of Faith* (Chicago: Moody, 1972), pp. 39-41.

[4] *Humanist Manifesto II* (Buffalo, New York: Prometheus Books, 1973), pp. 9, 13, 16.

10

The Exchanged Life and Worldwide Challenge

In the step of the Exchanged Life and Worldwide Challenge (the last step in the development of the disciple), all of the disciple's previous training becomes integrated in a more complete manner. All previous experience of trusting Christ through the Holy Spirit reaches a climax of understanding that enables the disciple to find confident rest. This is not a step that frees him from all sin, failure, or despair. But it brings him to the peaceful assurance that while *in himself* he does not have the power to gain victory, nevertheless *in Christ's Spirit* all things are possible. Jesus' disciples began to experience the Exchanged Life as a result of the final events and teachings of Christ's life, especially through the cross, resurrection, ascension, and the coming of the Holy Spirit on the day of Pentecost. They were then sent out with the challenge to reach the world.

THE DISCIPLES' INADEQUATE REALIZATION OF TRUSTING THE SPIRIT

From the beginning the disciples learned about the Holy Spirit. John the Baptist announced, ''After me will come one more powerful than I. . . . I baptize you with water, but he will baptize you with the Holy Spirit'' (Mark 1:7,8). On the day Jesus was baptized, the heavens opened and the Holy Spirit descended on Him like a dove. The voice of the Father said, ''You are my Son, whom I love; with you I am well pleased'' (Mark 1:11). Jesus was publicly declared to be the Christ, the Son of God, and His baptism was the public

153

anointing for His priestly ministry (cf. Heb. 5:4-6). From the initiation of His ministry Jesus was identified as the One who was anointed by the Spirit and as the One who would anoint others.

Jesus performed mighty miracles through the power of the Holy Spirit. In regard to His ability to cast out demons He said, ''If I drive out demons by the Spirit of God, then the kingdom of God has come upon you'' (Matt. 12:28). Later, Christ was also identified as the One who fulfilled prophecies concerning the Holy Spirit (e.g., Isa. 44:3,4; Ezek. 47:1-12; Joel 2:28,29). In John 7:37,38 He said, '' 'If a man is thirsty, let him come to me and drink. Whoever believes in me, as the Scripture has said, streams of living water will flow from within him.' By this He meant the Spirit. . . .'' The Holy Spirit was manifested in the ministry of the twelve apostles and later in the ministry of the Seventy, for they cast out demons and healed the sick through the Holy Spirit's power (Luke 10:17-20).

Jesus emphasized that *the Spirit* was *all important*. In John 6:63 He said, ''The Spirit gives life; *the flesh counts for nothing*.'' Yet even though Jesus pointed out that the flesh cannot please God, the disciples had not understood that only by the Holy Spirit working in and through them could they do God's work. These men had gone through many experiences that had thrown them into utter dependence on Christ. But they now felt a professional confidence. They were impressed with their ability to minister and to lead, and they felt very important to the movement. They expected to have prominent positions in the earthly kingdom of God. After all, they had helped build the movement that now involved many thousands.

EVENTS DESIGNED TO SHATTER CONFIDENCE IN THE FLESH

The events that led to the crucifixion were of such a nature as to undermine the disciples' subtle confidence in the flesh. That confidence was utterly shattered by the crucifixion.

When Jesus ceased His public ministry and started His last journey to Jerusalem, the disciples thought He would immediately establish an earthly kingdom and they would be primary recipients of its fleshly benefits. All the subsequent events were designed by Christ to help them see that flesh would fail. Only those things done in the power of the Holy Spirit would prevail.

Prediction of death and resurrection. Their confidence in the flesh should have been shaken when Jesus predicted that He would die and be raised at Jerusalem. But the disciples had little understanding of His words. Apparently, they only heard Him speak of his plans to go to Jerusalem. Knowing His popularity, they assumed that He would establish His kingdom immediately.

James and John had their mother approach Jesus to request that they be given the two most prominent positions in the new kingdom. When the other ten disciples heard of this, they were angered, for each of them wanted the honored positions. Using this situation to teach them, Jesus said, "Whoever wants to become great among you must be your servant . . . just as the Son of Man did not come to be served, but to serve, and to give his life a ransom for many" (Matt. 20:26-28).

Expectation of fleshly kingdom refuted by parable. As Jesus and His disciples passed through Jericho, two blind men cried out for help, "Lord, Son of David, have mercy on us!" (Matt. 20:30). "Son of David" was a messianic title. When these blind men called Jesus the Son of David, they were, in essence, calling him the great King. They appealed to Jesus as the king of Israel, and He healed them.

Following the healing, Zaccheus, a Jewish tax official for Rome, was converted. He resigned from his position and joined Jesus, taking Him to his home. (Zaccheus probably thought Jesus' kingdom would soon displace Rome.) Zaccheus's conversion impressed the crowds. These two events led the people to think that the kingdom would come immediately (Luke 19:11).

Jesus then told a parable of a nobleman who was going to a distant country where he would receive the authority to be king. Before he left, the nobleman called together his servants and dispensed his wealth. He charged them to invest his money faithfully while he was gone, promising to return and reward them after he had been made king. Clearly, Jesus was telling the disciples that He was departing to a place where they could not come. During His absence He would be crowned king and given authority to rule, and the disciples would be held responsible for carrying on the work He had begun. Later, when He returned, He would reward them for their faithfulness.

The human and divine plan for death to the flesh. The disciples in their self-confidence and optimism had been blind to the fact that Jesus Christ would soon die. The Sanhedrin had met and determined to put Him to death (John 11:47-53). At the same time, Jesus went to the house of Simon in Bethany. There Mary, a woman disciple, anointed Him for burial. This act disclosed that God Himself had determined that Christ should now go to the cross, and the Sanhedrin was only carrying out His preappointed plan (John 12:3-8).

Coronation for heavenly kingship. The day after Mary anointed Him for burial, Jesus made His triumphal entry into Jerusalem (Matt. 21:1-9; John 12:12-16). That event is generally misunderstood because it is not usually seen in the context of the Old Testament. Jesus' ride into Jerusalem reflected the Old Testament practice of crowning a king. First Kings 1:32-35 records what occurred after King David had been told that his son, Adonijah, was attempting to usurp the kingdom:

> King David said, "Call to me Zadok the priest, Nathan the prophet, and Benaiah the son of Jehoiada." So they came before the king. And the king said to them, "Take with you the servants of your lord, and cause Solomon my son to ride on my own mule, and bring him down to Gihon; and let Zadok the priest and Nathan the prophet there anoint him king over Israel; then blow the trumpet, and say, 'Long live King Solomon!' You shall then come up [to Jerusalem] after him, and he shall come and sit upon my throne; for he shall be king in my stead; and I have appointed him to be ruler over Israel and over Judah."

During a Jewish coronation ceremony, the king would ride into Jerusalem on a white mule to be proclaimed king of Israel. When Jesus, therefore, rode into Jerusalem on a colt, the crowds responded enthusiastically. Some threw their garments in the road, while others cut down branches and spread them along the way, shouting, "Hosanna to the Son of David." In effect they were saying, "Long live the king of Israel."

The triumphal entry fulfilled the prophecy of Zechariah 9:9:

> Rejoice greatly, O daughter of Zion!
> Shout in triumph, O daughter of Jerusalem!
> Behold, your king is coming to you;
> He is just and endowed with salvation,
> Humble, and mounted on a donkey,
> Even on a colt, the foal of a donkey.

The crowd expected Jesus to set up a kingdom in Jerusalem at that moment.

A careful study of the Scriptures, however, indicates that Jesus knew He would gain His crown *after* His death and resurrection. The day before, He had told them the parable of the nobleman who went away into a far country to get the authority to rule, leaving His servants to carry on his work for a period of time (Luke 19:11-27). In regard to Jesus' entry into Jerusalem and His fulfillment of the prophecy of Zechariah 9:9, John said, "At first His disciples did not understand all this. Only *after Jesus was glorified* did they realize that these things had been written about him and that they had done these things to him" (John 12:16, italics mine).

In 2 Samuel 7:12,13, God promised David that his descendant would sit on His throne forever. This promise was the hope of the Jews. It was the most eagerly anticipated promise in the Old Testament Scriptures.

In Psalm 110:1 David predicted the fulfillment of this promise. While debating with the Jewish leaders a few days after His triumphal entry, Jesus quoted David, showing that David called his descendant his Lord and prophesied that He would sit at God's right hand (Matt. 22:41-45).

On the day of Pentecost, Peter claimed that this promise to David was fulfilled in the resurrection and ascension of Jesus Christ (Acts 2:30-36). Peter and the other New Testament writers realized that He was crowned king in heaven, and the coronation ceremony in Jerusalem had simply been a public declaration of His kingship (cf. Ps. 110:1 with 1 Cor. 15:20-28).

Predictions of Israel's rejection by God and replacement by the worldwide church. Jesus knew that the Jews would reject Him and that His coronation in heaven was imminent. He denounced the nation of Israel for her failure to bear fruit for God. He predicted His rejection and the coming destruction of Israel. This emphasis during the final week of Jesus' earthly life should have shaken the disciples' fleshly confidence.

During that week Jesus again cleansed the temple, denouncing the apostasy of Jewish worship (Matt. 21:12-16; Mark 11:15-18; Luke 19:45-47). On this second cleansing of the temple, He emphasized it was God's intent for *all nations* to worship Him (Mark 11:17). He cursed the fig tree because of its fruitlessness, symbolizing God's impending destruction of Israel (cf. Isa. 5:1-7; Hosea 9:10; Micah 7:1,2; Matt. 21:18-22; Mark 11:12-14,20-25). He entered into bitter conflicts with Jewish leaders over His authority and their lack of response (Matt. 21:23-46; Mark 11:27–12:12; Luke 20:1-18). By asking questions concerning the Messiah, He countered their efforts to entrap Him (Matt. 22:15-46; Mark 12:13-37; Luke 20:20-44). Then He predicted that the prophecies of Jeremiah that God would forsake His house and leave it desolate would soon be fulfilled (Matt. 23; Mark 12:38-40; Luke 20:45-48; cf. Jer. 12:7; 22:5).

At this time Jesus told the Jews two parables that should be interpreted in light of the events and teachings following the triumphal entry: the rented vineyard (Matt. 21:33-46) and the wedding feast of the king's son (Matt. 22:1-14). Jesus warned that the vinegrowers (the Jews) who killed the owner's son would themselves be destroyed and the vineyard would be given to other vinegrowers who would be faithful stewards (Matt. 21:38-41). He expressly said to the Jews, ''The kingdom of God will be taken away from you and given to a people who will produce its fruit'' (Matt. 21:43), thereby pointing to the creation of the New Testament church (Eph. 2:11-19).

In another parable Jesus told of a king who invited his friends to the wedding feast of his son. Because they refused to come and killed the servants who delivered the invitation, he destroyed them. Instead of his friends, he invited strangers from the streets and highways (Matt. 22:7,9,10), indicating the inclusion of the Gentiles.

The Greeks who sought Jesus in the temple (John 12) represent the new vinegrowers and the guests from the streets. Jesus knew that the time had come for Him to die so that the harvest of the Gentile world might be reaped (John 12:20-33). His death at the hands of the Jews and His subsequent resurrection were linked to the rejection of Israel and the calling of a new nation. Many of the people of this nation would be Gentiles, and they would work for Him on earth while He reigned from heaven. His acceptance by the Greeks foreshadowed His glorification (John 12:23). The logical consequence of these teachings was Jesus' command later given to His disciples to make disciples of all nations and teach them all things that the heavenly King had commanded (Matt. 28:18-20).

The prophetic discourse in Matthew 24 and 25 constituted the final statement on Israel's rejection. Jesus foretold Jerusalem's destruction, predicting that not even one stone of the temple would be left upon another. He said He would leave His subjects with the task of feeding His household and expect them to be faithful stewards until His return in kingly power (Matt. 24:44-51). They would be like the servants of a man who was going on a long journey. He would entrust them with all his possessions to invest in his absence. At his return they could expect reward or punishment according to their service (Matt. 25:14-30). He promised to come again in great glory to judge the world, but His coming would be unexpected, like a thief in the night. And the disciples should be ready like wise virgins, expecting the groom to come with his wedding party (Matt. 25:1-13). He spoke of the signs that would indicate the imminence of His return: His coming would be at a time of growing evil, apostacy, and tribulation.

By this time the disciples' hopes for an immediate earthly kingdom should have been shattered. Like Abraham who pled for God to accept Hagar's son of normal fleshly birth or Jacob who sought God's blessing by his own sinful manipulation, the apostles continued to hope in the flesh and look for a worldly political kingdom. They had forgotten that Jacob could not overcome Esau. God had to perform a miracle to deliver him from Esau's hands. To remind Jacob that God must accomplish the victory, God changed his name from Jacob (which means "deceiver") to Israel (which means "Let God prevail," or "Let God do it!"). In the same way, the apostles needed to learn that God must prevail. He must establish the kingdom.

Last-day efforts to promote denial of the flesh in favor of trusting the power of God. Throughout the final day and evening of Jesus' life, He referred to His coming death. He symbolized the institution of the new covenant through His death by serving the Passover bread as His broken body and the wine as His blood. He announced His betrayal by Judas and predicted that He, the Shepherd of the sheep, would be killed and the sheep scattered. He warned Peter that he would deny Him three times before the next dawn was announced by the cock's crow (Matt. 26:20-33). When He girded Himself with a towel and washed the disciples' feet, He dramatically demonstrated that His followers were called to live as servants (John 13:1-12).

The disciples still had confidence in the flesh. They all insisted that they were willing to die with Jesus if necessary. Peter even boasted that though everyone else denied Him, he never would: "Even if I have to die with you, I will never disown you" (Matt. 26:35). The other disciples said the same.

That evening Jesus declared that He must soon go away to heaven in order to send them the Holy Spirit (John 14:1-3,12,16,17; 16:7). Three times He called Peter, James, and John to pray with Him and warned them not to have confidence in their own abilities: "Watch and pray so that you will not fall into temptation. The spirit is willing, but *the body* [Greek: *flesh*] *is weak*" (Matt. 26:37-46; Mark 14:33-42).

Hope for the flesh on the cross. When Jesus was arrested, tried, and crucified, the disciples saw their hopes demolished. They fled in fear. Their king and their vision of the imminent kingdom were gone. "We had hoped that he was going to redeem Israel," they said, but that hope died when the chief priests and rulers "handed him over to be sentenced to death, and they crucified him" (Luke 24:20,21). Human effort could no longer do anything to produce the kingdom. They were separated from His visible leadership and were afraid.

VISION OF NEW HUMANITY AND KINGDOM IN THE RESURRECTION

Through the cross the new kingdom was initiated. Jesus Christ was raised from the dead and declared with power to be the Son of God. A new creation was made possible; the second Adam became "a life-giving spirit" (1 Cor. 15:45,47). Over a forty-day period after His resurrection, He appeared to His disciples in His transformed body. After giving the Great Commission, He ascended to His position of authority at God's right hand (Heb. 1:3). On the day of Pentecost, Christ sent the Holy Spirit into the world to indwell the disciples (Acts 1,2). Since then Jesus has been calling men to Himself to be a part of His body, the church, over which He rules in the world.

He will remain in heaven "until the time comes for God to restore everything" (Acts 3:21; cf. 1:11; 2 Tim. 4:8).

After the death, resurrection, and visible appearance of the Lord Jesus Christ, the apostles gained a new perspective. In Gethsemane before His death, they had slept, even though Jesus had exhorted them that the flesh is weak and they should pray lest they enter into temptation (Luke 22:39-46). They had not fully understood that prayer was necessary in order to renew the Holy Spirit's power (cf. Matt. 17:21; Mark 9:29). After the resurrection they followed Jesus' instruction and went to Jerusalem to await the Holy Spirit. Here their actions reveal a changed attitude towards prayer: "They all joined together constantly in prayer" (Acts 1:14).

After the Holy Spirit visibly came on them on the day of Pentecost (the Jewish feast of First Fruits at the beginning of harvest), the apostles and their followers went forth different men. Peter, who had fearfully denied his Lord before the little maid and a few others at the house of the high priest (John 18:15ff.), now stood in the midst of the temple before all the Jews. Bravely accusing them of crucifying by wicked hands the Lord of Glory, he called them to repentance (Acts 2:14ff.). All the apostles were marked by new boldness (Acts 4:31). Instead of wanting to build a kingdom and seeking first place for themselves, they began to sell their earthly possessions and share with each other according to their needs (Acts 4:32-37). Their hope was in heavenly things.

The disciples now were led and empowered by the Holy Spirit, their source of strength and authority (Acts 1:15,16; 2:4; 4:8,31; 5:3,9; 8:14-17; 10:45-48; 13:2-4; 15:7-9, et al.). His working was always supported by the record of God's past working (cf. Luke 24:44-49; Acts 1:20; 2:16-21,25-28,34,35; 3:22; 4:11, 24-26, et al.). God had enthroned His Son in heaven and given Him all power. The apostles shared this power with Christ and saw themselves as sons of God. They looked at life from the perspective of Christ's throne and evaluated everything in the light of the eternal kingdom. They were now resting in Christ's ability to handle every circumstance of life, including their ministry. They trusted in the Holy Spirit rather than the flesh and, in fact, were willing to die for Christ. The disciples were experiencing the Exchanged Life with Christ. They began to be like the second Adam, Jesus Christ.

CARE IN UNDERSTANDING THE EXCHANGED LIFE

Care must be taken in teaching that the same things that happened in the apostles' lives during this step of growth can be duplicated in the lives of all believers. There are some essential differences in the way the Holy Spirit came upon the apostles and His relationship to believers today.

For one thing, the coming of the Holy Spirit on the day of Pentecost was a visible event marking a historical turning point never to be repeated. From Abraham's day God planned to pour out a blessing on all nations of the world (Gen. 12:3). Paul said that this promise was fulfilled in the coming of the Holy Spirit (Gal. 3:14).

The Old Testament prophets predicted God's coming judgment on the nation for its sins. They also spoke of the day when the Holy Spirit would be poured out on God's people of all flesh. Beginning from the altar of God (the cross, in the New Testament), the Spirit would go out like a great stream of water, reviving a people who were like a dry wilderness (Isa. 44:3,4; Ezek. 37; Joel 2:28; 3:18, et al.). This day the new covenant would be instituted. God would forgive His people and by the Holy Spirit write His laws on their hearts (cf. Jer. 31:30-34; Ezek. 36:25-27). When John the Baptist came filled with the Holy Spirit, the Jewish people, being aware of these prophecies, believed that the new day of the Holy Spirit was about to dawn.

The fact that Pentecost was an important turning point must be emphasized. However, *care must be taken not to create a discontinuity between the Old and New Testament working of the Spirit.* The Holy Spirit's work in the Old Testament gave intelligent meaning to the Pentecost of the New Testament. Bishop J. C. Ryle has said:

> When we read of the Holy Ghost being ''given,'' we must not think that He was in no sense in the church before the day of Pentecost. He was even in the hearts of Old Testament believers. No one ever served God acceptably, from Abel downwards, without the grace of the Holy Ghost. John the Baptist was ''filled'' with Him.[1]

The Holy Spirit worked in the lives of the Old Testament saints and in the life of John the Baptist, even as He worked in the New Testament. But in the New Testament His working had new meaning of far greater significance.

The Holy Spirit's working in the lives of Christ and His apostles was a prologue, while Pentecost was the pivotal point. Jesus had promised that all who believed on Him would receive the gift of the Holy Spirit, which would be like a river of living water. However, John was careful to point out that Jesus had been speaking of an experience that would happen *after* Jesus had been raised and glorified (John 7:37-39). On the last night before the crucifixion, Jesus spoke of the event as still being in the future. He said that it would mark a change in their relationship. He said:

> I will ask the Father, and he will give you another Counselor, the Spirit of truth, to be with you forever. The world cannot accept this Counselor, because it neither sees him nor knows him. But you know him, for he lives with you and will be in you (John 14:16,17).

Even after His resurrection the Scripture says:

> He gave them this command: "Do not leave Jerusalem, but wait for the gift my Father promised, which you have heard me speak about. For John baptized with water, but in a few days you will be baptized with the Holy Spirit" (Acts 1:4,5).

THE MEANING OF PENTECOST

What was the *new significance* of Pentecost? Jesus had indicated that because the Holy Spirit worked in His life the kingdom of God was already operating in the world (Matt. 12:28). On the day of Pentecost Peter said that Jesus Christ had been enthroned at God's right hand and that through His power He had poured out the Holy Spirit on them (Acts 2:25-28,32-36). *Pentecost testified that Jesus was Lord* above all principalities and powers. Peter's words agree with John's — the Spirit was given as a result of Jesus' glorification (John 7:39). Pentecost marked the point from which the glorified Christ began to give gifts by the Holy Spirit. Through the distribution of the gifts He could direct and govern His church from His throne in heaven (John 17:4-10; 1 Cor. 12; Eph. 4:8).

Pentecost also marked *a turning point in God's dealing with men*. Whereas before, He had dealt with the nations only through Israel, after Pentecost He accepted any man or woman who would come to Him in faith. Peter said that Joel 2:28 was fulfilled at Pentecost. God had given His Spirit to "all flesh." People of any strata of society, from bond servants to kings, old or young, men or women, could receive the Holy Spirit (Acts 2:16-21). Later, in the house of Cornelius, Peter and his party of Jewish Christians witnessed the signs given by the Holy Spirit and accepted the Gentiles into the body of Christ (Acts 10:34,35,44-48; 15:7-9). Peter and John came to Samaria and imparted spiritual sign gifts to those who had become Christians through Philip's preaching. This demonstrated that the hated Samaritans had received the Holy Spirit and, therefore, were to be equally accepted in the church (Acts 8:5-17). (The event related in Acts 19:1-6 is different, as discussed on page 82.)

Receiving the Holy Spirit was an *indication that a person was accepted into the kingdom of God* and was an heir to all its blessings. The Twelve and the Seventy had experienced the Holy Spirit's power to work miracles because Christ chose them and associated with them. At Pentecost the presence of the Holy Spirit became more distinctly a blessing expressed in individual gifts. Paul called the Spirit a *"pledge"* or "down payment" on the believer's inheritance in the kingdom of Christ. The Spirit is God's *seal* on the Christian, signifying that he is God's possession for eternity (Eph. 1:13,14). Indeed, the Holy Spirit is the very life of God in the believer that will continue into the eternal kingdom. The Old Testament individuals never saw this meaning concerning the working of the Spirit.

The coming of the Holy Spirit into every believer *changed the whole idea of worship*. In the Old Testament the "tent of meeting" or tabernacle of the wilderness was replaced by the temple in Jerusalem as the only place men could meet with God. God dwelt within the Holy of Holies and was manifested there by His Shekinah glory. People of other nations had come to Jerusalem to worship according to Mosaic law. In the New Testament, the ceremonial law and the necessity of worshiping in Jerusalem were replaced by a new form of worship — worship in *spirit* and in *truth* (John 4:21-24). A Christian or group of Christians anywhere could meet with and worship God. As Jesus Christ had become the Tabernacle for the Holy Spirit (John 1:14), so now every Christian is the temple of God. Paul said, "Do you not know that your body is a temple of the Holy Spirit, who is in you, whom you have received from God . . .?" (1 Cor. 6:19; cf. 3:16; 2 Cor. 6:16). Every Christian is indwelt by the glory of God, even as Jesus was (John 17:22). In this sense the Spirit is not only *with* the Christian or Christians, but is *in* them as a center of worship, a temple, which was not so of the saints before Pentecost (cf. John 14:16,17).

By way of summary, every Christian is the temple of God indwelt by the Holy Spirit who signifies the lordship of Christ over him. The Spirit is a pledge and seal of his acceptance and inheritance. He teaches and guides him. This relationship between the believers and the Holy Spirit was instituted on the day of Pentecost.

SPECIAL MEANING OF PENTECOST FOR THE TWELVE

The twelve apostles received a unique inspiration from the Holy Spirit that is not applicable to other believers. The apostles had been with Jesus and witnessed His ministry from His baptism to His ascension (Acts 1:21,22). Jesus said, "You also must testify [about me], for you have been with me from the beginning" (John 15:27). He promised, "The Holy Spirit, whom the Father will send in my name, will teach you all things and will remind you of everything I have said to you" (John 14:26). Their preaching would become the standard on which all succeeding generations would base their faith (John 17:8,20). No other Christians can have this privilege.

EXPERIENCING THE EXCHANGED LIFE IS FOR
THE TWELVE AND ALL CHIRISTIANS

The apostles stood in a unique place in history and experienced a unique role. Still, the evidence shows that *they progressed much like other Christians*. They grew to trust the working of Christ by His Spirit in their lives. Their development is the only clear pattern for subsequent believers. Jesus offered the new birth by the Holy Spirit to Nicodemus at the beginning of His ministry (John 3:3-16). Those already following Him must have experienced this, and Jesus had already given them the supernatural power of the Spirit to live and minister in His name while He was still with them (Matt. 10:1,20; Luke 10:17, et al.). But it has been shown that they had not learned to rest in the power of the Holy Spirit alone. Until the crucifixion they still had confidence in the flesh. Later they came to the point of resting in Christ by exchanging their lives in the flesh for His life through the Spirit. This was the step of faith that became the basis for all future growth and ministry.

That does not mean the apostles were perfect and never failed again. Peter returned to his old fear of men (Gal. 2:11,12). Paul admitted that he was not perfect but that he pressed toward the goal (Phil. 3:12). But there is no question that after Pentecost the Eleven came to a rest in the power of Christ never before experienced. All Jesus' teachings near the end of His life prepared them for this step.

Every Christian must come to understand the weakness of the flesh and rest in the Exchanged Life with Christ. In the early steps of growth the Christian is motivated to look to Christ for help. The new Christian is taken with the freshness of knowing his Lord. As he begins to witness and minister to others, he is afraid and looks to Christ for help. As he steps out in leadership for the first time, he relies on Christ. The challenge to forsake the earthly and live for the heavenly also causes him to look to Christ.

After a time the apostles became accustomed to working in the ministry. They *became professionals and trusted in themselves,* relying on their own importance. This is true of many Christians. Often God must bring Christians to a point of deep frustration. He must show them that they have not come to rest in the sufficiency of Christ through the Holy Spirit. He shows them that the ministry is not first theirs, but Christ's; their family is not first theirs, but His; their life is not first theirs, but His (Gal. 2:20). When they see that Christ is sufficient to cleanse, empower, and give wisdom and that they need nothing else (even if it means failure from the world's view), then they will enter into the Exchanged Life.

Also, as the apostles trusted in the visible evidence of Christ's physical presence, so today Christians get to depend on the *feeling of God's presence* and various *evidences* of the supernatural rather than trusting God the Spirit Himself. Just as the disciples had to see Christ die and had to give up Christ's visible presence, so Christians often have to be separated from fleshly *feelings* and *evidences* of the Spirit and learn to walk in obedience to the light of Christ's clear teaching alone. A little child needs to be spoken to often by his parents, but as the child grows older and knows the parents' will, he is expected to walk in obedience without having to be told. This does not mean the parents love the child less or are supporting him less. Just so, God sometimes stops giving evidences of His presence so His maturing child may learn to trust and apply His word. God is still for us and we can still trust Him.

This can be a very frustrating experience for the Christian, especially if threatening circumstances arise. David went through this feeling in the Old Testament and his experience pointed to the more real and threatening separation from the Father that Jesus experienced (Ps. 22:1,2,14,15; cf. Matt. 27:46; John 19:28). But David believed God was still there and trusted (Ps. 22:19-24) as did Jesus on the cross (Luke 23:46).

God once brought me to the point where I saw that even in failure Christ is sufficient whether I feel He is there or not. Out of that experience I came to understand the exchanged life. I have counseled with many in Christ's work who have had to learn this truth. One young woman who traveled and supervised other women in a ministry came to me with a sense of great frustration about her life and work. She knew of no sin in her life and had had several years of fruitful experience in Christian work. People often had said, "We like to have Susan around, because we sense the Holy Spirit's presence in her."

Yet she came to me in anguish, as if her whole world had collapsed around her. She could not explain why she seemed to lack a sense of God's presence in her life. I confronted her with the possibility that she may have become "professional" in her ministry or had come to trust fleshly evidences rather than the Lord. Through the Spirit she had learned how to do what was Christ's will but now had stopped looking to Christ's Spirit for the strength and wisdom to do it. Since she was not trusting Him, God withheld the Spirit's power and she began to fail to produce in her work. After prayer, she saw that she had really failed to trust Christ to be adequate no matter what came to pass. She had stopped looking to Jesus.

On another occasion a gifted young man drove two hundred

miles to talk to me. He said he had experienced many gifts of the Holy Spirit, including speaking in tongues and healing. He had built a church of fifteen hundred members and felt he had labored in the power of the Holy Spirit. Recently he had accepted a challenge to build another church but had come to feel totally incapable of doing God's work. He had lost the feeling and evidences of Christ's working. He knew of no sin in his life. He too had become a "professional" minister, doing things as he had learned how but without faith in the risen Christ. Like Susan, *ideally* he knew that in the flesh he could do no good thing. But now he was experiencing the reality of that. I pointed out to him that even if he totally failed, Christ was adequate for his need. He found rest in looking to Jesus as totally sufficient.[2]

Learning to *rest* in the power of God in Christ — a power available to the Christian through the Holy Spirit — is the last foundation stone for erecting a mature Christian life and for carrying out a joyful ministry. One may experience many things under the Spirit's control and influence and still not have learned to *rest* in His sufficiency.

One may be born again, be led of the Spirit in unusual ways, witness and minister in the power of the Spirit, exercise unusual gifts of the Spirit, be used of the Spirit as a leader, and even make great sacrifice of temporal blessings while trusting the Spirit, and still not have learned to rest in the sufficiency of the Spirit. That occurs only when the disciple has come to realize his total inability to please God in the flesh and the fact that he must consciously trust in the Spirit of Christ alone. When he learns this, he will know once-for-all that apart from exchanging his fleshly life for Christ's eternal life there is no joy or victory in life and service for the Savior. This is the seventh step.

The Worldwide Challenge

When the apostles had had their faith tested and had learned to trust the Spirit regardless of the circumstances, they were ready for the challenge to evangelize the world. A Christ with worldwide power should be known and worshiped by all nations. Therefore, Christ told them He would be present by the Holy Spirit and challenged them with the Great Commission of making Him known to the world (Matt. 28:18-20; Luke 24:46-51; John 20:21,22; Acts 1:8).

There is a preview of this already in the Old Testament. When David had gone through the test of his faith, he was given a vision of assembling all nations to worship God his King (Ps. 22:27-31). And after Christ's commission Paul talks about world proclamation to those who ''continue in [the] faith, established and firm, not moved from the hope held out in the gospel'' (Col. 1:23-27).

CONCLUSION

Today the last step of discipleship is a test of whether the Christian trusts in the flesh or in the power of the Spirit of God. When he has passed this final exam, he is ready for the challenge of a world ministry. He will believe in a sovereign Christ who is worthy of the worship of every creature.

This seventh step does not mean he will have reached a point of sinlessness, nor that he will never fail the Lord, nor that he will never have a time of depression. Indeed, he will know the impotence of the flesh and the sin principle in a profound way. But it does mean that having learned this truth of the exchanged life, he will from that point on know why he failed, why he was depressed, why he sinned, and he can quickly be restored to a state of joy and victory. He will know that he trusted in himself or in fleshly evidences of the Spirit's working and not in Christ Himself. He will know that the power of Christ can lead him through sin, depression, or failure to triumphant victory — even if there is a cross. Christ's life is always sufficient. This is the life of continually dying to self and yielding to the Holy Spirit (Rom. 6; 2 Cor. 4:7,8; Gal. 2:20).

Notes

[1] Bishop J. C. Ryle, *Ryle's Expository Thoughts on the Gospels* (Grand Rapids: Zondervan, 1956) 4:303.

[2] V. Raymond Edman's *They Found the Secret* (Grand Rapids: Zondervan, 1960).

III

Important Principles of Discipleship

11

Association for Communication

The way a teacher associates with a person (or persons) will determine how effectively he can communicate with him. It has already been suggested that the basic failure in discipleship in the American churches lies in this area. Through currents of change in education inside and outside of the church, the pastor now relates mainly as a lecturer and administrator. He is not involved with the congregation personally in such a way as to apply truth to their everyday life. Jesus' method of disciple building was in contrast to this. He progressively became associated in a more intimate way. Moreover, the nature of His association with people was designed to accomplish the particular objective of the successive steps of growth.

DIFFERENT WAYS OF ASSOCIATING TO ACCOMPLISH THE DESIRED OBJECTIVE

Casual association for Repentance and Faith. During the step of Repentance and Faith the objective is to sow the seed of the Word of God widely so that those who have been prepared by the Holy Spirit may be led to turn from their sins to trust Christ. The objective is to contact as many persons as possible with the call of God in a meaningful way. Since in-depth contact with people would limit outreach to only a few, most contacts must be done on a casual basis. When John the Baptist and Jesus led people to repentance, their association was in large crowds, small home evangelistic socials, and person-to-person evangelism. Even in the latter, it is doubtful whether Jesus was personally acquainted with the individuals prior to His conversations with them (e.g., the woman at the well, Nicodemus, and the rich young ruler). This does not exclude developing a meaningful relationship with people in order to win them to Christ when they are encountered on a day-to-day basis. But it does mean that when a person is engaged in an evangelistic ministry, his association will be more casual and less intimate. Today, the efforts to lead others to repentance should be similar. The leader will know them only casually and the person addressed need only have an interest to hear the Word.

Little or no demands and an open fellowship for Enlightenment. In gathering disciples for the step of Enlightenment, the relationship becomes more intimate. To understand who Jesus was and to trust Him as their leader, the disciples had to be associated with Him personally over a period of time. However, this group that Jesus had was tentative and open. The men who followed Him had *no initial commitment* to Him. They simply associated on a friendly level in order to learn. By this friendship association Jesus moved them toward the point of committing themselves to Him as their leader. Hence, Jesus made no requirements for those who met with Him at this point. They might be called "believing associates."

Often when seeking to gather a group of disciples, we make a mistake by establishing requirements for participation. Years ago I gathered a group of new Christians with the intent of helping them grow. Because I wanted it to be a group of high quality and deep commitment, I told them that in order to be a member of the group they must agree to attend two meetings a week, memorize two verses of Scripture each week, spend an hour a day in Bible study and prayer, and witness to someone at least three times a week.

Instead of producing a group with much commitment, I lost most of the disciples. Some decided the group was not for them. Others joined, but not yet being convinced in their hearts that these activities were important, they were not faithful to do them. This resulted in their feeling guilty and dropping out. A few others joined the group, were faithful, but were not joyful under these legal requirements. Their interest level was thereby greatly reduced, and they did not grow very fast.

These disciples were not ready to be locked into a commitment to me and my program. They needed to grow to trust me and become more excited about the Lord and His Word before they could accept and work happily under strong obligations. Jesus did not make this kind of mistake. His first group of followers was open to learn with no responsibility to Him other than the willingness to be publicly associated with Him.

When Jesus returned from His forty days in the wilderness after the baptism by John, He began to gather His first followers. At this time John the Baptist directed the apostles John and Andrew toward Jesus. Immediately, Andrew went and found his brother Simon Peter and brought him to Jesus (John 1:41). After Jesus had invited Philip to join Him, Philip found Nathanael and invited him also (John 1:43-46). A number of others began following Him at this time, but only the names of Joseph (Barsabbas or Justus) and Matthias are given (Acts 1:21-23). Shortly after these began following Him, Jesus invited Matthew (and perhaps others) to join Him. Some of these were, in a certain sense, selected by Jesus. Others probably just joined, and Jesus let them continue to come. During this early association, Jesus disclosed His identity. He claimed to be the Messiah.

The gathering of disciples follows similar lines today. Men are invited by the teacher or disciples to come to learn. No prior commitment is expected other than a willingness to attend.

This *open, friendly association that makes no demands but permits one to attend at will* allows for several things. It allows anyone to come without the teacher making any commitment to continue teaching the disciple. Hence, disciples can be evaluated as to their sincerity to grow and those with spiritual promise can be discovered and invited to continue. The group can also be expanded so that the teacher has a larger selection from which to choose those he wants to be involved in Ministry Training.

At the step of Ministry Training, the teacher actually begins to exercise selection. Jesus *chose* certain men and invited them to be in a group where they would "become fishers of men." Although Scripture mentions only a few of these whom Jesus called, there must have been at least twenty or thirty, since He later selected twelve of these as apostles. Jesus probably did not select all of these at once but added new men (e.g., Matthew) to be trained as the period of Ministry Training progressed. Those in ministry training might be called "full-time followers."

All of the steps from Leadership Development and following involved a closed, select group of twelve with an association that was intimate and permanent. They enjoyed this unique relationship even though others entered into different relationships with Jesus.

At the step of Participation and Delegation the association of the Twelve continued to be intimate but had to be shared with the Seventy. The Twelve were not over the Seventy except as assistants to Jesus, who seems to have directly supervised them. But the Twelve were still the most intimate group related to Jesus.

At the step of the Exchanged Life Jesus was beginning to teach the Twelve the things that would promote a severance of their direct personal association to Him in exchange for a dependence only on the Holy Spirit. That personal association was severed by the Cross, the Resurrection, and the Ascension. Today the leader and the disciples must also make this transition: the disciples exchanging their intimate association to the leader for a relationship to the Lord through the Spirit alone.

A Summary of the Development and Changes in Association Throughout the Seven Steps

Repentance and Faith
—casual association to reach the most people
—in mass public meetings, in home meetings,
or in person-to-person evangelism
Enlightenment
—an open, small, intimate group — but growing,
with people coming or going
—a friendship relationship without commitment
by disciple or teacher
Ministry Training
—a small, intimate, select group with others
being selected and added
—a team committed to learning and helping
the leader
Leadership Development, Reevaluation
—a select group of Twelve, closed to others
—permanent, intimate, daily association
—a team committed to the leader to continue
to learn and to help in the responsibility
of leading the people
Participation and Delegation
—same select group of Twelve — but less intimate
association, since leader is involved with
the Seventy
—helping leader instruct and direct the Seventy
The Exchanged Life
—select group of Twelve now over the Seventy
—being weaned from a personal association
to the leader to a dependence on the Lord
through the Spirit alone

—a close association and dependence of the
team of Twelve on each other in the Lord
—committed to leading the work

PROGRESSIVE SELECTIVE RELATIONSHIP

During His earthly ministry Jesus could be closely associated
with only a few persons, and His relationships with the groups of men
He selected became more and more intimate. This progressive selection can be traced as follows in the diagram on page 176. In the step of
Repentance and Faith, the general populace (the world) was
evangelized. John the Baptist initiated this outreach that Jesus (and
the Twelve) later took over. In the step of Enlightenment an *interested crowd* gathered from among those who had been evangelized. Andrew, Peter, Philip and others became *Christ's discipleship group* at this time. Those who were called to be "fishers of
men," that is, the *ministry group*, were selected in the step of
Ministry Training. As the ministry progressed into the step of Leadership Development, Jesus chose the *Twelve* from among the full-
time followers. The appointment of the *Seventy* came at the beginning of the step of Participation and Delegation. Like the Twelve,
they were chosen from among the full-time followers. The *120* (who
included the Twelve and the Seventy), seen in the upper room after
the Crucifixion and Resurrection, again must have come from the
same group as the Twelve and Seventy. As the diagram indicates,
there was a progressive numerical growth (with two major setbacks)
in the size of the interested crowd, the discipleship group, and the
ministry group.

QUOTES FROM EDUCATORS

Coleman, in speaking of association in discipling, emphasized
the relationship Jesus had with His men:

> Having called His men, Jesus made it a practice to be with them. This
> was the essence of His training program — just letting His disciples
> follow Him. When one stops to think of it, this was an incredibly
> simple way of doing it. Jesus had no formal school, no seminaries, no
> outlined course of study, no periodic membership classes in which He
> enrolled His followers. None of these highly organized procedures
> considered so necessary today entered at all into His ministry. Amaz-
> ing as it may seem, all Jesus did to teach these men His way was to
> draw them close to Himself. He was His own school and curricu-
> lum. . . . Jesus asked only that His disciples follow Him. Knowledge
> was not communicated by the Master in terms of laws and dogmas, but
> in the living personality of One who walked among them. His disci-
> ples were distinguished, not by outward conformity to certain rituals,
> but by being with Him, and thereby participating in His doctrine (John
> 18:19).[1]

Steps of Discipleship

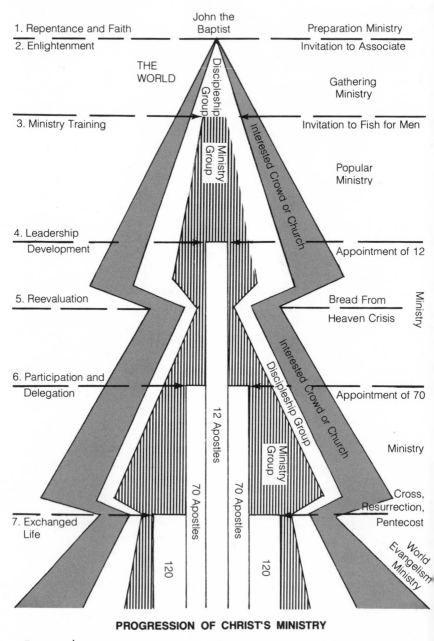

Steps of Discipleship		
1. Repentance and Faith	John the Baptist	Preparation Ministry
2. Enlightenment		Invitation to Associate
	THE WORLD	Gathering Ministry
3. Ministry Training	Discipleship Group	Invitation to Fish for Men
	Ministry Group	Popular Ministry
4. Leadership Development	Interested Crowd or Church	Appointment of 12
5. Reevaluation		Bread From Heaven Crisis — Ministry
6. Participation and Delegation	Interested Crowd or Church / Discipleship Group	Appointment of 70
	12 Apostles / Ministry Group	Ministry
	70 Apostles / 70 Apostles	Cross, Resurrection, Pentecost
7. Exchanged Life		World Evangelism Ministry
	120 / 120	

PROGRESSION OF CHRIST'S MINISTRY

Much earlier (1920) Herman Horne taught concepts similar to those of Coleman. In a chapter entitled "Education by Personal Association" He observed:

> What does this title suggest to you? It is a pedagogical truism that we teach more by what we are than by what we say. Such is the influence of personality. We learn by association with persons. All that goes by the name of suggestion and imitation is at work when one person is thrown in contact with another.

He pointed out that the great moral and religious teachers throughout history have followed this basic procedure. Horne continued, "Thus the main secret of the training of the twelve was association, and its main objective was service."[2]

THE VALUE OF THE SMALL GROUP IN PERSONAL ASSOCIATION

Although Jesus preached the gospel to big crowds and taught "interested associates" in fairly large groups, most of His teaching to develop His men was in small groups. People may often be together for quite a length of time in a large group without really relating to each other or communicating with each other. But within a small group the leaders and individuals can interact. Again, although a close personal association demands individual attention at times, involvement in a small group is also important. If a teacher's time is spent only with individuals, his influence will be limited.

The small group lends itself to meeting the needs of the individual while also meeting the needs of the group. The leader can focus on the individuals and on the group when the small group is set apart from the masses. This relationship is not possible in the large congregational meetings.

In a small group there can be both lecture and discussion. This is not possible in a large group. The small group gives the sense of belonging and intimacy. Within its structure questions can be asked and answered in greater depth and personal application can be stimulated. It is difficult to help a person apply truth when he is meeting in a large group, but in a small group the progress of the individual can be observed and individual application of the truth can then be made.

If a person can learn to function properly in a small group, he will be able to function properly in the family unit. If a father learns how to function in a small group of men, he will then know how to reproduce that model in his own family unit. This is important in our modern world.

The most important reason for using the small group is that it allows the leader to easily observe several individuals in such a way as to know what truth is needed in their lives. Also, it allows the leader to be intimate in showing the individual how to apply the truth to his life on a day-by-day, situation-by-situation basis. Much more will be said about this in chapter 17 — "Application of Truth to Obtain Obedience."

The interaction among the disciples in the small group also created an atmosphere where learning was stimulated. In John 4 while Jesus was talking to the woman at the well, the disciples returned from town and were amazed at the situation. They did not ask Him about it, but apparently had discussed the matter among themselves. This was just one instance when they were able to have this type of interaction.

The personal example of the leader in the small group does away with a great many legal rules that one would otherwise have to follow. Since the leader is intimately present and observing their conduct, the disciples will be careful to please him. The small group maximizes the ability of the group members to understand the thinking, vision, and methods of the leader.

Paul preached publicly and from house to house and ministered to the churches that met in houses (Rom. 16:5). These small groups differ from many modern churches in that they were informal and personal and they involved the leader in the life of the disciple.

A GROUP OF WOMEN ASSOCIATED WITH JESUS

There were a number of women who traveled with Jesus and with whom He also had a close association (Luke 8:1-3). It has been mentioned that some of these apparently had leadership responsibilities over other women (pp. 117,118).

Others He was closely associated with were Martha and Mary of Bethany. Mary apparently took a place with the men who were the small group that "sat at His feet" (Luke 10:39). The phrase "sat at the feet of" was commonly used to describe the close relationship between a rabbi and his small group of pupils (Acts 22:3; cf. the Greek text as translated in KJV). These women at times understood Jesus' teachings better than men did (Matt. 26:6-13; John 12:3-8).

JESUS' OTHER WAYS OF RELATING

Retreats. In building an intimate relationship to His men Jesus also took them away on retreats. He took them to a mountain, possibly the Horns of Hattin, where He selected the Twelve and preached the Sermon on the Mount (Matt. 5ff.). He also took them on retreats to Tyre and Sidon (Matt. 15:21; Mark 7:24), to the border of Decapolis (Matt. 15:29; Mark 7:31), Dalmanutha in southwest Galilee (Mark 8:10), the villages of Caesarea Philippi (Matt. 16:13; Mark 8:27), and to Perea east of the Jordan (John 10:40-11:54; Luke 13:22; 19:28). Because of the hostility in the area of Judea, He withdrew to Ephraim near the desert to spend time with His disciples (John 11:54).

Certain ones separated. At times Jesus would separate certain men from the others (Matt. 16,17; Mark 10:32). When He raised Jairus' daughter, Peter, James, and John went with Him. They also accompanied Him to the Mount of Transfiguration, the Garden of Gethsemane, and probably to other places also. On the night of His passion, Jesus took His disciples to the upper room, separating them from the crowds. After His resurrection, Jesus appeared to select people — first to individuals, then to small groups, and finally to a larger group. Basically though, He appeared to the same select group of people.

OTHER WAYS JESUS' CLOSE ASSOCIATION IS SEEN

In Jesus' statements about his disciples. Jesus' intimate relationship with these men is seen in His statements throughout the Gospels. He said, "You also must testify, for *you have been with me* from the beginning" (John 15:27). When the apostles decided to select someone to take the place of Judas, they emphasized that he must be one who had been with Jesus from His baptism until His ascension (Acts 1:21). In Luke 22:28-30 Jesus said, "You are those who have stood by me in my trials. And I confer on you a kingdom, just as my Father conferred one on me, so that you may eat and drink at my table in my kingdom and sit on thrones, judging the twelve tribes of Israel." He was reflecting on the intimacy with which they had suffered, traveled, and lived with Him. He pointed out that He had daily set an example for them: "I have set you an example that you should do as I have done for you" (John 13:15). Peter spoke of Christ as "leaving you an example" (1 Peter 2:21).

In His prayer for His disciples. This intimate relationship is also borne out by the compassion Jesus expressed for His men and the great burden of prayer He had for them. The events of the closing days and the words of Christ reflect how close their relationship was (John 17).

In post-Resurrection evidence. In Acts 4:13 Luke recorded that the members of the Sanhedrin were impressed by the apostles: "When they saw the courage of Peter and John and realized that they were unschooled, ordinary men, they were astonished and they took note that these men had been with Jesus."

PAUL'S CLOSE ASSOCIATION WITH HIS DISCIPLES

Paul developed very personal relationships with his disciples. In Galatia, on his second missionary journey, Paul met Timothy, the most outstanding of his disciples, and Timothy followed him. He trained Timothy to be a minister for Jesus Christ. Paul also traveled with others (undoubtedly a sizeable group), among whom were Silas and Titus. Besides those who traveled with him, Paul was closely associated with the elders in Ephesus. These were men whom he had trained. Perhaps among these leaders were some of the twelve followers of John whom he had discipled while in Ephesus (Acts 19,20). His frequent reference that he was an example to them showed his close association with his disciples.

Again he instructed Timothy: "And the things you have heard me say in the presence of many witnesses entrust to reliable men who will also be qualified to teach others" (2 Tim. 2:2). He mentions four generations of Christians: Paul, Timothy, the faithful men he will teach, and those whom they will teach. This is the principle of spiritual multiplication. Paul clearly envisioned that this training through close association would be passed on to succeeding generations.

When a close relationship is accompanied by personal teaching and application, strong disciples who can multiply themselves by teaching others will be the result. In the long run, more people will be available to do the work. In the modern church this would mean that the workload would shift from one teacher or leader to many.

MOVING WITH THE INTERESTED IN CLOSE ASSOCIATION

The key to successfully discipling others is finding those who want to grow and putting them in groups where they will be taught and personally built. In the average church the pastor spends a great deal of time trying to teach people who do not want to be taught and to change people who do not want to be changed. He tries to get people to work and minister who do not want to have a ministry. Often he spends more time trying to motivate the disinterested than he spends building those who are interested. But the disinterested are a drag on the whole church effort.

Howard Ball, president of Churches Alive, has called this the convoy syndrome. Ships traveling in a convoy have to wait for all the ships to be ready to move before the convoy moves. So pastors wait until a carnal or dissident group gets ready to do things. Hence, they seldom, if ever, move very far.

Jesus did not follow the convoy syndrome principle. He gathered those who wanted to move, and taught and led them. When a Christian leader learns to do what Jesus did — namely, to teach, motivate, and use the people who are interested — then things begin to happen. As these interested people grow, get excited about the Lord, and see things happening, they often awaken many who are not interested.

This principle of finding the interested and spending time building an intimate association with them is the key to Jesus' approach. It may be said that the whole success of a church, a movement, or any organization rests on it. This was the principle the apostle Paul used in his churches. The gifted leaders were to build up those who were interested so that they in turn might do the work of the ministry (Eph. 4:12).

DIAGRAM OF DRAWING DISCIPLES INTO CLOSE ASSOCIATION FOR MOTIVATION OF THE WHOLE CHURCH

The diagram on the following page shows how this probably worked organizationally in Jesus' day and how it should work today. After calling sinners to repentance and commitment of faith, Jesus began to gather a discipleship group (DG) around Him and teach them who He was (step 2 of Enlightenment). From these He invited some disciples to become full-time followers and receive ministry training (MT) so they could become "fishers of men" (step 3). Those who learned to help Him then became a permanent ministry group (MG) of men and women. From the ministry group He chose twelve to be in a leadership group (LG, step 4). As these worked with others in the ministry group then gained many new believers, who became a part of the church. Thus, the church had new people being added daily. From the interested people in the church a second generation of discipleship groups (DG) was formed of believing associates, Jesus' new leadership helping in these. This process would thus continue adding new people to the ministry group and new leaders to the leadership group (the 70, and later those who brought it up to 120). From these, new believers would be continually added.

The entire process is based on an intimate relationship of the pastor to the first discipleship group, then to the ministry training class and the ministry group, and then later to his leadership. These leaders then go through the same kind of intimate association with the succeeding groups.

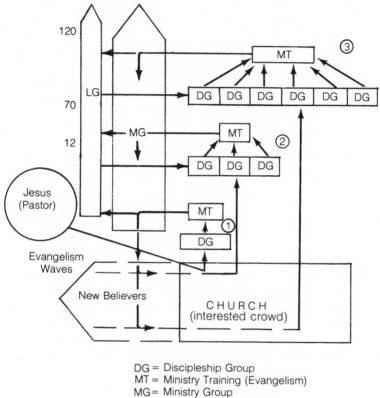

DG = Discipleship Group
MT = Ministry Training (Evangelism)
MG = Ministry Group
LG = Leadership Group

**NEW TESTAMENT ORGANIZATION FOR
DISCIPLE BUILDING AND CHURCH GROWTH**

The Scriptures indicate certain basic factors that contribute to the right relationship for the proper close association of the leader and his disciples. These will be considered in the next chapter on "Fellowship for Discipleship."

Notes

[1] Robert Coleman, *The Master Plan of Evangelism* (New York: Revell, n.d.).
[2] Herman Harrell Horne, *Teaching Techniques of Jesus* (Grand Rapids: Kregel, 1971), pp. 143,144.

12

Fellowship for Discipleship

The Meaning of Fellowship

When my son was married, he and his bride wrote their own vows and read them to each other in the wedding. One thing he promised her was, "Elsita, I promise to try to create the kind of environment and conditions that will help you to continue to grow into a lovely Christian woman, reaching all your potential. One cannot coerce a flower to grow and bloom in great beauty. But one can give that flower the warmth, the nurture, the protection, and pruning that enable it to be free to grow. So I promise to seek to do this for you in our home."

This is an important part of discipleship. A husband helping his wife and children grow is the most basic of all disciple building. So the church must create the right environment and conditions to allow its disciples to develop.

Developing the kind of fellowship that will be conducive to the spiritual growth of a disciple is one of the most important aspects of disciple building. The New Testament word *koinonia*, translated "fellowship," comes from the Greek verb *koinoneo*, which means "to share." Therefore, the word *koinonia* refers to those sharing — those who have something in common. *Koinos* means "common"; *koinonos* means a "partner"; *koinonoi* means persons who hold property in common, partners, or shareholders. The basic idea is people who share with each other.

In 1 John 1:3 John expresses a desire for Christians to fellowship with one another. He emphasizes that the source of their fellowship is their relationship with the Father and the Son, Jesus Christ. Fellowship, therefore, involves both a vertical and a horizontal relationship. In the *vertical* relationship, a person *shares in the life of God*. In the *horizontal* relationship, those who are sharing the life of God begin to *share it with each other*.

God initiates fellowship by the revelation of Himself in the Word of Life. Jesus was the Word incarnate who initiated that fellowship between man and God and among believers. During His earthly ministry, He called individuals into a relationship with Himself and also led them into a close fellowship with each other. His leadership determined the quality of their fellowship. His love for them and for others led them to share intimately with Him and with each other. With this kind of fellowship they found a security that allowed them to be free to grow as disciples.

In the New Testament the idea of fellowship implies the sharing of a common faith, a common salvation, and a common grace (Phil. 1:7; Titus 1:4; Jude 3). (Each of these phrases comes from the same Greek root.) The sharing of wealth, households, and food at a common meal is also prevalent in the New Testament (Acts 2:44-47; 1 Cor. 1:9; 10:16). The word *koinonia* or *fellowship* is also used in terms of sharing labor (2 Cor. 8:23; Phil. 1:7), sufferings (Phil. 3:10; 1 Peter 4:13; 5:1), common problems, and prayer. Clearly, fellowship involves sharing all of life in its various aspects.

FELLOWSHIP AND DISCIPLE BUILDING

Certain aspects of fellowship are important to disciple building. While "vertical" fellowship with God was initiated by the coming of God into history in the incarnation of the living Word (Jesus Christ), that fellowship since Christ's death, resurrection, and ascension is *maintained daily by the Spirit,* who reveals Him and His will *through the written Word,* the Bible. It is vital for Christians to gather together to hear the public preaching of the Word and to meet in small groups to read and discuss the Scriptures. Christians also need to spend time alone daily, reading the Bible, meditating on it, and praying. Every man is called to teach the Word to his family. Christians need to correct and exhort each other, openly sharing the Word and interpreting it, for every Christian is a priest for Christ and not a judge (Matt. 7:1; Rom. 14:1). Jesus is the only judge (John 5:22; Rom. 8:33,34). The pastor should be the principal man to declare the Word, but many among the Christian brethren should also be declaring it. In other words, the truth of God learned in the vertical relationship must be shared and put in practice in horizontal relationships.

HUMILITY AND FELLOWSHIP

Andrew Murray has said, "Humility, the place of entire dependence on God, is, from the very nature of things, the first duty and the highest virtue of the creature, and the root of every virtue." He points out that since pride was what caused the fall of Satan, the angels, and man, humility must be the first step to restoration of fellowship.[1] There can be no sharing of God's life with man or of one person's life with others without humility. "As we study the Word, we shall see what very distinct and oft-repeated instructions Jesus gave His disciples on this point [of humility], and how slow they were in understanding Him."[2]

Jesus calls His disciples to be humble so that they can serve one another. He used the example of His own willingness to humble Himself and become a servant in order to redeem man, to encourage His disciples to be humble (Mark 10:42-45; Phil. 2:3-11). Andrew Murray has pointed out that "humility towards men will be the only sufficient proof that our humility before God is real."[3]

One evidence that there is humility toward God and toward man is a willingness to confess our sin to God and to others we have wronged. Therefore, nothing will open the floodgates of fellowship so much as a willingness to confess our sin.

A young woman in Christian work was asked by a member of her staff team if she knew how to do needlepoint. She had never done any needlepoint, but since she was a home economics major she did not want to admit she had not. She lied, saying she had. Then, having read the directions, she showed the girl how to do it. The Holy Spirit convicted her of her pride in this lie, and, with much inward resistance, she went back to the whole staff team and confessed the lie she had told them. This led to confessions from other members of the team. That team developed an exciting and deep fellowship where there was great sharing of spiritual and material things. Without humble confession by this young woman, this would not have been possible.

HONESTY AND FELLOWSHIP

The above illustration also shows how important honesty (or truthfulness) is for fellowship too. Jesus was truthful even if it offended others (John 8:40). Paul said that we Christians "by the manifestations of truth [are] commending ourselves to every man's conscience in the sight of God" (2 Cor. 4:2).

Unless we have a good conscience toward others, we cannot share with them. Unless the leader is honest, his disciples will not be open to his teaching. Unless the disciples are honest with each other, they will not share with one another. Paul therefore argued that honesty is necessary for members of a body to relate to each other (Eph. 4:25).

Faith produces fellowship. If fellowship is to be conducive to spiritual growth, *faith must be present.* There must be faith if the body is to function correctly. Faith is the willingness to believe that the Holy Spirit can use any adverse situation or problem and the willingness to trust Him even to use evil for God's glory and benefit. When a person has this kind of faith, he accepts others as members of the body of Christ, believing that the Holy Spirit can work in another person's life. (Men learn to trust God to work in the lives of others during the step of Participation and Delegation, but the group leader should be demonstrating this trust from the beginning of the association.) If someone having this kind of faith meets with doctrinal differences, he can trust God for the solution. A Christian with this kind of faith will be open to seeing where he is wrong instead of trying to prove that he is right. Thus, sharing and growth through sharing become possible (cf. p. 205).

Love produces fellowship. Of all the qualities of life that must be present if fellowship is to be conducive to spiritual growth, the central quality is love. A more complete evaluation of Christian love is given in the chapter on applying truth to obtain obedience, pp. 238-40, but it must also be evaluated here as it relates to fellowship. We should love God foremost, for we are the recipients of His love. God has taken the initiative in *sharing Himself* by the giving of His Son. Thus, because we know that God cares for us, we can respond to Him and trust Him (2 Cor. 5:14). The consciousness of God's love is basic to the fulfillment of any fellowship. In like manner, Christians must have an attitude of love and a willingness to give themselves so that others may openly respond and share with them. Fear prevents Christians from opening their lives to each other, but the Scriptures say, ''Perfect love drives out fear'' (1 John 4:18).

Jesus said that Christian love would convince the world that God had sent Him, and because of it people would be led to believe in Him (cf. John 13:35; 17:21). This kind of love is the supreme witness of Christ's love. It produces unity among Christians. This unity is not that of the invisible link between the Spirit and the invisible church nor the unity of organizational structures. Rather, it is a unity that is expressed when Christians are concerned for and share with each other. (See pages 204-6 for a discussion of unity.)

This type of unifying love will be a forgiving love — a love that is willing to forgive and take the risk of being hurt. At the same time, it may be called "tough" love. It upholds that which is holy and right; it does not give in just for sentimental reasons or for approval. In other words, love is faithful to the truth and does not compromise principles. This love is firm, not out of stubbornness, but because of the conviction that the truth and biblical principles are best for the other person and for all people. Therefore, this "tough" love refuses to give in to the whims and desires of others. It is the kind of love that makes one willing to accept rejection and persecution from others because he knows that the love and acceptance of God are much more important.

God's type of love makes one accept a person as he is, with his own peculiarities and weaknesses. One who loves like that is willing to accept differences that do not alter God's principles. The more important the differences, the more careful love will be to evaluate and accept that person if no doctrinal or moral question is involved. Differences may be an asset to the body — the eye needs the very different organ of the ear in the body (cf. 1 Cor. 12:20-23).

This is *agape* love. It is willing to suffer for others, and it produces what the Scripture calls the "attitude of grace." That is, when a person is transformed by agape love, he will not have an attitude of criticism. He will not try to discover the faults of another, nor will he try to "get the best" of others. Instead, his attitude will be one of acceptance and forgiveness. He will care for others no matter what the cost. This kind of love is described in 1 Corinthians 13 and Ephesians 4:2,32–5:2. It is the kind of love that understands its liberty in Christ but does not use that liberty if using it will hurt someone else (Gal. 5:13-17). This kind of agape love must be imparted by the Holy Spirit (Rom. 5:5). This love frees a person to share himself at the deepest level.

HOSPITALITY AND FELLOWSHIP

Where there is genuine love, it usually leads Christians to open their homes to others. It is a fact that the first group of disciples who met with Him to be taught gathered together because He invited them into His home (John 1:38-42). It was a characteristic of the early church that they had fellowship by "the breaking of bread" together (Acts 2:42). Eating together may not insure fellowship, is open to abuse (cf. 1 Cor. 11:20), and may not involve hospitality at all. But a hospitable person is one who begins the sharing of his home and forms a climate for others to share in other ways. This is why Paul required hospitality of everyone who was to be a leader in the church (1 Tim. 3:2; Titus 1:8).

I have never seen true Christian fellowship without at least one person having the gift of hospitality. Grace Evangelical Church, of which I was the first pastor, has grown rapidly in recent years and has had a rich fellowship. Several people in the group have opened their homes to all of us, and encouraged sharing.

Organization and fellowship. Organization also affects fellowship. The wrong kind of organization may inhibit the qualities of love and faith and also be a direct hindrance to sharing. In a large church that has no small groups, the pastor may share with the congregation by preaching, but the members do not usually share with him or among themselves because they lack the opportunity. Because this kind of church structure is prevalent today, many churches do not offer a fellowship that facilitates growth.

Jesus Christ basically used three levels of organization in His ministry. He drew people into *groups of two to four,* appealing to natural affinities. For instance, the two brothers James and John were grouped together as were Philip and his friend Nathanael. When sending the disciples out to minister, He sent them in groups of two. It has been mentioned that often Jesus took Peter, James, and John aside to teach them.

The second form of organization is the *small group of about twelve.* Jesus chose twelve and He worked with them for several years. He taught and ministered to them as a group. The third level is that of *the congregation.* Jesus formed a congregation from those who constantly followed Him and listened to His teaching. All three levels of the church of Jesus Christ had a ministry to the community, and the believers talked about Jesus with each other within these three group levels.

The large group is basically the place where vision is imparted. Through the preaching of the pastor (like that of the apostle in the early church) common information is transferred to the whole congregation. The large group creates a sense of the importance of a movement and it makes possible a greater influence among the people. Although the larger congregation is impersonal and does not demand much from the individual, it does serve a function in disciple building. Therefore, Christians should continue these larger meetings, for they do have a vital place.

History shows the importance of small groups for fellowship. Historically any revitalization of the church has taken place when the importance of sharing in small groups has been rediscovered (see pp. 177,178). In eighteenth-century England the Methodist movement was made stronger by the rediscovery of the importance of small groups (the Holy Club and class meetings). A similar revitalization occurred as a result of the praying societies of Scotland. More recently, the East African revivals have gone hand in hand with the Christians' meeting together in small groups.

In his book, *Plain Account of the People Called Methodists,* John Wesley described the Methodist class meetings:

> Many now [in the class meetings] happily experienced that Christian fellowship of which they had not so much as an idea before. They began to bear one another's burdens and naturally to care for each other. As they had daily a more intimate acquaintance with each other, so they had a more endeared affection for each other.

George Whitefield (a Methodist leader at that time) in his letter to the religious societies (or class meetings) said:

> To this end you would do well, as others have done, to form yourselves into little companies of four or five each, and meet once a week to tell each other what is in your hearts; you may then also pray for and comfort each other as a need shall require. None of those who have experienced it can tell the unspeakable advantages of such a union and communion of souls. . . . None I think who truly loves his own soul and his brethren as himself will be shy of opening his heart in order to have their advice, reproof, admonitions, and prayers as the occasions require.[4]

The Methodist groups were between the size of Jesus' smallest group (two to four members) and His group of twelve members.

Jesus apparently appointed the groups of two so each person would support the other as they evangelized, organized, and promoted together. These small groups also met for prayer and for encouragement. Jesus took the three (Peter, James, and John) aside *for prayer* both on the Mount of Transfiguration and in the Garden of Gethsemane.

A person is usually less threatened in a very small group of two or three. He is usually more open to share, and intimate sharing between two or three will promote sharing in the larger groups. As they share their witnessing experiences with the larger group, the entire group will be encouraged to share their faith. This willingness to share will often spread from the small group to the larger congregational groups.

Today it is common to call small groups "supportive groups." While those in such groups do support each other as they share life together, there is a danger in this name. It seems to create the idea that Christians are to rely on each other rather than on the Lord working through each other. I prefer the terms "discipleship group" or "fellowship group."

EXERCISE OF SPIRITUAL GIFTS AND DEVELOPMENT OF DISCIPLES

Much is being said today about the recovery of "body life" — Christians building each other by the exercise of their gifts. Unfortunately, many churches are structured so that only the gift(s) of the pastor or priest is expressed. Certain basic gifts of individuals within the church are neglected. But when members are allowed to express their different spiritual gifts, thereby performing different functions, they testify to and serve one another.

Christian witnessing has often been presented as a Christian sharing with a non-Christian. But when Christians regularly share with other Christians what Christ is doing in their lives, they will also share naturally with non-Christians. As Christians exercise their different gifts, witnessing will be natural and creative.

As Christians recognize the value of each of the spiritual gifts and the value of the individual ways of expressing those gifts, they can better appreciate each other. As agape love prevails and Christians accept each other, they will be free to manifest their gifts. Paul wrote:

> There should be no division in the body, but . . . its parts should have equal concern for each other. If one part suffers, every part suffers with it; if one part is honored, every part rejoices with it (1 Cor. 12:25,26).

This unity will be realized as the different members of the body understand that the other members exist for the common good (1 Cor. 12:7). The service each member performs for the others draws the body closely together. Moreover, it reminds them of Jesus Christ, the Head and controlling Person of the body. When the individuals know and exercise their gift(s), proper growth in discipleship results. Just as the human body will not grow unless exercised, so the body of Christ will not grow unless its members exercise their God-given gifts. Unless the members use their gifts to share benefits to the body, the purpose of the gifts is aborted.

PASTORAL LEADERSHIP FOR FELLOWSHIP

As the qualities of humility, honesty, faith, love, and hospitality are exhibited in the pastor's life, people will be open with him. Since he must organize and lead the small groups, he should know the proper methods of working with them. Unfortunately, many pastors are not educated in these techniques. In order for individual needs to be met, the small group must provide an atmosphere in which a person feels free to discuss himself and his problems. In small groups laymen often respond better to each other than to the pastor (who may tend to dominate the discussion). Pastors need to form a leadership group from among their laymen so that they can teach these men to lead small groups of their own. They should turn the leadership over to the laymen as soon as possible. In these leadership groups pastors need to both know and practice discussion-group techniques in order to teach them to these leaders. Because most pastors are taught to be the "authority" in the church, using such techniques involves new attitudes.

The importance of sharing not only the spiritual but also the material must be taught and practiced by the pastor as well. One of the great churches of America is Briarwood Presbyterian Church of Birmingham, Alabama. The pastor and his wife constantly have people in their home. This has encouraged other leaders to open their home to groups of the congregation. While the pastor cannot invite everyone into his home, showing hospitality to the group of leaders he is training will set an example for them.

Men are often too busy today to take the time to minister to people's needs. But the pastor must show attention and concern for others and encourage the lay leaders to show the same personal attention and concern throughout the church. This necessitates the pastor's training laymen to help overall and lead the people.

As he trains leaders in his small group, he should assign them the responsibility of discipling small groups within the congregation. These small groups within the church are best formed on the basis of common interest; e.g., young married adults, young single people, high school students, and married older adults. If these suggestions are followed, a greater sense of fellowship will develop in the church and more disciples will experience proper growth and development.

Notes

[1] Andrew Murray, *Humility, The Beauty of Holiness* (Fort Washington, Pennsylvania: Christian Literature Crusade), p. 12.

[2] Ibid., p. 14.

[3] Ibid., p. 34.

[4] Wesley's and Whitefield's quotes were taken from an unpublished paper by Jon Braun.

13

Involvement and Disciple Building

Proper involvement in the ministry is one of the most important aspects of leading and nurturing an individual. There are two aspects to involvement. First is the increased involvement in teaching and learning that produces an increased acceptance of the ideology and goals of the movement. The second aspect of involvement is an increased commitment to the activities and work of the movement. The first produces the second but the second helps maintain interest in the first. This chapter focuses primarily on the latter.

THEORIES OF INVOLVEMENT

Within the worldly theories of involvement are two basic poles: "utilitarian" and "humanitarian."

Those who have a "slave" or "utilitarian" viewpoint see the leader as using others for his own ends. The individual does not matter, and the leader is interested in him only insofar as he can be used to accomplish the leader's goals. This concept is one of slavery.

The "humanitarian" concept of involvement is the other pole. From this viewpoint the individual is all-important. Every action focuses on helping the individual. In other words, the individual's involvement is for self-benefit — not for God. One who holds this philosophy inevitably is faced with a dilemma: who should benefit — his neighbor or himself? Since the individual is setting the standard, self takes precedence over the neighbor. As a result, the "humanitarian'' concept becomes in reality the ''slave'' or ''utilitarian'' viewpoint. Communism has demonstrated this. The leadership of Communist countries is a privileged class.

Unfortunately, some Christian organizations or leaders seem merely to use the people who work for them with no concern for them as people. Also, some have overemphasized the individual and have not been concerned for the glory of God.

The ideal Christian view is radically different from these worldly views. Christ was concerned with developing individuals, but not for their sake alone. Here, chapter 2 on Goals becomes important. The Christian seeks to build others into the image of Jesus Christ so that they may experience all God's blessings and bring glory to God. The Christian's goal is to help a person develop into all that God intends him to be, for he believes that the individual achieves his God-given destiny and has the most meaningful existence when he glorifies God by his life. In short, one is happiest and most fulfilled when he carries out the law of love for God and his neighbor.

One of the goals of the Christian movement is to carry out the law of love, so when individuals are fulfilling this law, the movement is developed as well. In building disciples who in turn help to build the movement, the Christian will glorify God and will feel fulfilled.

COMMON MISTAKES

A pastor must be careful about how and when to get a person involved. Giving a person too much responsibility too soon will have bad effects for both the individual and the movement. In 1 Timothy 3 Paul discusses the qualifications of an elder. He specifically mentions that the leaders should not be novices, that is, new converts. The reasons for this guideline are clear. If a leader is not mature enough to do the job, he will become discouraged and may ''tube out.'' On the other hand, if he is capable and he does handle the situation well, he may become proud. In that case the result will be just as harmful as the first. I know many tragic incidences where new converts who excel as leaders in sports, in the academic arena, in business or some other area are pushed into leadership roles before they are mature enough. Unable to cope with the job, these people become discouraged. Or they may perform well, but their life will be too shallow for the job and become unreal.

On the other hand, a leader can be too slow in getting a person involved. If he fails to give him enough responsibility to keep him involved and challenged, the individual will not continue to develop and will become discouraged.

The manner of involvement is just as important as the timing.

Some leaders have put their disciples in situations that were too bold for their particular stages of maturity and development. A young convert may become discouraged and withdraw if he is attacked or maligned for his beliefs.[1] Conversely, if there is no challenge, if a disciple is given nothing but the routine and mechanical, he will become bored and feel unimportant. Again, he will want to withdraw from the movement.

The Progression Toward Deeper Involvement

Jesus Christ knew how to involve people. In chapter 11, concerning Association, involvement for the purpose of learning was discussed. This chapter deals with Jesus' methods of involving people in the actual activities of ministry. (Note that involvement for the purpose of learning and involvement for the purpose of ministering are so interrelated that they cannot be entirely separated.)

In the chapter on association we noted the way in which the disciples' relationship to Jesus changed. The diagram on page 176 illustrates how their involvement in the ministry progressed from a minor role to completely directing the ministry themselves. As the diagram indicates, the Twelve became central and controlled more and more people, with increasing levels of participants dependent on them. Finally, they led the whole church in its worldwide expansion.

If Jesus had given the three simple fishermen (Peter, James, and John, who became His "executive committee") the responsibility of leading this large group of people at the beginning, they would have drawn back. The task of leading this large crowd of believing associates and full-time followers would have been too much. They would have felt inadequate. They could never have seen themselves in that kind of leadership role. Gradually, Jesus drew them into this kind of involvement. As the movement developed, they became more and more involved, until they were the core of a very large movement and had tremendous responsibilities.

Survey of Steps

The following is a simple survey of the way Jesus involved His disciples at each of the successive steps. In the step of Repentance and Faith, Jesus challenged people to openly confess their sin, to admit their wrongdoing and to entrust themselves to God publicly. He challenged them to be publicly baptized — an act that would symbolize their cleansing and their forgiveness through the power of the Holy Spirit. Basically, being baptized did not demand much understanding on their part. The disciples were not called to challenge other people, but they were called to stand up before the world, admit their wrong, and take part in a sacrament that associated them with God and His people.

The step of Enlightenment led to other kinds of involvement. This period was especially strong in teaching, but at the same time Jesus gave His disciples specific jobs. Sometimes these jobs were quite menial; sometimes they were simple rituals. For instance, in John 4:8 Jesus gave His disciples the task of procuring food. They also baptized people (John 4:2).[2]

In the step of Ministry Training, the disciples continued doing many of the mechanical jobs, such as rowing Jesus from one place to another. This job was a simple kind of involvement — much like getting ready for a meeting by setting up the chairs. But Jesus now began to involve His disciples in other tasks. He challenged them, saying, "Come, follow me. . . . and I will make you fishers of men" (Mark 1:17). Jesus showed His disciples how to preach, how to talk to people, and how to win them to the kingdom of God. He also demonstrated how to pray for the lost. The disciples learned primarily by His example. He also took them on a tour of Galilee, showing them how to make an evangelistic tour. In other words, in this stage they observed and helped Jesus as He ministered.

In the step of Leadership Development, Jesus went farther. He selected twelve men to be leaders and publicly announced that they were to be responsible for the kingdom of God. He taught them the various principles of leading a ministry. He began to teach them how to pray and continued showing them how to preach. He demonstrated the various ministry tasks, and they performed these tasks with Him. At this time Jesus actually gave them responsibility and authority, sending them out into the villages to minister on their own. By this fourth step they had identified themselves with Christ's ministry and shared the responsibility of failure or success. Jesus did not send them out on their own until He had trained them and until they had sufficient skills to do the job.

In the step of Reevaluation Jesus called His disciples to sacrificial service. He gave them some mechanical jobs as well. For instance, when He fed the five-thousand, He used the disciples to help Him organize the people into groups of fifty. Then He gave the food to the disciples, and they distributed it. More importantly, the disciples dealt with people's spiritual needs. For instance, in one situation the disciples tried to cast a demon out of a boy. Although they were unable to do so, the context seems to indicate that they had previously done so (Mark 9:14-27).

Jesus appointed the Seventy during the step of Participation and Delegation. The Scriptures indicate that the Twelve were still the predominant leadership group and that they helped Jesus train the Seventy. They were gaining experience in training new leaders. In the later stages of their ministry, the disciples were involved in rather bold actions, such as leading the crowd into the hostile city of Jerusalem at the Triumphal Entry.

After Pentecost the disciples entered into the experience of the Exchanged Life — the experience of resting in the Holy Spirit. Christ left them on their own. Under the guidance of the Holy Spirit, they continued to minister even though Christ was not physically present. They were involved in every aspect of the ministry on their own.

The disciples had gradually become involved in the movement. They began with a simple public commitment to follow Jesus and they finally became involved to the point of having an independent ministry. They began under constant supervision with little responsibility. In the end they ministered the kingdom of heaven in the power of the Holy Spirit and they were responsible for many people.

TRANSFER OF RESPONSIBILITY

In transferring responsibility, Jesus took His disciples through four basic stages, beginning with their involvement at the stage of Ministry Training and ending with their release as independent workers. Jesus at first said to the disciples, "Follow me . . . and I will make you fishers of men" (Mark 1:17). They simply traveled with Jesus, *observing* what He did. When He took them on an evangelistic tour, they watched Him carry on His ministry. Thus, they learned by association. The second stage was learning by *participation*. Jesus chose the Twelve, and they ministered with Him. Third, they learned by delegation under Christ's *supervision*. Jesus sent His disciples out on a missionary tour, and He followed them up to see how they were doing. Finally, after the day of Pentecost, the disciples learned by having an *independent ministry*.

The apostle Paul also went through these four stages of leadership involvement. When Barnabas was at Antioch, he recruited Paul. Paul then worked with Barnabas, watching what he did in the city of Antioch. Then the time came when the Spirit said, "Set apart for me Barnabas and Saul for the work to which I have called them" (Acts 13:2). They were sent out together. In the first part of their journeys Barnabas is listed as the leader, and "Saul" is listed as accompanying him. However, later in their journey Saul, now called Paul, is listed as the leader, and Barnabas is listed after him. Finally, Paul and Barnabas separated, and Paul took Silas with him, while Barnabas started over again training John Mark.

There are, then, four steps: that of watching and assisting the leader, that of accepting official responsibility and working with the leader, that of leading under supervision, and, finally, that of accepting independent leadership responsibility.

The biblical data indicates that a disciple's involvement greatly affects his growth. The way Jesus and Paul involved their disciples should become guidelines for leaders today. However, we must look to the Holy Spirit to guide the individual disciple.

Notes

[1] This was probably one of the reasons Jesus avoided going to Jerusalem for about a year after the Jewish leaders determined to kill Him. A year later His disciples were much more mature and committed to the work.

[2] At that time the ceremony of baptism was not considered to be a clerical function as it is today. Its importance lay in the fact that it was a symbol of identification, and any Christian could perform it. Paul apparently left the task of baptism to others also, for in 1 Corinthians 1:17 he said that he was not sent to baptize but to preach the gospel.

14

Motivation and Momentum

Two of the most important aspects of Jesus' ministry of building men are motivation and momentum. Without proper motivation and continuous momentum, neither individuals nor the movement will grow significantly.

DEFINITIONS

Motivation is the impelling desire to move toward a goal or an objective. Whereas the term *motivation* is used primarily in relation to the individual, *momentum* is used primarily in reference to an organization or a movement. Momentum is the actual progression toward the goals and objectives of an organization or movement. Motivation is a vital part of momentum, for without motivated people, momentum cannot be created or sustained.

Motivation is either extrinsic or intrinsic. When it is extrinsic, pressure to accomplish some goal is applied from the outside. (For instance, if you were commanded at gunpoint to do something, you would be motivated extrinsically!) Intrinsic motivation, on the other hand, comes from the inside. It is a person's inner desire to accomplish a goal. Extrinsic motivations are obviously short-lived. They last only as long as the external pressure exists.

Jesus Christ was a master of building momentum. His movement began with a few chosen men and continued to grow until it became a dominant force in Palestine. The expansion of Jesus' movement did not stop in Palestine but continued until its influence had permeated all of the Roman world. It continues to expand and grow to this very day. During Jesus' ministry the movement itself was the ideal in terms of momentum. Jesus Christ knew how to motivate men and how to keep the momentum of His movement consistently growing.

INNER RELATIONSHIP BETWEEN MOMENTUM AND DISCIPLE BUILDING

Jesus Christ recognized the direct relationship that exists between an individual's spiritual growth and the momentum of the movement in which he is involved. If the movement is exciting and progressive, the individual will be caught up in that excitement and will want to be involved. His interest will be focused on what is happening, and he will begin to grow as an individual. On the other hand, if a movement is indecisive and stagnant, the individual will lose interest and will not grow.

The reverse is also true. If an individual is growing, he will communicate his excitement to others. In so doing, he will help motivate other people and stimulate both excitement and growth within the movement. Again, if the individual is not growing, he will become stagnant. He will not be interested in what the movement is doing, and so the movement also will begin to stagnate and become indecisive. Therefore, motivating people so that they become excited about what they are doing is very important for building momentum.

Many people try to debunk excitement. But people learn best under a certain amount of emotional excitement. If that emotional excitement is worked up through fleshly means, motivation may result, but it will lack sufficient moral *control*. However, if the truth is presented in a dynamic way, an emotional excitement that motivates and produces controlled moral action may be produced. And what is learned will be long remembered.

When the truth is presented properly, it produces the best motivation. Momentum affects the motivation of a disciple, and at the same time the disciple's motivation affects the momentum of the movement. Therefore, as a disciple affects momentum through his growth, momentum will in turn affect the growth of others. The key is to motivate individuals by truth first and then to keep them motivated. Then momentum will be built. The result will be sustained momentum.

SUSTAINED MOMENTUM

The momentum that characterized Christ's movement grew continually and led to the expansion of His movement. While there were times in His ministry when the momentum seemed to die down, Jesus actually used these times to lay the foundation for an even greater momentum. By changing the motivations of His men and seeking to strengthen their new motivations, He created a far greater momentum in the long run.

It is important to establish a sustained momentum and not an erratic one. Actually, erratic momentum arrests any progress toward the goals. It leads to confusion and discouragement. When one young man found how readily high school students responded to his ministry, he focused on reaching this age group. With the help of some students with leadership ability, the group grew quickly. Because the governor's daughter became involved, the meetings were moved to the governor's mansion. The crowd exploded. In a short time over four hundred high school students attended, and many accepted Christ. And the spiritual babies needed personal care — their spiritual diapers needed changing and they needed the milk of the Word. But there were not enough mature disciples to help care for so many. The meeting turned into a social gathering and was intruded by drug pushers. Many of the so-called converts fell aside, and the Lord was dishonored. The Christian workers and a few earnest young people became discouraged. How much better it would have been to build a core of maturing and established disciples along with building the outreach! Then there would have been enough mature leaders to support the growing number of converts.

I once spoke at a series of church meetings for a week. The meetings were enthusiastically promoted by both the pastor and people, and many attended. Each night the house was crowded, and the number of interested people grew. But no preparation was made and no instruction given to the Christians in how to build the new people. After a few weeks had passed, most of the new people fell aside, the church had gained little visible strength, and the people were more discouraged than ever.

Sometimes it is good for momentum to diminish for a short time if the purpose is to strengthen commitment and motivation. On the two occasions in which Jesus' ministry seemed to lose momentum, Jesus had planned the recession. It had a specific purpose. If the objective of creating a sustained momentum is visibly reached, other people will be influenced and motivated by the movement. The diagram on page 176 illustrates the development of Christ's ministry. All areas of involvement grew continually except for the two times clearly marked on the diagram. But immediately following those two points, the growth rate exploded, creating a greater momentum than ever before. As a general rule, however, consistent motivation and thorough training lead to both the growth of disciples and a constant momentum.

I have a plaque on my wall from the Latin America Mission containing significant words by the late director of that mission, R. Kenneth Strachan. They emphasize the relationship of an expanding movement to the involvement of its people:

> The successful expansion of any movement is in direct proportion to its ability to mobilize and involve its total membership in constant propagation of its beliefs, its purposes, and its philosophy.

In other words, the expansion of a movement is based on its ability to motivate all of its members to achieve its particular goals and objectives. Unless individuals are continually motivated, and unless they are thoroughly indoctrinated and trained to accomplish their goals, momentum will not be consistent.

QUANTITY AND QUALITY AS THEY RELATE TO MOMENTUM

In maintaining momentum in His movement, Jesus kept a delicate balance between quantity and quality. Although He continued to sow the seed of the Word widely and to draw large crowds to Himself, He carefully aimed at producing a quality in His disciples that would attract others to the movement as well as provide leadership to continue to reach an increasing number of people.

In my ministry with high school students I have discovered that they easily become excited about Jesus Christ. Using proper means, a large number can be assembled in a short period of time. However, if there is not adequate leadership to teach these young people, to help them with their problems, and to relate to them personally, their enthusiasm soon cools and they forsake the Christian movement. This has been one of the tragic lessons of the recent Jesus Movement in America. What is true of young people is also true of adults. One should be careful to have the leadership to teach, along with the ability to evangelize, if there is to be sustained momentum.

Immediately following His dramatic baptism, Jesus could easily have mustered an enthusiastic following. A great multitude witnessed the event. They must have been excited by the manifestation of the Holy Spirit. But rather than drawing an immediate, superficial following, the Spirit led Him into the wilderness for forty days to be tempted of the devil. When He returned, most of the ecstatic crowd that would have immediately followed Him had gone home.

After the temptation, John the Baptist pointed Jesus out to two of his disciples (John 1:36). As a result of John's witness, Jesus gained His first disciples. It was with these and a few others whose interest was growing that Jesus began His ministry. Had Jesus begun with a large number of superficial followers, many, no doubt, would have forsaken Him and returned home. His movement would have seemed to be losing momentum rather than growing. With this impression, He would have had difficulty creating any kind of momentum in the future.

After feeding the five thousand, Jesus again put quality above quantity. The multitude was so impressed with His ability to provide food for them that they wanted to make Him their earthly king. They wanted Him to go to Jerusalem and be crowned. But that kind of popularity and power would not have produced the kind of kingdom He wanted. For that reason He rejected the invitation and rebuked the people for laboring for that which would perish rather than for that which would endure for eternal life. Jesus sought quality of commitment more than a large following.

After His rejection of an earthly kingdom, the multitudes began to forsake Him, and even His intimate followers appeared ready to leave Him. However, as a result of this experience, these disciples were brought to the point of an even greater commitment. This new commitment led to an immediate numerical increase that more than compensated for what He had lost earlier.

Jesus' example was followed by the early church. Numbers are mentioned throughout the book of Acts. Three thousand souls were added to the church on the day of Pentecost (Acts 2:41). Five thousand men believed after Peter's message at the portico of Solomon (Acts 4:4). According to Acts 6:1, the disciples were increasing in number regularly.

Then in Acts 5 a purging is recorded. Ananias and Sapphira were stricken dead because they had lied to the Holy Spirit. As a result, the numerical growth of the church came to a temporary standstill: "No one else dared join them [the apostles], even though they were highly regarded by the people" (Acts 5:13). However, soon after this, the church began another phase of rapid growth. "More and more men and women believed in the Lord and were added to their number" (Acts 5:14). This record shows the concern of the early church leaders for both quality and quantity. The chapter on evangelism expounds this principle in detail.

Four Essential Elements of Motivation

Four elements are essential in motivating people and creating a sustained momentum. In establishing His movement, Jesus Christ involved these elements of motivation.

1. In order to accomplish His primary goals, Jesus established primary and secondary *goals*. (The primary goals and objectives were discussed in chapter 2.)

2. The *individual* is a vital part of the ministry. Christ focused on reaching the individual, involving the individual, and developing the individual according to God's plan for him.

3. In order to reach the goals, a *strategy* is necessary. Jesus' strategy is revealed in His method of developing people and is outlined in the Seven Steps. As Jesus envisioned the progressive outreach of His movement in Acts 1:8, He commanded His disciples to continue His strategy. His planned program was the practical implementation of His strategy.

4. *Unity* is essential. If Christ's disciples had not been of like mind and if they had not been moving in the same direction, their movement would not have gained momentum.

All four elements are important and are vitally interrelated. Goals are useless without individuals who will work toward them. Even with adequate manpower, goals are not reached without a strategy. And, of course, individuals in conflict do not move towards a single goal, and so on. The key is to have individuals who are in proper relation to the goals, the strategy, and to the other individuals. The individual must be of primary concern, for the ultimate goal is to bring glory to God by building individual persons into the image of God. The program is aimed at meeting that goal. The one element not discussed before in this book is that of unity.

LACK OF UNITY TODAY

In spite of the emphasis on Christian unity in recent years, there is little agreement as to what Christ actually demanded. Everyone agrees that Christ wanted His disciples to be united (John 17:21). Most evangelical Christians agree that believers should be united in their love for each other (John 13:34,35) and that all Christians should be united in a common faith based on the apostolic teaching of the New Testament (John 17:20-23).

However, there are two questions much in debate: (1) To what extent should Christians be united under one organizational structure and what are the requirements for being a part of that organization? (2) To what extent should Christians be in agreement on the interpretation of the apostolic New Testament teachings? In this brief discussion only a few observations can be made.

In the history of the church, united organizational structures have been greatly abused. In the past, as in the Roman Church and as a result of the clerical movement of the second to fifth centuries, ordained leaders of such structures have tended to compel individuals and groups to conform, even when those individuals and groups did not feel that the leaders were following Christ's teachings or submitting to His leadership. In forcing others to conform, these leaders were denying the Holy Spirit's leading and teaching of the individual. An extreme example is the persecution during the Inquisition. Denominational leaders today at times try to require their constituents to follow denominational policies, programs, and materials. This happens even though some within the denomination feel that these disagree with the teachings of Christ and His apostles.

While Jesus apparently expected most of His followers to work together cooperatively, He clearly taught that some individuals — those who showed loyalty to Him and worked so as to give glory to His name — should have the privilege of working independently (Mark 9:38,39; Luke 9:49,50). Therefore, Christ could not have meant complete unity of organization and program when He spoke of unity.

Most evangelical churches agree on the major doctrines concerning the person of Christ: His deity; salvation through His death, resurrection, and ascension and the gift of new life through His Holy Spirit; and His lordship over the church. But on the details of these doctrines and on other doctrines, they differ sometimes to the point of hostility. Many do not feel Christ expects unity on the interpretation of the Word.

The crux of the problem lies here. People have become cynical. They do not believe that Christ through His Holy Spirit can lead them into greater agreement. Christians should stop trying to prove that they are right. If humility is the mark of one who has Christ's mind (Phil. 2:5-10), they should *be open to Christ's showing them where they are wrong.* Christians should be open for their brothers and sisters to help them understand where they may be wrong. Then they will be able to believe that the Holy Spirit can give greater unity.

Christians should also *try to communicate more effectively* so that a greater confessional unity can be attained. The apostle Paul was largely independent of the other apostles in his work. However, he was concerned that all recognize that what he preached was in agreement with the preaching of the other apostles (Acts 15; Gal. 2:2-10). He submitted his teachings to the apostles in Jerusalem even though he had no question about the accuracy of his teaching (Gal. 1:11,12).

Dr. Henry Van Dusen, president of Union Theological Seminary in New York and a leader in America's ecumenical movement, once observed that the efforts to bring organizational unity were hypocritical because they did not produce a unity at the grass-roots level — there is not unity in the work and ministry of the local churches. This is obviously true. Love, desire for communication, and efforts to cooperate by people in the local churches and among the various local church groups is necessary if significant momentum is to be gained in Christ's work. As a witness for Christ, local unity is perhaps even more important than denominational unity.

TEN ASPECTS OF MOTIVATION

Jesus was a superb motivator. If we follow His example, we too can learn specific ways to motivate people and thereby promote momentum.

1. The individual feels a great sense of value when he knows he is working toward a *goal of great importance*. Jesus presented the greatest goal that can be offered to man — seeking the kingdom of God. In seeking this kingdom, people bring glory to God and are restored to the position of children of God, and in the fulfillment of this goal the greatest blessing for all people is promised (especially for those who are workers for the kingdom). Jesus preached, "Repent, for the kingdom of heaven is near" (Matt. 4:17). He called people to turn back to God because the kingdom was about to be established. Jesus taught that the kingdom is like a treasure found in a field — one should sell all he has to gain it. It is like a pearl of great price. It is worth selling everything to obtain it (Matt. 13:44-46).

A common adage states, "Small plans seldom inflame the minds of men." Offer people a big challenge, and they will respond. When Jeremiah was in prison and had lost his vision and hope, God said to him, "Call to me and I will answer you, and will tell you great and hidden things which you have not known" (Jer. 33:3). God wanted the prophet to see the greatness of what was to be done for His kingdom.

William Carey, often called the "founder of modern missions," grasped the significance of seeking great goals. While he was a member of the Minister's Association of Nottingham, Carey had a vision. On May 31, 1792, as he read Isaiah 54:2,3: "Enlarge the place of your tent . . . ," he saw God's family being enlarged. When children are born to a family of nomads living in the desert, the parents add sections to their tent. Just as they would spread their tent out, strengthening the stakes and lengthening the cords, so William Carey saw the family of God expanding to include all people of all nations.

William Carey acted on the basis of this vision. By October 2, 1792, he had formed the first mission board, the Baptist Missionary Society. He himself went to India where he translated the Bible in whole or in part into twenty-four languages and dialects. Under his direction, the Surampu Press made the Bible accessible to 300 million people. William Carey sought and aimed at big goals. He said, "Expect great things from God; attempt great things for God."

2. In showing how *intermediate goals* can be attained, Jesus motivated people by *creating hope that final goals can successfully be reached*. Reaching every person in the world with the gospel and making disciples of all nations is such a big goal that it appears to be impossible. Christ's strategy was to assign the Twelve and the Seventy to certain cities at various times in His ministry. In three years they had preached in almost every place in Palestine. Then when Jesus talked about reaching the world, the task did not seem insurmountable. Again Jesus outlined intermediate goals: Jerusalem, all Judea, Samaria, and beyond (Acts 1:8). The disciples had learned that they could reach some communities, their disciples could reach others, and *their* disciples could reach still others.

One organization working with high school students effectively uses this principle of motivating students by setting up intermediate goals. For instance, in a school of one thousand, the staff explains that if a hundred students can be won to Christ and each one be trained to witness to ten others, the school can be reached quickly. The Christian students in that school can then see how all the students of the city and eventually all the students of the world can be reached.

Feasible intermediate goals help a person see that the ultimate goal can be reached. If the ultimate goal seems impossible, who will work for it? Hope of attainment is essential if one is to be motivated to try.

3. Jesus gave His disciples *confidence in their source of power*. They were assured that this power was adequate to help them reach the goal, for whenever obstacles were great, He disclosed the power of God.

For example, the night before Jesus rebuked the crowds and they began to leave Him, He showed the disciples that He Himself was God by walking on the water (John 6). There was also a time of tension and confusion during the step of Leadership Development. John the Baptist, Jesus' friends, and His family all doubted Him. The religious leaders (the Pharisees and Sadducees) opposed Him. But Jesus encouraged His disciples by an amazing display of His power (Matt. 8:18,23–9:34; Mark 4:35–5:43; Luke 8:22-56). Then, after the shattering experience of the cross, Jesus displayed His risen body and proclaimed, "All authority in heaven and on earth has been given to me. Therefore go . . ." (Matt. 28:18-20).

Christians must be reminded that all God's power is behind His church. From time to time that power must be displayed by answers to prayer offered in faith.

4. Jesus gave His disciples *an understandable and workable program* for reaching their goals. He demonstrated many techniques, such as how to gather the crowds, how to carry out personal evangelism, and how to hold home evangelistic meetings. These aspects of the program worked; they saw results. To be motivated, people must see the program operating successfully.

The leader must be humble. If the program is not working, he needs to reevaluate and correct the problems or weak points. When the multitudes began to look for an earthly king and when they began to look upon Jesus purely as One who could satisfy their physical needs, Jesus made an adjustment in His strategy and began to change their way of thinking.

5. In order to motivate His disciples, Jesus *created a limited sense of urgency*. He preached, "The time has come. The kingdom of God is near . . ." (Mark 1:15). Because Jesus warned them that the kingdom was coming soon, the people were urged to respond. A limited sense of urgency offsets laziness and procrastination, and Jesus skillfully used this motivational tool.

Today, those who seek to motivate disciples need to emphasize the nearness of Christ's return in glory. They should tell of the coming judgment of the nations and the difficult times that are approaching because of our growing sin.

If the sense of urgency that is created is too great, people will become discouraged and not be motivated. If they are convinced that Christ will return tomorrow, they will tend to sit down to wait. They will feel that there is no time left to accomplish the goals Jesus has given us. At the same time, if people think that the return of Christ is far off, they will not be motivated at all.

6. Jesus made *the individual worker* feel that he was *important* to the kingdom of God. At times He addressed individuals specifically, saying, "Follow me" (Matt. 4:19; 8:22; Mark 1:17). He communicated the idea that their talents could be used more fully in His ministry, saying, "I will make you fishers of men" (Mark 1:17). Jesus utilized and developed Peter's outspokenness, and Peter became the great confessor and preacher of the gospel. Judas had an interest in money, so Jesus gave him the responsibility of being the treasurer of the group.

To be motivated, the individual must know that his position and his qualities are unique. He must have the assurance that he has something to contribute to the success of the work. While "of the flesh,'' the worker has little to offer, yet the Spirit of God can use him to God's glory. When the disciples had problems or needs, Jesus spent time with them and helped to direct their focus. We can show others that God has a plan and a place for them and their talents. The fact that the Holy Spirit called them into God's work is evidence that He wants to use them.

Jesus seems to have given His men as much responsibility as they could reasonably assume. He sent them out on their own, allowing them to have a ministry without Him. Thus, He was preparing them for the time when He would no longer be present. It is best not to do for a disciple what he can do for himself. He must be given an opportunity to act independently and responsibly.

The program and strategy should never take priority over the individual. If you are so intent on carrying out a strategy and a program that you cannot give attention to the individual, motivation will be undercut.

7. The *individual* also needs to *feel accepted*. He needs approval. In the parable of the talents Jesus said that the master said to his servant, ''Well done, good and faithful servant'' (Matt. 25:21 et al.). Jesus also told His twelve disciples that they would sit on the twelve thrones of the twelve tribes of Israel because they had been loyal to Him (Luke 22:28-30). We need to encourage our disciples by telling them when they have done a job well.

On the other hand, if the disciple has failed, we should be honest with him and correct him. When the disciples feared they would perish in the storm, He asked them, ''You of little faith, why are you so afraid?'' (Matt. 8:26). When Jesus foresaw Peter's failure, He warned him that Satan would sift him like wheat. But He also encouraged him by saying that He had prayed for him that his faith would not fail.

Denouncing or condemning a disciple will discourage him, but correction and instruction will be an encouragement. By taking the time to instruct the disciple, the leader shows that he loves him. This kind of loving instruction motivates a person.

8. When motivating people, we should put them in circumstances that will *help* them *see their needs*. They need to be personally exposed to real situations that show their need for development and growth. Then they can begin to meet that need.

In Matthew 17, Mark 9, and Luke 9, Jesus used a situation His disciples could not handle. A father had brought his demon-possessed son to them to be cured, but they were not able to drive out the demon. When Jesus returned from praying on a mountain, He drove out the demon. He then explained to His disciples that this type of demon could only be driven out by prayer (and fasting). Consequently, they were motivated to develop in these areas so that they would be able to meet such obstacles when encountered again.

9. Jesus emphasized *the love of God* and the care for the individual. He exhorted His disciples not to be concerned about money or clothes or food. God feeds the sparrows of the air and clothes the lilies of the field. Would He not take care of those who were of far greater value in His sight (Matt. 6:25-34)?

Those in leadership positions should emphasize the aspect of God's love manifested in the death of Jesus Christ on the behalf of His church. This love illustrates the worth of the individual and God's concern for the individual. The knowledge of this love will motivate the individual disciple more than anything else.

The parables of the lost sheep, the lost coin, and the lost son in Luke 15 illustrate God's love for lost people. As the disciple understands that God loves all people and wants to redeem each person, he will be motivated to find people who need Christ and witness to them.

10. *Prayer* is the most important motivational tool. The Holy Spirit is the One who truly motivates people. Jesus Christ constantly prayed for His disciples. The person who wants to create momentum must spend time in prayer, beseeching the Holy Spirit to work in the hearts of his group of disciples, motivating them and helping them when they have problems.

Proper motivation is important if momentum is to be created and disciples are to grow. From time to time, leaders should review some of these principles of motivation and see where they may be falling down or what they can do to motivate their people more adequately.

15

Evangelism and Discipleship

In the chapter on goals, I compared evangelism to the task of procuring tomato plants from the greenhouse and planting them in the garden. Evangelism involves taking people from the kingdom of Satan and placing them in the kingdom of Christ.

Just as evangelism is analogous to putting plants out in a garden, so disciple building is analogous to tending a garden. An inexperienced gardener might feel a great sense of accomplishment in planting a tomato garden. But if he only planted new plants and neglected to care for the plants that already grew in his garden, soon he would have problems. His tomato plants would either begin to die from lack of fertilizer or water, or they would be smothered by weeds or eaten by insects. On the other hand, if the gardener only tended his plants, not making any provision for planting more tomatoes the next season, he would also be without fruit.

Evangelism and disciple building must work together. Each is essential to the other.

THREE FORMS OF EVANGELISM

Jesus engaged in three forms of evangelism and trained His men in these. Each promotes the others, and all contribute to the process of disciple building.

Personal evangelism. In the ministry of Christ, personal evangelism was not so much a skill to be learned as an enthusiasm about Christ and sharing that enthusiasm with others. No doubt, Christ's disciples learned how to deal with people personally by watching Him. They observed His interview with Nicodemus, the rich young ruler, and others. And He undoubtedly related some of His conversations, such as the one with the woman at the well, to them. From His example they learned technique. But if they had not been excited about who He was and what He came to do for people, the disciples would not have been motivated to share with many others.

The modern church has rediscovered the importance of personal evangelism. Much training is offered in the different techniques of witnessing. Campus Crusade for Christ, the Southern Baptist Church (Win Program), and the Coral Ridge Church are some of the prominent groups that offer excellent training. But even when people are trained, the results are sometimes meager. For instance, a thousand attended a course in personal witnessing at one church. But less than a year later the pastor told me that no more than a handful were still sharing their faith. Often the problem lies in not adequately linking evangelism to disciple building. But sometimes the problem is motivational.

All the techniques in the world cannot motivate someone to witness. Why did Andrew search for his brother Peter and bring him to Jesus? Because he had heard John the Baptist testify of the descent of the Holy Spirit upon Jesus at His baptism. And after having associated with Jesus, he was convinced that Jesus was the Messiah (John 1:29-42; cf. also Philip bringing Nathanel, 1:45).

Why did Nicodemus come to Jesus? Undoubtedly, he had witnessed Jesus' cleansing of the temple and recognized Him as the divine rectifier whom Malachi predicted (cf. Mal. 3:1-5 with John 2:14-23; see also 3:2).

Why did the woman of Samaria leave the well in order to tell her friends about Jesus and bring them to Him? Because He had disclosed her sin and revealed who He was (John 4:16,19,26,27-29,40-42).

Why did the 120 go into the streets on the day of Pentecost to proclaim the wonderful works of God? Because they had seen the risen Christ and experienced the presence of His Holy Spirit (Acts 1,2).

Why did the lay Christians who were forced to leave Jerusalem go everywhere preaching the Word? Was it not at least in part because they knew that just before he died Stephen had seen Jesus Christ alive and exalted with all power at the right hand of God? (Acts 7:56; 8:1,4; 11:19-21).

People not only need to be trained in personal evangelism, but also to become aware of the presence and working of the risen Christ. Then they will enthusiastically talk about Him. How can this awareness be gained today, for "we live by faith, not by sight" (2 Cor. 5:7; cf. 1 Peter 1:8)? Certainly not by a human program! This happens only if Jesus Christ sovereignly chooses to manifest Himself and His power through His Spirit.

Scripture reveals that He chooses to work only under certain conditions. God's people need to confess and forsake their sin both individually and as churches, crying to Christ to make Himself known to them in His own way. Then He will manifest His love, drastically change lives, and heal hearts. Then they will have something to talk about! And non-Christians will be attracted to the churches to learn more about the Christ church members have been sharing.

When Christians witness personally, they grow as disciples. Non-Christians will ask them questions that will compel them to look for answers. They will be forced to formulate truth in their minds in such a way as to share it, and they will thereby gain a clearer understanding of truth themselves. As they share the truth of God with others, they become more involved publicly and more deeply committed emotionally to Christ and His movement. Then not only is the Christian strengthened, but the movement is made more vital.

Home or party evangelism. Jesus held meetings in the homes of His converts or in the homes of those who were interested in Him. After Matthew was converted, he invited many of his friends into his home to hear Jesus. There Jesus had personal contact with these nonbelievers, and many heard His message. He was found in the home of the Pharisee (where the prostitute wept at His feet) and in the home of Martha and Mary. In fact, His frequent home visits often caused gossip. People said that He had come eating, drinking, and partying. But He used the opportunities these parties provided to get close to people and draw them to Himself. Evangelistic teas, coffees, and socials accomplish the same purpose today. In small social gatherings, Christians can relate to people and present Christ to them.

Party evangelism is a very effective way for a new convert to reach his friends. Soon after his conversion he is still closely associated with his old friends, and they still feel an attachment to him. Experience has shown that after he has been a Christian for a while, their life styles will differ appreciably, and they will no longer be close. But if he has an evangelistic party soon after becoming a Christian and invites a mature leader to present Christ to his friends, many of them will attend, and some will be reached for Christ.

Home evangelism can also be helpful to the new convert. By immediately letting his friends know about his conversion, he is challenged to trust the Lord to help him live a more holy life before them. And, if some of his friends accept Christ, a home Bible study might develop. The natural affinity between him and his friends in this discipleship group will furnish a good environment in which to grow. Thus, discipleship is forwarded as well as evangelism.

Another great advantage in home evangelism is that of promoting the conversion of entire families.[1] Peter's meeting in the home of Cornelius, the centurion, resulted in the conversion of his entire family and friends (Acts 10:24,33,44). Paul's meeting in the home of the Philippian jailer had the same results (Acts 16:31-34).

The family is the basic unit of society and until the fourth century was the center of the church. The Western world has become so centered in thinking about *the individual* that it has basically denied the social nature of man and the importance of the family. Ralph Winter, Dr. Donald McGavran, and others have pointed out that in many places of the world whole families or groups turn to Christ at once.[2] This is not meant to deny that every individual must be personally related to God through faith in Christ, but it is also to recognize the biblical emphasis on the importance of family ties and influence.

Preaching or mass evangelism. This kind of evangelism began when John the Baptist preached in the area of Aenon by the Jordan River. Later Jesus preached in the same area, on the sea shores of Capernaum, and on the mountainsides of Galilee. When He was in Jerusalem, many people came to hear Him preach and teach in the temple. Jesus also preached in the synagogues. The apostle Paul preached in synagogues, in public assembly places, and in rented halls where crowds gathered nearby.

Mass evangelism allows the presentation of the gospel to large numbers of people at once. In a large group of people great excitement and interest can be generated in a way that cannot be done in personal or home evangelism. An emotional desire to participate and belong can be created in the individual. While many do actually accept Christ in mass evangelistic meetings, many others begin their desire to know Christ there and later find Him alone, in church, or by having someone share with their prepared heart and mind.

Mass evangelism was an essential part of the revivalistic movement that began in the eighteenth century. (This movement involved more than a mass evangelistic outreach, however.) George Whitefield and John Wesley preached to crowds in the fields, outside the mines, and in the streets. The nineteenth and twentieth centuries witnessed the building of a movement centered more strictly on mass evangelism. Dwight L. Moody, Billy Sunday, Wilbur Chapman, Oral Roberts, and Billy Graham and his team are among the leaders of this movement. Many individual and denominational evangelists have had fruitful ministries.

These mass evangelistic efforts can cause great interest in Christian disciples, and this encourages them to want to grow. They of course win new converts, who become disciples. Christians should practice mass evangelism more today. If churches cooperate in their evangelism efforts, they can use mass media more effectively to present Christ to the public.

INTERRELATIONSHIP OF DIFFERENT FORMS OF EVANGELISM

Local churches could hold evangelistic meetings with more success if accompanied by personal and party evangelism. The people contacted through the latter would most likely attend the larger meetings. If Campus Crusade for Christ would link its efforts to mobilize a whole city for personal evangelism with a Billy Graham crusade, the impact would probably be much greater than either alone could generate, and the cost would not be much higher than one of the efforts would be alone. In all of these evangelistic endeavors the greatest need is to link them with a plan to build the converts. Then a progressive momentum will be obtained in the evangelism movement.

Each of these forms of evangelism supports the others. Often personal evangelism leads to party or mass evangelism, and vice versa. After the woman at the well talked with Jesus and believed in Him as the Christ, she hurried into the city to tell her friends about Him. They, in turn, went out to hear Him, and the personal interview was suddenly turned into a public meeting. As a result of party evangelism and mass evangelism, individuals became interested in Jesus and sought Him out. Then He dealt personally with them. After they had placed their faith in Him, Jesus could challenge them to follow Him.

Personal evangelism and public preaching should be used to complement each other, as in the example of the woman at the well (John 4:7-42). When Jesus sent out the Twelve (Matt. 9:37; 11:1) and again when He sent out the Seventy, He apparently followed up their witness with a mass meeting in the area (cf. Luke 10:1). This same technique was demonstrated on the day of Pentecost. On that day the 120 were baptized with the Holy Spirit and began witnessing to "the wonders of God" (Acts 2:11). As a result of their sharing the gospel personally, multitudes came to the temple, where Peter stood with the Eleven to preach (Acts 2:1-41).

After the scattering of the church (Acts 8), the Christians witnessed personally to many (Acts 11:19-21). Thus, Barnabas, and later Saul, had the opportunity to preach the gospel publicly in Antioch (Acts 11:22-26). According to Acts 8:5-25 a similar situation apparently arose in Samaria.

Paul and other believers preached from house to house and publicly in the temple (Acts 5:42; 20:20). They witnessed in the synagogue (Acts 19:8) and in the school of Tyrannus (Acts 19:9). Home churches, which probably started from home evangelism, are mentioned in Acts 10; 12:12; Romans 16:3-5; 1 Corinthians 16:19; and Philemon 2.

Need for Balance in Evangelism and Disciple Building

As mentioned earlier, the movement of evangelism will not continue to gain momentum unless it is accompanied by disciple building. New workers must continually be trained. Their involvement in evangelism will directly contribute to their growth as disciples. Consequently, there must be a balance between evangelism and disciple building. Thus, in Jesus' ministry there was a wave of evangelism and then disciple building close to every six months.

Jesus masterfully achieved a balance between evangelism and disciple building. In seven successive waves, He evangelized and then built disciples.

1. The first major evangelistic outreach occurred during the step of Repentance and Faith. At this time, John the Baptist and Jesus preached in the area of the Jordan River. Afterwards, Jesus concentrated on building disciples, gathering a group of men around Him. He left the area of His evangelistic activity and traveled to the small towns of Cana and Nazareth where He could freely teach His disciples. During this period of Enlightenment, He performed only a few miracles. But through these He demonstrated the truth He had taught them about Himself.

2. This disciple-building effort was followed by another major evangelistic outreach as Christ traveled to Capernaum. There He performed mighty miracles and spoke to large crowds. Continuing His evangelistic activities (during Ministry Training), He traveled to the cities and villages of Galilee and then returned to Capernaum and Jerusalem. As He evangelized, Jesus continued to teach and build His disciples. Then He withdrew from Capernaum because of opposition. At this time (Leadership Development), Jesus selected the Twelve and, in the presence of the many who followed Him, delivered the Sermon on the Mount.

3. After the selection of the Twelve, the evangelistic outreach continued. Jesus returned to Capernaum and then traveled through Nain preaching by the Sea of Galilee. The multitudes now crowded

around Him so much that His teaching of the Twelve was hindered. Therefore, as Jesus began to concentrate on building His disciples, He taught them in parables. The unbelieving crowds were excluded, while the disciples learned a great deal. Before finally withdrawing to the area of the Gadarenes (across the lake), Jesus taught in His own home in Capernaum. Although Jesus did continue to evangelize during all His periods of disciple building, His main emphasis was not on outreach.

4. This period of concentrated disciple building was followed by another major evangelistic outreach beginning again in Capernaum. Here Jesus healed the woman with the issue of blood. He also raised Jairus' daughter and performed other miracles. Although He was rejected in Nazareth at this time, elsewhere His popularity grew. He sent the Twelve out to many cities and then followed them, preaching throughout Galilee. At the end of this period of Leadership Development, Jesus crossed the lake. Here He fed the five thousand (near Bethsaida).

At the beginning of Reevaluation Jesus was rejected by a great number of the multitude. Afterwards, Christ spent time building His disciples. He withdrew to Tyre and Sidon, to the Decapolis, and elsewhere. This was followed by another evangelistic campaign. Although not a major campaign, there was extensive evangelism among the Greek people in the Decapolis where He healed many and fed four thousand. The discipleship period that followed the feeding of four thousand occurred in Dalmanutha. Next He went across the lake to Caesarea Philippi, then to the Mount of Transfiguration, and then secretly returned to Galilee. At this time Jesus intensely taught His disciples.

5. The period of Participation and Delegation included another evangelistic campaign. Again, the campaign started from Capernaum and was continued en route to Jerusalem and the Feast of Tabernacles. After Jesus appointed the Seventy, He sent them out two by two to participate in the evangelization of Judea and Perea. After this campaign He withdrew to the Jordan area to spend time building His disciples. Following the raising of Lazarus, He again withdrew to Ephraim in order to avoid hostility and continue building His disciples.

6. It is not clear where the evangelistic campaign of Luke 13:22 occurs, but this verse does mention another tour. Perhaps it is linked with the campaign that began on the border of Samaria and Galilee, continued through Perea and ended in Jerusalem just before Passion Week. During the final week, Jesus was seen in public, but most of His time was spent teaching His disciples.

7. On the day of Pentecost, Jesus initiated the last evangelistic thrust by sending the Holy Spirit.

The chart on page 182 (see page 181 for description) demonstrates how a continuing outreach program of successive waves of evangelism increased the church members and how successive waves of discipleship groups were taught. From these new disciples, new people were trained for ministry and from them new leaders were chosen. With new leaders and others trained for ministry, a new and stronger wave of evangelism could be launched.

INTERRELATIONSHIP OF EVANGELISM AND DISCIPLESHIP

Because of the seven successive waves of evangelism, the number of people following Jesus constantly increased. In each of the periods of concentrated outreach, the disciples assumed a different role. As they matured, their responsibilities and involvement changed. They themselves were evangelized in the step of Repentance and Faith. In the step of Ministry Training, they helped Christ evangelize. From the step of Leadership Development onward, they both evangelized and led others in evangelistic efforts. In other words, at each step of growth their level of involvement in evangelism played a part in helping them mature. Also, as shown previously, different kinds of evangelism contribute differently to the disciple-building efforts. Thus, evangelism in all forms is an integral part of the disciple-building process, as well as being the means of gaining new disciples.

The task of building disciples takes longer, is more demanding, and is harder to publicize and sell. People are more impressed with statistics on evangelism than with those on disciple building. Statements such as, "We had five hundred at a meeting and eighty made decisions," or "We personally talked to one hundred people and twenty made decisions," are more exciting than, "In the last three months I have spent several hours daily working with ten boys." It is more dramatic to have a baby than to care for a child. But the former is tragic without the latter. The former gives little satisfaction to the parent without the latter. While some may not be easily impressed with disciple building, it pleases Christ to see His children walk in obedience. It should also please Christians (2 John 4, 3 John 4).

GROWING TENSION BETWEEN EVANGELISM AND DISCIPLESHIP

In recent years the relationship between evangelism and discipleship has not been understood. Many have considered these different aspects of the Christian ministry to be almost antithetical. The fact is, they are interdependent. One affects the other. In some cases, a brief time lag occurs before the effect is evident.

I foresee a crisis over evangelism in the church in the near future. If the United States moves further toward moral collapse, churchmen will be less satisfied with the kind of evangelism that leads people to profess Christ as Savior but produces "converts" who do not follow through by active membership in the churches, or if they join the churches, do not produce the fruit of the Spirit in their lives. There is the possibility that this might even lead to widespread rejection of evangelism altogether. This would be tragic.

Sentiments against public evangelistic efforts are growing even in the Southern Baptist Church, which does more of it than most organizations. Toby Druin, Editor of News Services, Southern Baptist Home Mission Board, recently completed a study on Southern Baptist evangelistic efforts and spoke out strongly about superficial results. He said, "We have too many nonresident members today . . . people who feel they have made the one-time decision, walked to the altar in answer to that appeal, and yet are not aware of what they were doing and what is expected of them."

HISTORIC POINT OF DIVISION BETWEEN EVANGELISM AND DISCIPLESHIP IN AMERICA

Satan has tricked the church into making a distinction between evangelism and disciple building. Where in the Scriptures do Jesus or the apostles separate the two ideas or debate one against the other? Evangelism is the process of winning men, enabling them to enter the kingdom of God. Disciple building is the process of teaching the new citizen how to obey the laws of the King and how to win and train others to do the same. Both evangelism and discipleship are necessary if the government of God is to be established in the hearts of men.

Not until antisupernatural philosophical thinking gained a stronghold in the church around 1850 was evangelism thought of as a separate enterprise. The word *evangelism* did not even exist before then. Mendell Taylor says:

> The proclamation of the good news of the gospel has been an integral part of the ever-expanding Christian religion through the centuries. However, the word *evangelism,* from which the terms gospel and good news were derived, was not incorporated in the terminology of Christian theology until the recent past.

Charles Adams was one of the first to use the word in the year 1850.[3]

William Warren Sweet pointed out that the church at that time was caught up in revivalism and "had largely ignored the law of

Christian growth. . . ."[4] Horace Bushnell, in his book *Christian Nurture* (first published in 1846 and revised in 1861), called the church back to disciple building. Bushnell's liberal views, which included an erroneous view of the atonement, undercut the motive for evangelism. Others with more liberal or antisupernatural theology followed Bushnell's example by emphasizing growth in the Christian life. Because they pointed out evident needs, these men gained a strong following in the Christian community. Thus, by the church's neglect of disciple building, modern unbelieving theology found an entrance to and gained influence in the church. The emphasis on Christian nurture eventually became identified with modern unbelief.

Believers avoided being associated with it lest they themselves be identified as liberals. Hence the area of disciple building, or, more broadly, Christian education, was more or less abandoned to more liberal and unbiblical thinkers. This led in practice to treating evangelism and disciple building as two separate processes.

The neglect of Christian nurture by evangelicals also left the door open for more liberal men to interpret the Christian life and society in terms of their purely humanistic values. These humanists led the church into error in social and political action, and she continues in error today. Since social action also became identified with liberal thought, evangelicals abandoned this aspect of ministry to the liberals just as they had done in the area of Christian nurture.[5]

Some church leaders still try to separate evangelism and discipleship. C. Peter Wagner in an article in *Christianity Today* called disciple building a "torpedo" to evangelism, implying that it hinders the fulfillment of the Great Commission.[6] In his thinking, it is similar to the political and social action efforts of the humanists. In contrast, Jesus considered the teaching of disciples to be as much a part of the Great Commission as winning them. He said, "Make disciples of all nations . . . *teaching them to obey everything* I have commanded you" (Matt. 28:19,20). It is possible that some leaders of evangelism feel one should make as many converts as possible without providing for their nurture. Such a singular emphasis on evangelism will likely be the thing that hinders evangelism in the long run.

THE NEED TO REUNIFY THE TWO

The two aspects of the Great Commission must be reunified in our minds as one task. Only as evangelism and disciple building are thought of as one united task and converts are taught what is involved in being a part of the kingdom of God will the social and political issues be grounded again on a biblical basis. Then Christians will be taught that social and political activity is a product of the Christian life. How do we accomplish this reunification? By returning to a proper emphasis on disciple building.

Although most evangelistic organizations have made genuine efforts to work with the churches in their programs, most evangelistic programs are not designed by the church to give long-term results for the church. Sometimes few if any permanent members are gained. Many evangelistic campaigns cost thousands of dollars and require hundreds of hours of work but produce little benefit or only indirect benefits for the churches. While these efforts doubtlessly offer worthwhile gains, even if doing nothing more than getting Christ's name before the public, they could be better designed to be more directly productive for the churches.

One large evangelical organization has planned an extensive evangelism program that will involve many churches across the nation and will cost Christians thousands of dollars. Of the ten men planning the program only one had ever been a church pastor, and he had served one small church for less than four years.

One evangelist who holds large meetings in many big cities makes almost no effort to work with churches. He has television programs in a big city for some time before going there and draws his crowds primarily through this medium. For several years I held large "city-wide" youth crusades, speaking to from one to four thousand young people and training many of them to share their faith. When I found that the churches did not follow through and get the students involved in the church, I stopped. At the time I blamed the churches. After all, I genuinely tried to work with them. But the problem lay in the fact that I had designed the evangelism program and asked the churches to work with it, rather than working with the churches to design an approach to evangelism that would benefit them by drawing people into the church.

No evangelist or evangelistic organization can effectively build disciples unless they assign permanent local staff to do this. A parent who lives somewhere else, but sends food occasionally cannot really care for a baby. Local churches can do this much better. Those in positions of evangelistic leadership desperately need to adopt the position and attitude of a servant by working with local church leadership in designing evangelistic programs that will draw more people into active church participation. If a tomato plant never gets planted in a garden, how can it ever have the gardener's care? If people who are evangelized never join a church, how can they ever be effectively discipled?

Some evangelists, such as Billy Graham, have funneled more converts into churches than others. Those getting more of these converts into the churches usually have worked harder at church cooperation. With rare exceptions, most evangelists need to work more closely with the churches in designing the way evangelism is done, and the churches need to work more with evangelists in doing this. Evangelistic programs need to be designed to help assimilate the converts and help them grow as well as to win them.

A return to New Testament methods of evangelism and to the New Testament balance and integration of evangelism with disciple building would produce considerable improvement. An understanding of the interdependence of the two will provide a good foundation for creative thinking.

FAILURE IN KNOWING HOW TO BUILD DISCIPLES

One of the biggest problems in encouraging converts to become church members lies in the fact that few churches know how to disciple. Recognizing this failure, evangelistic groups have developed their own disciple-building programs, which they either implement themselves or train churches to administer. Many evangelistic groups have designed "follow-up" or disciple-building programs for the churches, but in many cases these have not been effective. The reason is that most evangelistic organizations do not understand the problems of the pastor nor the problems involved in assimilating new people. Unless churches establish vital disciple-building programs and unless evangelists work with the churches to draw converts into these programs, maximum efficiency in building the kingdom of God will never be achieved.

Notes

[1] See Gene Getz, *Sharpening Focus on the Church* (Chicago: Moody, 1974), pp. 44,45.

[2] Ralph D. Winter, *The Twenty-Five Unbelievable Years 1945-1969* (South Pasadena: William Carey Library, 1970), pp. 90,91; and Donald McGavran, *Understanding Church Growth* (Grand Rapids: Eerdmans, 1970), pp. 296-315.

[3] See Mendell Taylor, *Exploring Evangelism* (Kansas City: Beacon Hill, 1964), p. 19.

[4] William Warren Sweet, *The Story of Religion in America* (New York: Harper, 1950), p. 342.

[5] Dr. Carl F. H. Henry, *The Uneasy Conscience of Modern Fundamentalism* (Grand Rapids: Eerdmans, 1947).

[6] C. Peter Wagner, "Lausanne Twelve Months Later," *Christianity Today*, vol. 19, no. 20 (July 4, 1975): 8.

16

Prayer

Prayer is one of the most important aspects of building disciples. If one is to help men grow in the knowledge of Jesus Christ, he must pray. Indeed, *if he does everything else right in terms of building disciples, yet fails to pray, nothing significant will happen.* The reason is simple. God acts in response to believing prayer, because through prayer He is glorified rather than the worker. Prayer must accompany every step of spiritual growth. While Christian teachers may minister to disciples in different ways, only God gives growth (Mark 4:27,28; 1 Cor. 3:6; Col. 2:19).

The Scriptures are quite clear about the essential nature of prayer in the life of every believer. Our tendency is to give up rather than look to God for the fruit of our labor. Through the parable in Luke 18:1-8, Jesus showed His disciples "that they should *always pray* and not give up."

Paul instructed Christians to "pray continually" (1 Thess. 5:17). In other words, Christians should maintain a constant sense of prayer to God. Paul also said, "And pray in the Spirit *on all occasions* with all kinds of prayers and requests" (Eph. 6:18). Then in Philippians 4:6 he said, "Do not be anxious about anything, but *in everything, by prayer* and petition, with thanksgiving, present your requests to God. And the peace of God . . . shall guard your hearts and minds in Christ Jesus."

223

ESSENTIAL TO THE MINISTRY OF JESUS CHRIST

Prayer was an essential part of Jesus' ministry. Every major event in His life was accompanied by prayer. For instance, at the time of His baptism, Jesus was found praying (Luke 3:21,22). Immediately after this introduction into His ministry, He went into the wilderness for forty days. Luke says that during those days He ate nothing (4:2). He was fasting, which for the Jew was always accompanied by prayer.

Later, Jesus' decision to leave the area where His ministry was very popular to go to an area where there was no existing interest was preceded by prayer. While He was praying in the early morning hours, His disciples came to Him and He announced that He must go to other cities, for He had been sent to them also. The timing of this sequence of events suggests that this vision of outreach had come from Jesus' time of prayer (Mark 1:35-39; Luke 4:43, 44).

Jesus spent an entire night in prayer before He selected the twelve disciples and preached their ordination sermon — the Sermon on the Mount. Luke wrote, "One of those days Jesus went out into the hills to pray, and spent the night praying to God" (Luke 6:12). After this night of prayer, He selected His disciples.

Later in His ministry Jesus had become very popular. He had fed the five thousand, and because He could feed them, the people wanted to make Him their king. But before He responded to the crowds, He went alone to a mountain to pray (Mark 6:46; John 6:15). The next day He made a crucial decision. He refused to be an earthly king who would satisfy only the physical needs of people. Claiming to be the true bread from heaven, He pointed them to an eternal kingdom. He exhorted the people to labor not for that which perishes but for that which endures unto eternal life.

Before Jesus sent out the Twelve, He said to them, "The harvest is plentiful but the laborers are few. Ask the Lord of the harvest, therefore, to send out workers into his harvest field" (Matt. 9:37–10:42). Again, His actions were attended by prayer and an urging of His disciples to pray.

Before Peter's declaration that Jesus was the Christ, the Son of the living God, Jesus had been praying (Luke 9:18-20; cf. Matt. 16:13-16). A week later Jesus was transfigured while He was praying (Luke 9:28,29). As Jesus returned from the Mount of Transfiguration, He found that His disciples were unable to drive a demon out of a child. Rebuking them for their unbelief, He said, "If you have faith as small as a mustard seed, you can say to this mountain, 'Move from here to there' and it will move. Nothing will be impossible for you." Then He said, "But this kind does not go out except by prayer and fasting" (Matt. 17:20,21 [some MSS]).

Jesus was in an attitude of prayer when the disciples came to Him and asked Him to teach them to pray (Luke 11:1), and through prayer Jesus raised Lazarus from the dead (John 11:41).

On the last night that Jesus spent with His men, He promised them the Holy Spirit, saying that He would pray to the Father and the Father would send the Holy Spirit to them (John 14:16; 16:7). In the "high-priestly prayer" (John 17) Jesus prayed that God would keep His followers from the evil one and that they might be united in love as a testimony to Him. Later when He went to Gethsemane, Jesus again prayed (Matt. 26:36-44). He also exhorted His disciples, saying, "Keep watching and praying, that you may not enter into temptation" (v. 41, NASB). Apparently, Judas knew that Jesus went often to the garden to pray, and he expected Him to be there that evening. So he chose that opportunity to betray Him.

On the cross, our Lord cried out, "My God, my God, why have you forsaken me?" And at the last He said, "Father, into your hands I commit my spirit" (Matt. 27:46; Luke 23:46). Christ remained in prayer to God even while dying on the cross.

ESSENTIAL TO THE MINISTRY OF THE EARLY CHURCH

The early church followed Jesus' example in prayer. It is not mere coincidence that Luke, when writing the book of Acts, records the times of prayer along with the works of the apostles. After the resurrection appearances of Jesus, His disciples met to pray (Acts 1:14). After Pentecost the disciples continued to pray (Acts 2:42). When Peter and John went to the temple *to pray*, they were threatened by the Sanhedrin and were told not to preach in the name of Jesus (Acts 4:5-22). The apostles once more came together to pray, and while they prayed the Holy Spirit came upon them again. The importance the apostles placed on prayer is again emphasized by the circumstances recorded in Acts 6:1-4: The apostles appointed deacons to take care of the ministry of food for the Grecian widows so that they (the Twelve) might devote their time "to prayer and the ministry of the word."

When Philip went to Samaria to preach, the Samaritans heard the gospel and believed on Jesus. Peter and John came from Jerusalem, and there prayed and laid hands on the Samaritan Christians, imparting the Holy Spirit to them (Acts 8). Prayer was essential to the inclusion of the Samaritans in the church. Because of Cornelius' prayers, God spoke to Peter who was praying and sent him to

Cornelius' house. The doors were thereby opened to spread the good news of the gospel to the Gentiles (Acts 10). Barnabas and Paul were sent on their first missionary journey because of God's instructions given while they prayed and worshiped (Acts 13:1-4).

The book of Acts is replete with examples of prayer preceding evangelism.

ESSENTIAL IN THE EPISTLES

The writers of the New Testament constantly mention how they are praying for the Christians and urging them to pray likewise (cf. Rom. 1:8-10; 1 Cor. 1:4; 7:5; Eph. 1:15-19; 3:10-21; 6:18-20; Phil. 1:3-6; 4:6; Col. 4:2,12; 1 Thess. 1:2; 2:13; 1 Tim. 2:1; 5:5; Philem. 4; 1 Peter 4:5). There are many other references, but these will give some idea of how important the apostles thought prayer to be. It was not only essential for their work, but it also played a vital part in the growth of the Christians.

REASONS WHY WE MUST PRAY

Christians must pray. Praying is not merely something we ought to do, or something we would enjoy doing, or even something that would be helpful. It is essential. It is as essential for the Christian as air, water, and food are for any person.

By prayer the Spirit gives understanding of spiritual truth. Prayer is essential to personal growth, evangelism, and disciple building. The carnal mind cannot discern spiritual truth. It is God who must reveal truth; He must give understanding. The unbeliever is under the control of Satan and his heart is set on satisfying the desires of the flesh and mind. Unless the Spirit of God draws him, he will not turn to Christ. The Christian still possesses an old nature, and the Holy Spirit must enable him to discern spiritual things. When we pray, God gives us understanding. He reveals His truth.

Scripture teaches a unique interrelationship between prayer and the knowledge of God's will and understanding of His truth. The Holy Spirit is said to pray for us with "groans that words cannot express" (Rom. 8:26,27). Another function of the Holy Spirit is to guide believers into truth. Jesus said, "The Counselor, the Holy Spirit, whom the Father will send in my name, will teach you all things and will remind you of everything I have said to you" (John 14:26). The Holy Spirit will help people understand the things of God. Paul also said that man cannot naturally understand spiritual truth but must have the Spirit of God within to teach and help him evaluate (1 Cor. 2:8-16).

The parallel passages of Matthew 16:13-20 and Luke 9:18-27

afford a good illustration of a person's mind being enlightened as a result of prayer: "Once when Jesus was praying in private and his disciples were with him, he asked them, 'Who do the crowds say I am?' . . . 'But what about you?' he asked. 'Who do you say I am?' '' (Luke 9:18,20). "Simon Peter answered, 'You are the Christ, the Son of the living God.' Jesus replied, 'Blessed are you, Simon, son of Jonah, for this was not revealed to you by man, but by my Father in heaven' '' (Matt. 16:16,17). Apparently, Jesus had prayed that God would disclose His deity to Peter. And when He did so, Peter understood and proclaimed it. When the natural man does not understand the things of God, it is because God has not revealed them to him. Unless the teacher or disciple asks God to show the disciple the truth from His Word and to reveal Himself to him, he will never understand about God, nor will he know God.

By prayer Satan's control is limited. Christians can have control over Satan only through prayer. Therefore, we must pray. In Luke 22:31 Jesus says, "Simon, Simon, behold Satan has asked to sift you all as wheat. But I have prayed for you, Simon, that your faith may not fail. And when you have returned to me, strengthen your brothers" (cf. 2 Tim. 2:25,26). In 1 Thessalonians 1:2 Paul wrote that he was praying for the Thessalonians. Later (3:5) he revealed that he had been fearful that the tempter had tempted them and his labor would have been in vain. When instructing the Ephesians to take their stand "against the devil's schemes" Paul encouraged them to be constantly in prayer (Eph. 6:11,18).

Jesus taught His followers to pray, "Lead us not into temptation, but deliver us from the evil one" (Matt. 6:13). For Jesus, prayer was the way to avoid the snares of Satan. Satan's power can be restrained and his influence limited only through the power of prayer. Therefore, Christians must pray if they are to escape the snares of Satan and continue to grow. They must also pray if their disciples are to remain faithful. "My prayer," Jesus said to the Father, "is not that you take them out of the world but that you protect them from the evil one. They are not of the world, even as I am not of it" (John 17:15,16). Through Jesus' prayers the disciples were kept from the power of Satan.

By prayer God's leading is made clear. The Holy Spirit works through prayer to lead and direct both the individual and the church. Many times Jesus and the apostles were led into specific actions and were given power and authority as a result of prayer. Prayer is especially essential for the Christian to be led by the Spirit of the ascended Christ. Paul said, "Those who are led by the Spirit of God are the sons of God" (Rom. 8:14). Paul went on to say that even though Christians often do not understand the will of God or do not know how to pray as they should, the Spirit will lead and intercede for them. Through prayer God's will is made known and is carried out in the Christian's life. He may study the principles and truths of God found in Scripture, but only as he seeks God in prayer is the Christian convinced that certain things are right and should be done for God and His glory.

By prayer God demonstrates His truth. The leader's teaching a disciple the truths of God is not enough. The Holy Spirit must demonstrate God's presence and power in the disciple's life. The leader needs to pray that Christ will make Himself known to the disciple. As the disciple experiences the reality of Christ's presence in his life, he will continue to grow.

When Jesus was baptized, the Holy Spirit demonstrated before all that He was God:

> Jesus was baptized too. And *as he was praying,* heaven was opened and the Holy Spirit descended on him in bodily form like a dove. And a voice came from heaven: "You are my Son, whom I love; with you I am well pleased" (Luke 3:21,22).

The preaching of John the Baptist and of Jesus Himself would not have been very convincing if God had not openly endorsed His Son. And that very likely happened as a result of Jesus' prayer.

Jesus said that we could do greater works than He did if we believed in Him. He also said, "And I will do whatever you ask in my name, so that the Son may bring glory to the Father" (John 14:13). As a result of prayer, God gives His credentials to His ministers, showing that they are His chosen vessels to teach the truth. There are other reasons why one must pray, but the reasons mentioned are very important in terms of disciple building.

In modern times those who have made great impacts for Jesus Christ have all been people of prayer. Martin Luther once said, "I am so busy I cannot manage unless I spend at least four hours a day with God in prayer." Hudson Taylor, the well-known missionary to China, used to arise at four o'clock in the morning to pray. Adoniram Judson, a missionary to Burma, prayed at seven specific times each day. David Livingstone died while he was kneeling with an open Bible in front of him. When Charles Haddon Spurgeon, the great Baptist preacher of London was asked the secret of his ministry, he immediately responded, "I have always had a praying people." One author concluded that Billy Graham's ministry stood out above all others in modern times because of his efforts to get men to pray for him. It is not a coincidence that all of these men were both outstanding Christians and great men of prayer. They became great men of God as a result of the outworking of prayer.

PRAYER IN EACH STEP OF GROWTH

In each of the chapters on the seven steps of Christian growth, the importance of prayer at that particular stage in a person's development is emphasized. If one knows how Jesus prayed, he can pray in the same way, with the assurance that God will hear and answer his prayers. One can pray in faith and see God do amazing things. The following are illustrations from each of the seven steps.

The step of Repentance and Faith involves the proclamation of the gospel to an individual, group, or community, calling them to turn back to God and receive forgiveness. God usually sends someone to proclaim the gospel as a result of the prayers of His people. John the Baptist was born as an answer to the prayers of Zacharias, Elizabeth, and others. The apostle Paul asked specifically that the Colossians pray "that God may open a door for our message, so that we may proclaim the mystery of Christ . . . that I may proclaim it clearly, as I should" (Col. 4:3,4). In Ephesians 6:18-20 he exhorted the Christians to pray on his behalf that he might declare the gospel fearlessly. So Paul asked for an open door, for clarity in presentation, and for fearlessness to preach against idolatry and to urge people to turn to God.

The step of Enlightenment involves gathering a group of people and teaching them who Jesus Christ is. Many leaders have experienced difficulty in beginning a study group. Remember Jesus' words in John 6:44, "No man can come to me unless the Father who sent me draws him." On many occasions Jesus spoke of His disciples as those whom the Father had given Him (John 6:39; 10:27,29; 17:6-9).

Jesus recognized that it was God who both drew people to Him and opened their eyes to His identity (Matt. 16:16,17). And He prayed for their increasing enlightenment (John 17:20-26). Paul likewise prayed that the eyes of the Ephesian Christian might be opened to God's truth and that they might understand the greatness of the living Christ (Eph. 1:17-21). When training men for the ministry (step three), we should observe Christ's prayers for His men and pray as He did. If God answered specific prayers for Jesus, we can believe that He will answer the same ones for us.

During His popular ministry in Capernaum, Jesus performed a miracle that astonished the disciples. When He had told them to take their boats out into the deep water and let down their nets, they caught so many fish that two boats were filled to the point of sinking. Being moved, Simon Peter fell down at Jesus' feet saying:

"Go away from me, Lord; I am a sinful man!" For he and all his companions were astonished at the catch of fish they had taken, and so were James and John, the sons of Zebedee, Simon's partners. Then Jesus said to Simon, "Don't be afraid; from now on you will catch men" (Luke 5:8-10).

These men made a lucrative living as fishermen. Getting them to leave their jobs in order to become involved in Christ's ministry was difficult. Apparently Jesus had been praying that God would humble them and break them of their self-sufficiency. He did so by proving His superiority and by showing them that His task was more important than catching fish. God had answered His prayer by guiding Him in this miracle, and it had a tremendous impact in the lives of His disciples. The disciple builder needs to pray that God will show his disciples how unimportant their worldly activities are in comparison to becoming fishers of men and having a ministry for Christ.

During this time of ministry training, it is important to pray that one's disciples will clearly understand Jesus' power to forgive sins and change lives. Luke 5:16 records that Jesus often slipped away to the wilderness to pray. Right after this (Luke 5:17-26) Scripture records His encounter with the paralyzed man. By commanding him to take up his bed and walk, Jesus was demonstrating His power to forgive sins. Men need to see lives changed. As they see God work in their own lives and the lives of those around them, they will become excited that Jesus has the power to forgive sin. Then they will want to share the good news with others (Ps. 51:10-13).

When one is seeking to have a ministry, it is imperative that God guide the individual or group into and out of a particular city or area. As a result of prayer, Jesus left Capernaum and went on a missionary tour around the villages of Galilee (Mark 1:35-39).

Jesus asked God to choose the men who were to be the leaders (step of Leadership Development). "One of those days He went out into the hills to pray, and spent the night praying to God. When morning came, He called his disciples to him and chose twelve of them" (Luke 6:12). The right choice for leaders is important in any type of work. In a ministry situation it becomes crucial to ask wisdom of God because natural leadership characteristics and the characteristics of a spiritual leader are sometimes quite different.

In the step of Reevaluation Jesus challenged the crowds to believe that He had come to give eternal life and not just to feed them. When He challenged them to labor not for the meat that perishes but for that which endures to eternal life, all but His disciples left Him. Jesus had prayed all night before challenging the crowds, and the fact that the disciples remained faithful was an answer to His prayer.

Therefore, as Christians challenge their disciples to stop living for the temporal and to begin trusting in the eternal, they can confidently pray that their disciples will remain faithful to Him.

After Jesus had appointed the Seventy in the step of Participation and Delegation, He taught them how to pray (Luke 11:2-4). He taught concern for someone else and how to importune God to meet the needs of others through intercessory prayer (Luke 11:5-13). During this step of Participation and Delegation, one should pray that God will teach the leaders to intercede for each other and for those whom they lead.

In the step of the Exchanged Life, when the disciples were being taught that the flesh is weak and cannot produce the kingdom of God, Jesus prayed for them that they would be sanctified by the truth and be kept from the evil one (John 17:15,17). He took the three leaders with Him to a private place of prayer in Gethsemane and warned them to "keep watching and praying, that you may not enter into temptation; the spirit is willing but the flesh is weak" (Matt. 26:41, NASB).

Specific prayers should accompany every stage of development. Christians can gain a vision of the importance of prayer in disciple building from the seventeenth chapter of John. Jesus poured out His heart in concern for the men who belonged to Him. Jesus knew how to build disciples. He realized that disciples cannot be built in the power of the flesh but that they are built as a result of prayer. Then the Spirit of God Himself works in people's hearts.

SUMMARY

Throughout the seven steps it has been repeatedly mentioned that God confirmed the teaching given the disciples by His supernatural working. This divine demonstration continues to be crucial for teaching disciples today. One who trains other disciples must be a person of prayer. He must have a vigorous faith so that he can lead others to step out and trust God to uphold His truth. Without God's manifest presence and working, Christian teaching will be dead and unproductive.

In one sense, God's manifest presence and miraculous working is wholly dependent on His sovereign will. On the other hand, God's Word indicates that when people love and obey Him, He will reveal Himself and do mighty works for them (John 14:21,23). In many cases it is when God's people realize their insufficiency, humble themselves, and seek God's help that He acts miraculously in their behalf (cf. Exod. 2:24,25; 3:7-10; 1 Sam. 7:2-11; 2 Chron. 7:14). God desires that His truth be heard, obeyed, and demonstrated.

17

Application of Truth to Obtain Obedience

Our world is threatened because people everywhere have very little commitment to responsible action. In biblical times obligations were often bound by a solemn covenant agreement. In our modern world the most common form of a covenant (and it is degenerating) is that of marriage. The biblical idea of a covenant between two parties always involved a commitment of obligation of one to the other. The New Covenant (or New Testament) is one of grace whereby God freely pardons all of a believer's sin through His Son's substitutionary death on the cross. Having thereby justified him, God makes him a child and heir of eternal life on the agreement that he will acknowledge Him as his Lord and his God and seek to obey Him in loving others as God has loved him. While the Christian's acceptance and justification is not *conditioned on* whether he lives a life of sacrificial love to God and others, his membership in the New Covenant is *revealed* by his life. Such love for God is not relative to circumstances, but is defined by the Ten Commandments and demonstrated by Christ's obedient death on the cross. All discipleship efforts aim at building up a Christian until he manifests the sacrificial love of Christ by doing good deeds. It aims at enabling the disciple to keep his covenant obligation.

From the outset of the Protestant Reformation there was an inherent danger. Martin Luther turned the course of history around by his scriptural declaration that "justification is by faith alone." But Luther had a disdain for an emphasis on good works of obedience. He once said that he wished he might "shout to all the world and might pluck the little word 'good works' out of all men's hearts, mouths, ears, and books" (Church Postilla). He called the Epistle of James "that right strawy epistle" because he thought it spoke too much about good works.

Succeeding Protestants have somehow looked on "works of obedience" as second-class doctrine. That is one reason evangelism has often gained *undue prominence* over disciple building, and why a humanistic emphasis on social action has been able to take the place of obedient Christian living.

Unfortunately, the Protestant mind generally did not fully embrace and forthrightly declare that the faith that produces obedient works is the only true saving faith, that faith and love that are only a profession are really hypocrisy. Faith and love must issue not only in words but also in deeds (James 2:17,26).

If the real cause is applied, a corresponding real effect will result. If a certain chemical will transform a solution into an acid, the resultant solution will always turn litmus paper from blue to red. If this indication does not occur, then the chemical change from base to acid has not occurred. If real saving faith has occurred in the heart, the indication of obedient works will always follow. Of course, this does not mean a believer will be obedient at all times. But Jesus said, "By their fruit you will recognize them." (Matt. 7:20).

The aim of all discipleship must be obedience. The church today needs to emphasize this, *but with care that it does not swing the pendulum too far* so that it ignores "justification by faith alone." That is the doctrine that motivates the Christian to obedience. It was Luther himself who once said that when a man falls off the horse of truth on one side, the Devil wants to help him back on so he can push him off on the other. Luther let this happen to him in belittling good works in favor of justification by faith. May we return to an emphasis on good works without canceling out the great doctrine that Luther recovered.

THE OBJECTIVE OF OBEDIENCE

Obedience and Ministry Goals. In chapter 3 it was shown that evangelism leads to church building, that church building should result in disciple building, and that disciple building should produce Christlike sons, who will give glory to God. If in building disciples the teaching does not aim at applying the truth to the life so that obedience occurs, people will not grow in love and the image of Christ, and so they will not bring glory to God, but will dishonor Him. Thus the whole purpose of evangelism, church building, and the teaching of disciples will be frustrated. The practical goals will not culminate in the ideal goals.

Why take the tomato plant out of the hothouse of Satan, plant it in the garden of God, tend it with care, and obtain water and sunshine for it through prayer if no fruit ever forms? All effort is wasted! There is nothing for the gardener to pick, eat, and enjoy. Andrew Murray has said, "The whole redemption of Christ consists in this, that He brings us back to the life of obedience, through which alone the creature can give the Creator the glory due to Him, or receive the glory of which his Creator desires to make him partaker."[1]

THE BIBLICAL EMPHASIS ON OBEDIENCE

The Scriptures of both the Old and New Testaments are filled with the emphasis on obedience to God.[2] In this chapter the desire is to bring these teachings to focus on New Testament discipleship. The idea of New and Old Testaments or Covenants center on the idea of obedience as man's part in the covenant.

Also, we have pointed out (p. 112) that in the Old Testament the obedience or disobedience of the people was primarily charged to the leadership. Jesus' strongest emphasis on obedience occurred at the steps of Leadership Development (the time of training the Twelve) and Participation and Delegation (the time of leadership development for the Seventy). He also strongly emphasized it in His final discourses in the upper room the last night and in connection with the Great Commission. Apparently He wanted both the Twelve and the Seventy to understand the importance of obedience for disciples in His kingdom and to see the lack of obedience as the major failure of the false leaders.

OBEDIENCE AND THE COVENANT IDEA

The two times Jesus taught most extensively about obedience were in connection with the establishment of the *new covenant*. The first time was in the Sermon on the Mount and the second was on the last night in connection with the celebration of the Lord's Supper. We have pointed out (p. 112) that at the time of the giving of the Sermon on the Mount Jesus was probably duplicating the renewal of the covenant and the kingdom as done by Joshua at Mount Gerizim and Mount Ebal. Joshua was renewing the covenant made at Mount Sinai. At the Lord's Supper Jesus specifically said, "This cup is the new covenant in my blood, which is poured out for you" (Luke 22:20; cf. Matt. 26:28; Mark 14:24).

The ancient tradition of making or "cutting" a covenant is clear from the Bible and from archaeological discoveries (at Nuzi, Quatra, et al.). A covenant between two persons or groups involved several things: stating the agreement between them in a book; the slaying of a sacrificial animal and sprinkling blood on the book, indicating that the violator was to incur the death penalty; and then the eating of a communion meal, whereby bread and wine were eaten as symbols of the broken body and shed blood of the covenant.

God had "cut" a covenant with Abraham whereby He promised to be his God, bless the world through his seed, and give him the land of Canaan eternally, and Abraham agreed to command his children and his household to keep the way of the Lord by doing righteousness and justice (Gen. 15; 18:19). This was renewed with Isaac and Jacob.

At Mount Sinai Israel had agreed to keep the ten commandments of God as He audibly spoke them and as they were written on tables of stone, and God agreed to treat Israel as His own possession among all the people of the earth (Exod. 19:5–20:17). This covenant was "cut" between God and the leaders of Israel on Mount Sinai, where the sacrifice was slain, the blood sprinkled, and a communion meal celebrated (Exod. 24:5-11). (Cf. also 2 Chron. 34:31-33; Jer. 34:18-20). The ten commandments of the covenant were applied in statutes and judgments first to the culture of the wilderness and later reapplied to the settled culture of Canaan (in Deuteronomy, which means "second giving of the law"). The enactment of the old covenant established the idea of *God as king* over His people Israel.

The work of the prophets was to point out to the people their violations of the covenant and to warn of impending death for violation of it. Years later, when the nations of Israel and Judah utterly departed from the Lord in disobedience, the prophets told how God would destroy the nations. But the prophets also foresaw a future day when God would make a *new covenant* with those of all flesh who were not His people and with Judah and Israel. This would be an eternal covenant (Hosea 1:10,11; 2:19-23; Joel 2,3, esp. vv. 28ff.; Jer. 30:18ff.; 31, esp. vv. 31-34; Isa. 55:3-7, esp. vv. 4,5; Ezek. 36:21-28, et al.).

THE TRANSITION FROM THE OLD COVENANT TO THE NEW

Jesus indicated that the dispensation of the old covenant in the law and the prophets extended until John the Baptist. John was the last great prophet in the tradition of Elijah (Matt. 11:11,12; Luke 16:16; cf. 1 Kings 19:13 and 2 Kings 1:8 with Matt. 3:4; 17:12,13; Mark 1:6; 9:13). As the ministry of John the Baptist was phased out, Jesus was teaching and explaining the meaning of the new covenant of His kingdom that He came to institute.

Jesus first began to proclaim that the kingdom of God was at hand immediately after John was imprisoned and his public ministry ended (Matt. 4:12-17; Mark 1:14,15). It has been shown (p. 111) that right after the Jews first decided to put Jesus to death, He withdrew to a mountain, proclaimed in the Sermon on the Mount the new code of righteousness demanded by the covenant of His kingdom, and appointed, instructed, and sent the Twelve out to proclaim the kingdom everywhere. At the time the Twelve returned and reported their results, John the Baptist was slain by Herod and his disciples joined Jesus, ending the old order (Mark 6:25-30).

Immediately afterward, Jesus rejected the appeal of the Jewish people to be an earthly king, saying He had come to be the bread of eternal life. Eating His flesh and drinking His blood, referred to later at the final Passover meal as the elements of the new covenant, was proclaimed then as the only way to have eternal life in His kingdom (John 6:4,15,27,40,51,53; cf. Luke 22:15-20). He stated that the eternal life of the kingdom could begin in this life now for all who would trust Him as their Messiah (John 5:24). It was during the step of Reevaluation that He clearly taught that His covenant had to do with eternal life in an eternal kingdom.

THE NATURE OF THE NEW COVENANT COMPARED TO THE OLD

Not a releasing from the requirements of the old but a fulfillment of them. Jesus made it emphatically clear that the demands of His new covenant would not release men from even one of the smallest of the moral demands of the commands of the old covenant, but would lead to fulfillment of them. He said, ''Do not think that I have come to abolish the Law or the Prophets; I have not come to abolish them but to fulfill them'' (Matt. 5:17). The Greek word *kataluō*, translated ''abolish,'' literally means ''release away from,'' and is used twice. Jesus indicated every ''jot or tittle'' of the law would be ''fulfilled'' or ''come to pass.'' He warned that if anyone breaks one of the least of the law's commands and teaches others to do so, he will be called least in His kingdom. But those who ''*practice*'' them will be called great. Jesus is not talking about the imputed righteousness He would give His followers but about the righteousness He expected them to ''practice'' (The Greek word is *poieō*, ''to do'') and to teach others (Matt. 5:19).

Jesus later summarized these demands of the law and the prophets in the requirement to love God totally and to love your neighbor *as yourself* (Matt. 22:37-40). He demanded the law of love to be practiced (Mark 10:17-22; Luke 10:25-37). This He also put in the form of the Golden Rule: ''Do to others as you would have them do to you'' (Luke 6:31).

Paul says Jesus Christ "gave himself for us to redeem us from all wickedness [literally, "lawlessness"] and to purify for himself a people that are his very own, eager to do what is good. These, then, are the things you should teach. Encourage and rebuke with all authority" (Titus 2:14,15). Paul makes it clear that fulfilling the law of love by keeping the ten commandments is expected of Christians (Rom. 13:8-10). Since Jesus Christ claimed that He was the God of Abraham (John 8:56-58) and that Moses wrote of Him (John 5:45-47), it is not surprising that the old covenant commands are still binding in the new covenant. God is unchanging, and His covenant commands of the old reflect His unchanging character, revealed also in the new.

The new supercedes the old by demanding heart obedience by the Spirit before God. Jesus taught that His followers should have a righteousness that goes beyond the legal outward obedience of the Pharisees and Sadducees. The difference is emphasized by Jesus' repetition of the phrase, "You have heard that it was said . . . long ago. . . . But I tell you. . . ." The Christian should have the right motive of the heart or mind and not just outward conformity to law. For the Christian, anger in the heart is the same as murder (cf. also 1 John 3:15). Lust of the heart is the same as adultery. One's intent to keep his word should eliminate swearing falsely in the name of the Lord. Demands for vengeance against an enemy should be replaced by doing good instead of evil when one is wronged. The aim of those under the new covenant is to be perfect as the heavenly Father is perfect (Matt. 5:20-48).

This obedience from the heart was predicted by Jeremiah (31:31) and is possible only because God will give people His Spirit, who writes God's laws in their hearts (Heb. 8:6-12). Therefore the ten commandments will continue in this new covenant. (cf. also Heb. 10:16-18). Thus the Christian's objective is to bring every thought into obedience to Christ (2 Cor. 10:5). Through the Spirit the Christian should seek the mind of Christ (1 Cor. 2:16, Phil. 2:5ff.). Christ's mind was set on obedience. The Christian's mind has been one of disobedience (Eph. 2:2) and therefore needs to be reprogramed or renewed (Rom. 12:1).

The people of God failed to keep the commands under the old covenant because they trusted in their own fleshly ability. However, Paul says, "What the law was powerless to do in that it was weakened by our sinful nature, God did by sending his own Son in the likeness of sinful man to be a sin offering. And so he condemned sin in sinful man, in order that the righteous requirements of the law might be fully met in us, who do not live according to our sinful nature but according to the Spirit.'' (Rom. 8:3,4). Through the law of the Spirit of life the Christian is set free from the law of sin and death (Rom. 8:2).

Man's violation of the old covenant is punished by the sacrifice for the new. Jesus took the bread and wine of the passover, symbolic of the old covenant, and said that they represented His broken body and shed blood, which were for the remission of man's sins under the old. At the same time He said that they were the sacrifice instituting the new covenant. The author of Hebrews tells us that by the offering of Himself, He made available the benefits of the new covenant (9:16-28). The once-for-all voluntary sacrifice of Himself removed the old covenant and instituted the new (10:9-11). Because Jesus Christ bore the penalty for the violation of the commands of the first covenant, those who become a party of the new covenant receive grace, and God continually forgives their sin. Through Jeremiah God had promised under the new, ''I will forgive their iniquity, and I will remember their sin no more'' (31:34). Therefore, though the law was given by Moses, grace and truth came by Christ (John 1:17). Christ, who gave the Law to Moses and has now been made the Judge, ever lives to intercede for us on the basis of His shed blood (Rom. 8:34-39). His death not only justifies us from transgressions of the old covenant, it brings us into a relationship of grace for living by His life (Rom. 5:9-11).

The old covenant focused on obeying a legal code before men, the new on pleasing the Lawgiver personally. In the step of Ministry Training Jesus taught His disciples to follow and obey Him as the Lord of the Sabbath above keeping the Jewish code on Sabbath observance. Paul taught that Jesus was raised from the dead in order that He might be the Lord over the dead and the living. Therefore, men should not judge each other in regard to legal interpretations because they live before the risen Christ who indwells them by His Spirit (Rom. 14:3-10). The only one they must please is the Christ who died for them and now intercedes in heaven for their sin. Christians are therefore not under law but under grace. ''In Christ'' they are free from the law and under the ''law of Christ'' (Rom. 7:3,7; 1 Cor. 9:21; Gal. 2:19; 5:18). The phrase ''in Christ'' meant that they belonged to Jesus as their king. The idea of Christ risen and personally reigning over His people is central to the New Testament.

The new exceeds the old by commanding to love by giving of self rather than to love as self. At the same point where the Lord's Supper and the blood of the new covenant appear in the Synoptic Gospels, John's Gospel records as a substitute how Jesus girded Himself with a towel and washed the dirty feet of the disciples. He then commanded them to become like servants of one another and said, "A new commandment I give you: Love one another. *As I have loved you,* so you must love one another. *All men will know that you are My disciples* if you love one another" (John 13:34,35). Shortly thereafter in the same discourse Jesus explained the extent of His love. "No one has greater love than the one who *lays down his life* for his friends. You are My friends if you do what I command" (John 15:13,14).

The demand of the old covenant, "Love your neighbor as yourself," is made new in that it takes love to its ultimate possible limit and bases it on the work of Christ in expressing that love for us on the cross (1 John 2:7,8; 3:11,12,16; 4:19-21). Under the old covenant the people of God were expected to love Him with their total beings and to love their neighbor *as* themselves. Under the new covenant the member of the kingdom is expected to love God so that he is willing to die to self and even be put to death to maintain obedience to Him. He is to love so that he is willing to give up all he has, even his life if need be for his neighbor. Obedience to the ten commandments under Christ's personal rule for the glory of God and the good of others is absolute and complete. Moreover, this love is offered gladly, freely, and voluntarily.

Obedience to the new covenant is based on faith in the resurrection. The old covenant was based on the belief that the one God who created all things had controlled the forces of nature in such a way as to deliver the Israelites out of Egypt miraculously and make them His peculiar people (Exod. 20:2). Their very existence as people and as a nation was possible only because of Him. Therefore, He deserved to be loved and worshiped with all their heart, mind, and soul. Since God created all men equally valuable in His sight, one should love his neighbor as himself. The Hebrews were taught to leave vengeance against their enemy to God (Lev. 19:18; Deut. 32:35; Prov. 20:22; Ps. 109; Matt. 5:38-48, esp. v. 43). Though it was difficult to love an enemy who threatened one's security and perhaps even his life, all was based on God as *Creator* and sustainer in this life.

The new covenant is based on faith that God the Father who created all things also raises the dead. He is the *Recreator.* While belief in life after death was a doctrine of the Old Testament people of God, it was nebulous and never clearly demonstrated. The account that records Jesus' act of girding Himself with a towel, demonstrating self-giving love, was preceded by a strong declaration of Jesus' faith in His own resurrection. "Jesus knew that the Father had put all things under his power, and that he had come from God and *was returning to God*, so he got up from the meal, took off his outer clothing, and wrapped a towel around his waist. After that, he poured water into a basin and began to wash his disciples' feet'' (John 13:3-5). Jesus believed that the Father would raise Him from the dead and restore Him to His place of authority (cf. Matt. 16:21; 17:9,23; 20:19; John 17:4,5, et al.). It was because Jesus believed He would be raised that He was able to love to the point of giving up self-interest for service, even to death on the cross (Phil. 2:6-11).

Paul bases the ability of the Christian to live the Christian life on our believing that we are identified with Christ not only in His death for our sins but also in His resurrection (Rom. 6:4-11). Being identified with Him in His obedience that led to resurrection leads us to obedience with the same hope through Christ. (Rom. 6:12-23). Peter also linked the obedient Christian life to the hope of the resurrection at Christ's return (1 Peter 1:13-25; 2 Peter 1:3-7,14,15), as did John (1 John 3:2,3ff.).

If one believes that God so loves him that He will forgive his sin and raise him from the dead, he can still have hope even if he forfeits everything. If I believe God will raise me from the dead and give me glory, then I can be free and give my life for my neighbor. If I believe I will be raised, I can even love my enemy who might kill me. So faith enables us to work by love (Gal. 5:6).

The ethical demand of the new covenant, which is sacrificial love, is possible only to those who believe in Christ's resurrection for them. It is uniquely Christian. The old commandment to love my neighbor as myself, which is based on created values (and the miracle of the Exodus for Israel) may be found in other religions and ethical codes. In a number of religions the golden rule, or love for others as oneself, is found in a negative way; in the Old Testament it is clearly and positively stated.[3] But Jesus lifts it from the Old Testament and makes the law of love central and prominent.

In no other religion is there found the ethic of the new covenant of Jesus Christ, which is to love God and others to the point of giving up one's life for them. While there are reincarnations and the idea of rebirths, there is nowhere the teaching of the resurrection of the body as in Christianity. Only in Jesus Christ is life and immortality brought to light (2 Tim. 1:10). Therefore the demand of the new covenant to love others as Christ loved us is possible only for Christians. It is the unique mark of a Christian.[4]

Scripture teaches that man's fear of death is what has kept him in bondage to Satan (Heb. 2:14,15). He *must* look after self-interest or he may die. Since death is threatening him, he must seek to eat, drink, and be merry while there is time (1 Cor. 15:32). The great surge of hedonism in our time is due to the fact that the secular humanism that permeates our society has rejected the idea of the eternal and the

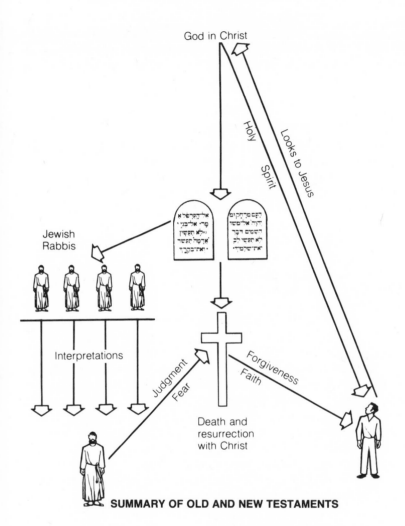

SUMMARY OF OLD AND NEW TESTAMENTS

A. Old Testament

1. Looks to Law before men.
2. Ten Commandments summary
   is to love as self.
3. Law shows sin and judgment.
4. Weak through the flesh.
5. Flesh rebels.

B. New Testament

1. Christ as judge forgives, intercedes,
   promises resurrection.
2. Dead to Law and risen with Christ.
3. Looks to Lawgiver, Christ.
4. Summary: Sacrificial servant love as Christ's.
5. Constrained by Christ's love to want to obey.
6. Holy Spirit writes laws on heart
   and empowers to daily practices.

possibility of resurrection from the dead to participate in a future life. The only adequate counteraction to this is a life that demonstrates by sacrificial love that it believes in being raised from the dead. As such love is shown, it persuades men to believe in the risen Lord who will also liberate them from Satan's power. Then the believer will from the heart obey the risen Lord (Rom. 6:16-18).

SUMMARY DIAGRAM OF THE OLD AND NEW COVENANTS

The diagram on page 241 summarizes in part the transformation from the old to the new covenant. The man in position A is under the old covenant. He looks to the law as interpreted by his leaders and tries to keep it in the flesh. Under the fear of death he puts self-interest above God and others and rebels against God's law. He then hears the good news that Christ died for him, was raised to represent him, and offer him new life by the Holy Spirit. He then identifies himself with Christ and becomes in Christ under the new covenant. He then moves to position B. There the law is still valid or good as an expression of the character and will of God. But he does not look to the letter of the law but to the Lawgiver who died for him and now sends the Holy Spirit into his heart to teach and empower him. Therefore, freedom from the Law of the old covenant is in order that he might become an obedient responsible servant to the One who purchased that freedom.

Obedience as a principle or attitude of commitment. To the Christian, obedience involves accepting the principle of being able to die to self once and for all in an identification with Christ on the cross. The Christian's desire is to please God. He delights in the law of God and in the will of God (Pss. 1:2; 37:4; 119:11,14,16,20, et al; John 14:15). As Andrew Murray has pointed out, the obedience of Christ was a life principle.[5] He came knowing that He was going to the cross to die. His first declaration in Jerusalem was about His awareness that the Jews would put Him to death (John 2:19). The author of Hebrews says that Jesus came to replace the sacrificial animals by a *voluntary* offering of Himself. When Jesus said, "Here I am, I have come to do your will," He set aside the first (covenant) in order to establish the second (covenant). "By that will we have been made holy through the sacrifice of the body of Jesus Christ once for all" (Heb. 10:9,10). Since we as Christians identify with Christ's cross as ours, we are called to die to our own self-will and also to delight in doing the will of God. In this sense Paul says, "For just as through the disobedience of the one man [Adam] the many were made sinners, so also through the obedience of the one man [Christ] the many will be made righteous" (Rom. 5:19). By identifying ourselves with His obedient death, we commit ourselves to the principle of obedience. This begins with step one and makes possible growth through the other steps. When a Christian becomes carnal, he has forsaken this principle of obedient love and begins to act like a non-Christian or natural man (1 Cor. 3:1-3).

Obedience as a daily practice. Jesus showed through the washing of His disciples' feet that the *principal* attitude of obedience must be put into practice in our daily relationships. He taught that the cross must be taken up "daily" if we follow Him (Luke 9:23). Paul, having discussed the once-for-all identification with Christ in Romans 6:1-10, goes on to show that this must be *daily practiced* by the Christian as an act of His will. He says,"In the same way, count yourselves dead to sin but alive to God in Christ Jesus. Therefore, do not let sin reign in your mortal body so that you obey its evil desires. Do not offer ("do not go on offering," NASB) the parts of your body to sin, as instruments of wickedness, but rather offer yourselves to God, as those who have returned from death to life; and offer the parts of your body to him as instruments of righteousness" (Rom. 6:11-13; cf. also vv. 17,19). By walking in the Holy Spirit, the Christian daily practices obedience and puts to death the deeds of the body (Rom. 8:2-13).

THE MOTIVE OF OBEDIENCE

The acceptance of the principle of obedience is what occurs at the step of Repentance and Faith. The truth that motivates a person to turn to God and want to be obedient is God's love. ''God's kindness should lead you to repentance'' (Rom. 2:4). It is because we believe that He died for us and was raised for us that we are motivated to want to live in obedience to Him (2 Cor. 4:14ff.). While conversion is motivated by grace through faith, it involves a turning to Him as Lord with a desire to please Him. Otherwise, conversion has not occurred. To say that a person can be converted and saved without accepting the lordship of Christ shows a lack of understanding of what conversion is. By faith we confess Him as Lord and begin to trust Him to help us practice obedience daily.

The love of God, which constrains us to turn to Him, accepting the principle of obedience, is also the truth that motivates us to practice obedience and love our brethren daily (1 John 4:7-21). ''We love because He first loved us,'' and this leads us to want to love our brethren. Peter tells us that when a person fails to practice obedience and have the moral qualities that lead to expressing love, he ''has forgotten that he has been cleansed from his past sins'' (2 Peter 1:5-9). As we *trust* God's love and power offered to us in the cross, we then are enabled by the Holy Spirit to be obedient even as Jesus was obedient. "Obedience is the loving response to the divine love resting on us, the only access to a fuller enjoyment of that love."[6]

ERRORS IN REGARD TO OBEDIENCE

There are many satanic traps into which Christians fall. We may be deceived in such a way as to intend to be obedient when we actually are not. Some seek great knowledge about God and His will and are satisfied with this rather than trusting God and acting on that knowledge. Others get busy doing religious things established by the traditions of men rather than seek to live in the power of the Lord through His Holy Spirit. Others seek a mystical appropriation of the working of the Holy Spirit without going on to set their minds on the means of grace whereby the Holy Spirit works.

Distinction between knowing and obeying. Of very great significance is the obvious distinction Jesus makes between knowing the will of God in His commandments and doing it. The modern world in which we live is obsessed with obtaining knowledge and storing it up. This is the source of pride in this humanistic generation. Man wants to think he is as wise as God (Gen. 3:5,6). We write multitudes of graduate dissertations, fill great libraries with more and more books, cram information on minute microfilms, load our computers full of data, and make multitudes of tapes and videotapes. The emphasis is on knowing.

Unfortunately, Christians have been led along by the world's ways. We too attend our seminars in great crowds, go to our conferences and world congresses, and return home with shining eyes demonstrating our packed notebooks, our accumulation of tapes, and the hosts of printed volumes we have purchased. Far too often they are put on our shelves and forgotten. To attend and know much has been interpreted as a virtue. But for the Lord of the church, the only purpose of knowing is to lead to doing.

The only way knowledge *about* things can become knowledge possessed by a person is for that person to act on that factual knowledge and thereby discover for himself it is true. Theoretical knowledge becomes experiential, or real, knowledge by obedience. Faith or trust is the link between the two. For example, from information about the construction of a footbridge across a river, one may believe intellectually it will hold his weight. But only when he walks across, trusting himself to the bridge, will he *know* it is reliable. I studied how to fly for several months, but only when I got into a plane with an instructor and took off did I really *know* how to fly.

Jesus said to the Jews who began to believe on Him intellectually, "If you *hold to my teaching*, you are really my disciples. Then you will know the truth, and the truth will set you free" (John 8:31,32). The Psalmist said, "I *understand* more than the aged, for I *keep* thy precepts" (119:100; cf. 111:10). One knows God personally only as he trusts and obeys what he intellectually knows about God.

Growth into new knowledge is based on trust and obedience to the knowledge one is confronting. It is like a series of bridges across several successive rivers on a road one is traveling. Unless one crosses the first bridge, he cannot get to the next, and the next, and so on. To fail to act on one aspect of knowledge about God keeps us from getting to others.

To ignore, rationalize, or disobey truth God has taught us keeps us from progressing. Being willfully blind to one truth keeps us from seeing others. Moreover, we tragically influence others to follow our blind ways (Luke 6:39; Rom. 2:19; 2 Cor. 4:4). Paul says the disobedient are "ever learning and never able to come to the knowledge of the truth" (2 Tim. 3:7-9; cf. Rom. 1:21-23).

Andrew Murray has said, "A heart yielded to God in unreserved obedience is the one condition of progress in Christ's school, and of growth in the spiritual knowledge of God's will."[7] Robert Coleman agrees: "Obedience to Christ thus was the very means by which those in His company learned more truth."[8]

Religious deeds in the flesh rather than seeking to know and obey God by the Spirit. From the time of Cain men have tried to worship God by deeds of their own thoughts and efforts (Gen. 4:2-8; 1 John 3:12). Men can even carry out the religious forms God has instituted without a heart that delights to please Him. While doing these things, they continue in their own sins and pursuit of the flesh, so that their religious works become useless. God became sick of this in the Old Testament (Isaiah 1:11-17; 61:8; Jeremiah 6:20; 7:21-23; 14:12; Hosea 6:6; Amos 5:21-24; Micah 6:8). Prayer, fasting, and almsgiving were used to get the praise of men, but Jesus taught that these were to be done to please God alone (Matt. 6:1-18). Jesus warned that many would profess Him as Lord and do many religious deeds in His name, but still not know Him (Matt. 7:21-23).

Jesus was emphasizing in those statements that it is by the fruit of one's life rather than by doing religious deeds that a person can be recognized as His disciple (Matt. 7:20). In His last discourse to His disciples, Jesus emphasized that it is by abiding in His truth that one bears fruit. He said, "I am the vine; you are the branches. If a man *remains in me* and I in him, he *will bear much fruit*; apart from me you can do nothing" (John 15:5). The apostle Paul, in Galatians 3, chides the Galatians for having begun by trusting the Holy Spirit, but then, having turned away from looking to the risen Christ through the

Spirit, going back to looking at the Law itself and trying to do things in the flesh. He tells them that to have the fruit of the kind of character that Jesus had, it must be the fruit of the Spirit as the result of walking in the Spirit (Gal. 5:16ff.).

Today there are multitudes in the churches who go through perfectly good religious rituals and deeds without knowing the living Christ and without seeking His will. They think they are pleasing God. They go to church, to prayer meeting, committee or board meetings, teach Sunday school, participate in the women's or men's work, take communion, give to the church, and do many other activities. But these are often done as conformity to human traditions or for other selfish reasons.

Often there is no real understanding of the cross, heart devotion, or commitment to the risen Christ involved. So these actions become a stench in God's nostrils. The actions are not wrong, but they are done in the flesh. These are no substitutes for daily keeping the commands of Christ at home, work, or school, out of love for Him. Some people involved in this error have even had an experience with the Holy Spirit, but don't know what it is to walk in the Spirit.

The error of seeking a mystical experience without seeking the things of the Spirit. There is no question that the New Testament writings show that Christians have the privilege of experiencing the mystery of the working of the power of the Holy Spirit in their lives. This has been taught in connection with the Seven Steps. One may think of this as ''appropriating the Spirit by faith'' or in terms of being ''filled'' or ''baptized'' with the Spirit, accompanied by unusual feeling or signs. While the idea of the mysterious inner working of the Spirit is valid, that is not the complete biblical teaching. Christ described the Spirit's working in terms of remaining in Him (John 15:4-11) and Paul talks about keeping ''in step with the Spirit'' (Gal. 5:25). Both imply *a continuous process*. What is this process of walking or abiding?

Paul says that those who walk according to the Spirit and not according to the flesh *''have their minds set on what the Spirit desires. The mind of sinful man is death, but the mind controlled by the Spirit is life and peace''* (Rom. 8:5,6). The mind of the natural man, or the first Adam's nature, has been completely perverted by his depraved nature and must be completely reprogramed or renewed. Paul besought Christians to be transformed by the renewal of their minds by turning away from the standard of the world to that of the will of God (Rom. 12:1,2). This process of renewing the mind in knowledge to become like Christ is a continuous process from the time of conversion (Col. 2:10).

But what are the "things of the Spirit" on which the Christian's mind should be set? Jesus talked about *His words* abiding in the disciples in connection with abiding in Him (John 15:7). Paul says that the Scriptures were given by the Spirit to teach, reprove, correct, and equip the disciple for every good work (2 Tim. 3:16,17). They should be carefully studied to be rightly understood (2 Tim. 2:15). Paul indicates that the things of the Spirit include all things that may be counted as true, honorable, right, etc. by the standard of God's Word (Phil. 4:8,9). The fullness of God's Spirit comes from experiencing God's Word and sharing it by talking and singing in fellowship with God's people (Eph. 5:18; Col. 3:16). Prayer is associated with the Spirit's working (Luke 11:13; Eph. 6:18, et al.). Witnessing is also an activity involving the Spirit (Acts 1:8). Thus as one involves himself daily in personally studying the Word of Christ and things that agree with it, in sharing that word in Christian fellowship, in seeking Christ and His will through prayer, and in sharing the Word of Christ in witnessing, he is putting his mind on the "things of the Spirit." There is room here for Christian art, literature, and the like.

As the believer seeks Christ in the Scriptures as an example, the Holy Spirit thereby forms Christ in his heart and enables him to witness to Christ in his attitudes, words, and deeds. The Christian does not just seek to know certain legal demands of Christ in the Word, but His attitudes, mind, and manner of life as well. The Holy Spirit makes the living Christ known to the Christian so that he is aware that Christ is abiding with him. Therefore, the Christian does not "imitate" Christ as an example. Rather, he beholds the example of Christ in Scripture and the Spirit forms Christ in him (Gal. 4:19) and enables him to live the Christlike life. But the Christian must love Christ and *be willing to obey* Him before this occurs (John 14:15-17,21,24; 15:10-12).

I have known many people who have known the mystery of the Spirit's presence in their lives but they have not "set their minds on the things of the Spirit" and soon discovered that Christ was no longer real to them. Their profession of truth went far beyond their obedience to it, leaving a hollow vacuum that led to a spiritual collapse. This happened to a well-known pro-football player, a prominent Pentecostal pastor, a student body leader, and others. There is a great need for the leaders of the church to help disciples know how to be involved in the things of the Spirit and help them apply Christ's Word to their lives in a daily way.

How to Apply the Truth to Obtain Obedience

While it is true that the primary teacher to apply truth to men's hearts is the Holy Spirit (1 John 2:26,27), He does so by giving the Christian discernment as to which human teachings are of the world and which are of God (1 John 4:6). The Scripture emphasizes the important ways human teachers are used to help the disciple apply truth. On His last night Jesus looked back on His work for the Father as being complete (John 17:4). It consisted principally of teaching and applying the word of God to His disciples so that they could teach others also (John 17:3,8,14,20). Those three years of teachings were the basis on which the Holy Spirit would sanctify them in the days that lay ahead when Christ would be bodily absent from them (John 17:17). Pentecost would have been useless without that teaching. The way church leaders teach and apply the truth in discipling men today is equally crucial.

How Should Men Apply the Word of God Which the Holy Spirit Uses?

Chapters of this book related to applying truth. All of the chapters in the last section of this book aim directly at helping us understand the application of the Word of God in the process of disciple building. The chapter on association was specifically trying to help a teacher understand how to rightly relate to his disciples in order to be able to communicate and apply truth to their lives. The chapter on fellowship specifically aimed at helping to know how to establish the kind of Christian fellowship that would be conducive to having individual Christians share with each other and be open to receive from the leadership so that the truth could be applied to their lives.

The chapter on involvement aimed at trying to help a leader understand how to get a person involved with the truth and begin to act and obey the truth in such a way as to help him grow. As has been stressed, knowledge alone is not enough. Being obedient to be involved in a ministry in other people's lives is a part of growth. The chapter on motivation and momentum was designed to help one see how specific truth can help motivate people to act in obedience. The chapter on evangelism and disciple building gave a better understanding of obedience in evangelism, which gains disciples and contributes to growth as believers have a part in evangelizing. The chapter on prayer specifically aimed at helping understand how to invoke God's working of His Holy Spirit to enlighten and motivate people to obey the truth that we apply.

THE BIBLICAL EMPHASIS ON APPLYING THE WORD
SPECIFICALLY AND DAILY

Scripture makes it abundantly clear that it is necessary for human teachers to apply the Word of God *daily* to the lives of individuals and to *specific situations* in life. This is the great failure in the modern church.

Jesus' specific application. We have pointed out that Jesus, with His disciples, daily applied the Word of God in evangelism to individual lives in specific ways, calling men to confront the law and their specific sins (Mark 10:19-22; John 4:16-19, et al.).

In dealing with His disciples on an intimate basis as individuals and in groups, Jesus made specific application of the truth. When they were fearful in the storm and did not trust God, He rebuked them. When they argued about who would be great, He taught them the Scripture that called them to humility. When Peter was tempted by Satan to rebuke Christ for His commitment to go to the cross and die, Jesus corrected him and told him that he was following men and not God. He called Peter and all the other disciples to die to self. When Satan was attacking Peter to cause him to deny Jesus, Jesus specifically warned Peter about his weakness and encouraged him. Many passages of Scripture show that Jesus made specific applications of the Word of God to definite situations on a daily basis.

Specific application to God's congregation. Paul points out that every Christian should be careful in his conversation, so that he would speak "only such a word as is good for edification *according to the need of the moment,* that it may give grace to those who hear" (Eph. 4:29, NASB). This passage shows that all Christians should be alert to apply God's Word at any moment as they relate to each other in Christian fellowship. In his own ministry, Paul said that he was exhorting and encouraging and imploring each one "as a father deals with his own children" (1 Thess. 2:11). In other places he implies that he regularly taught and applied truth to the lives of people with great concern for their holiness of life, not only in his public preaching, but by going into their homes, meeting with them, and being involved with them. (Acts 20:31; Col. 1:28,29).

Specific application in the home. In Ephesians 6:1ff., Paul makes it quite clear that it is the responsibility of the parents to bring their children up in the nurture and admonition of the Lord. The duty was especially put on the father, as the priest of the family, to teach his wife and children. For the Jew this meant a heart commitment and devotion to God to do His will and then to apply the commandments to his children's daily lives. God said to Israel,

You shall love the Lord your God with all your heart, and with all your soul, and with all your might. And these words which I command you this day shall be upon your heart; and you shall teach them diligently to your children, and shall talk of them when you sit in your house, and when you walk by the way, and when you lie down, and when you rise (Deut. 6:5-7).

Today this would mean that we should teach and apply the truth of God to the lives of our children at the dinner table, when we are sitting in our family room watching T.V., when we are riding in our automobiles, or in whatever situation of life. Since more time is spent in our homes than any other place, even in modern transient America, the home is still the vital place where the application of Scripture must be carried out (cf. Deut. 4:9-10; 6:6-7).

WAYS OF COMMUNICATION TO PROMOTE APPLICATION

Be an example. There are certain definite ways of communicating God's Word to people so they can see how it should apply to their lives. Most important of all is the idea of *setting an example* of obedience in our own Christian lives. Jesus, after washing the disciples' feet, said to them, "I have set you an *example* that you should do as I have done for you" (John 13:15). Paul strongly emphasized that the Christian leader should be an example as he relates and associates intimately with his disciples. He wrote to the Philippians: "Join with others in following my *example*" (Phil. 3:17). To the Thessalonians he said, "We did this . . . to make ourselves a *model* for you to follow. (2 Thess. 3:9). Paul enjoined the men who were to be leaders not only to follow his example but also to teach others by their example. He advised Timothy saying, "Set an *example* for the believers" (1 Tim. 4:12).

Many other passages might be given to support this truth. Generally speaking, most of us are horrified at the idea of having to set an example for others. We even assume that it is arrogant to ask people to follow our example. But for the Christian leader this is imperative. He must set the example, and he must call men to follow his example in Christian living.

Identification by sharing. Another way is that of identifying with an experience heard from a Christian who shows what God is doing in his life. For example, as the Holy Spirit shows a person a sin that is in his life, he confesses it and is cleansed from it. If he then shares this with other Christians in small groups or in large group meetings, the people there who may have the same sin in their lives will then see how Christ has dealt with this repentant brother. By identifying with him, some will apply the same truth to their own life and repent. The truth shared does not have to be negative only. As a person shares truth that God has shown him and praises God for the experience of obeying Him in that truth, this also can be a means whereby others personally identify and learn that same truth.

Direct command. A third way in which we help people apply the Scriptures to their lives is that of direct command. This is usually given by one in an official capacity of leadership, such as a parent to the child in the home. In the fifth commandment children are told to honor their fathers and mothers and therefore obey them. The authority to command is also given to the official leaders of the church, namely the elders or pastor, who have oversight. Jesus frequently pointed out the commands of the Old Testament and urged the people to obey them (Matt. 19:7; Mark 10:3). Jesus Himself did not hesitate to give direct commands to His disciples, and He based their continued fellowship with Him as His friends on obedience to the commands He gave (John 15:14,17). In matters of conduct where Paul had a clear, direct command from Jesus Christ, he commanded the congregations to do those things (2 Thess. 3:4,6,11,12). Moreover, Paul put some teeth into this by urging disciplinary action taken against those who did not respond (vv. 14,15). In doing this Paul was, of course, acting in behalf of Christ, in His name, just as Jesus had planned. Jesus said to His apostles, "He who receives you receives me" (Matt. 10:40; John 13:20).

Proclaiming and teaching. Another way of applying the truth was the simple proclamation of the will of Christ and teaching the things Jesus had enjoined upon His disciples. Ministry commonly associated with prophecy in the early church was a ministry to edify by presenting the positive teaching to the people. (1 Cor. 14). So is the modern preaching ministry. As people hear the teaching of the will of God, the Holy Spirit of God applies it to individual lives in the congregation.

Correcting, rebuking, and encouraging. A last and very important way to apply the truth to people's lives is closely akin to the teaching ministry and in a sense is a part of it. It is that of correcting, rebuking, and encouraging people in regard to sin and obedience.

The Greek word *elengchō*, "to convince" or "convict," is translated "*rebuke.*" The task of *rebuking* people who were wrong also belonged primarily to the official leadership and was done in love (2 Tim. 4:2; Titus 1:13; 2:15; Rev. 3:19). But laymen were also to rebuke each other. Rebuke for a sin was to be first between an individual (an elder or a church member) and the person who was involved in sin. If the brother continued to persist in sin, then two more were to go and rebuke him and urge him further to repent. If, however, he did not repent then, he was to be publicly rebuked. An elder should first be respectfully entreated. (Matt. 18:15-17; Luke 17:3ff.; 1 Tim. 5:1,19,20).

The Greek word for "encourage" or "exhort," *parakaleō*, means "to call to one," "summon," or "admonish." The matter of exhorting was especially the job of the elders who did the teaching. Unless a man was capable of doing this, he was not really qualified to be an elder (1 Thess. 4:1; 2 Tim. 4:1,2; Titus 1:9,10). Leaders were especially guided to give particular exhortation to various groups of people who had certain tendencies toward sinning. For example, the young men were to be exhorted to be sensible (Titus 2:6); servants were to be exhorted to be obedient to their masters (v. 9).

Correcting, rebuking, and encouraging were often a special gift given to certain individuals in the body, as well as perhaps to those who had official leadership (Rom. 12:8; 1 Cor. 14:3). One of the major purposes for Christians gathering together regularly in the congregation was to receive exhortation and teaching and to exhort each other individually lest they grow deeper into sin and be deceived (Heb. 3:13). This was the great key to the Ruanda revival in central Africa.[9] There the Christians began gathering together in small groups, and in love they corrected, reproved, and encouraged each other in the Lord. One of the most important ways for the members of the congregation to help one another is that of lovingly exhorting each other (1 Thess. 5:14; Heb. 3:13).

CARE TO MAINTAIN THE AUTHORITY OF CHRIST

The church today is vulnerable to men who would assume authority to themselves that belongs to the Lord Christ. Because the pastor has often become a lecturer and administrator removed from a close relationship where he can apply truth and because there has been a vacuum of meaningful teaching both in the old-line denominations that have emphasized the intellectual ideas and in some charismatic groups, many of the people are in great need of a word of authority to help them with their problems and sin. As mentioned in chapter one, there is today a neoclerical movement that is ready to supply that authority without a clear word from Christ.

The crown and glory of Jesus Christ is that He died for our sins and then was raised to the right hand of God that *He* might be *Lord* over His body, the church, and rule over every individual life within His church. Paul says in Romans 14:9, "For this very reason Christ died and returned to life so that he might be the *Lord* of both the dead and the living." Paul was combating a new trend of legalism within the church (Rom. 14). In the Old Testament, human authority had come between God and His people and Jewish leaders put the traditions and teachings of men above the Word of God. Paul saw that in certain matters a new and similar legalism was creeping into the church. Some of the human teachers were making pronouncements beyond what the Holy Spirit had indicated in the Scriptures. They were giving their opinions without showing the truth to their brethren from the Word. Paul calls them in to question, ''Who are you to judge someone else's servant? To his own master he stands or falls; and he will stand, for the Lord is able to make him stand'' (Rom. 14:4). Where the Scripture does not give clear guidance in certain details, it is not the right of a human teacher to do more than apply related principles of the Word and ask the individual to seek the Spirit's leading. If he tries to spell out minute legal details for the Christian life, he will step between Christ and Christ's servant.

In Paul's day there were men who were trying to make decisions in terms of practical Christianity as to whether or not they should eat meat offered to an idol and if they should observe one day or another day. Paul says one may do it one way, and he does it for the Lord; another may do it another way, and he is doing it for the Lord. He says, ''For none of us lives to himself alone, and none of us dies to himself alone. If we live, we live to the Lord; and if we die, we die to the Lord. So, whether we live or die, we belong to the Lord.'' He emphasizes, ''You, then, why do you judge your brother? Or why do you look down on your brother?'' (Rom. 14:1-12).

In the same manner James calls all men to humble themselves before the presence of the Lord. Then he warns, ''Brothers, do not slander one another. Anyone who speaks against his brother, or judges him, speaks against the law and judges it. When you judge the law, you are not keeping it, but sitting in judgment on it. There is *only one Lawgiver and Judge,* the one who is able to save and destroy. But you — who are you who judge your neighbor?'' (James 4:10-12). James is saying that a human teacher must not go beyond the clear statements of the Word of God in seeking to help a person apply the Word of truth to his life. The responsibility of the human teacher is to show the Christian what the Word of God says, and then to say to that person, ''This is Christ's Word to you and He would have you obey it.'' Thereby the human teacher points them to the living Christ, and the living Christ then, through the Holy Spirit, will speak to their hearts. No human teacher has the right to go beyond what is written by the Holy Spirit.

If a person fails to respond to the Word of Christ, Christ is perfectly capable of chastening and correcting him for his disobedience. He can cause trouble and hurt to come upon him (Rom. 14:4;

Heb. 12:6). Men do not have to take over for Christ.

Special rules when authoritatively giving specific application. There were special considerations that seem to have been kept in mind in regard to an elder commanding, exhorting, and rebuking specific individuals. One was that before a leader or a member of the church exhorted another member of the church, he was to be careful not to set himself up as a judge. He was first to humble himself and to see if he had a log in his own eye before he tried to take the speck out of his brother's eye. This meant that any exhortation or rebuke was always to be carried out with great humility and with great care not to become involved in the same sin in which the brother was partaking (Matt. 7:1-5; Gal. 6:1).

It is interesting that most of the passages that deal with the elder, pastor, or teacher commanding, exhorting, or rebuking a member of the congregation are surrounded in the context by a certain restriction to avoid the abuses mentioned above. Peter reminds the shepherd of the flock that he is not to act like the Lord (1 Peter 5:1-5). He is to take a position of humility, prove himself as an example to the flock, and not set himself up as a judge, because he knows that the Chief Shepherd, who is Christ, will one day return and judge his work.

Paul says to Timothy that he should prove himself as an example and read the Scripture publicly as the basis for his exhortation (1 Tim. 4:12,13). Even when Paul commands others, he urges them to look to the Lord and let the Lord direct their hearts (2 Thess. 3:4,5). He reminds them that the commands he is giving are based on the teachings of Christ that he has received with the apostles (2 Thess. 3:6). Paul is quite careful to base his commands, his exhortations, and his reproof on the Lord Himself. At times, he says that he is doing these things in the name of the Lord Jesus Christ or "by the authority of the Lord Jesus Christ" (1 Thess. 4:1ff.).

Paul is careful to distinguish when he is giving an opinion of his that is to be received as advice and when he is giving a command that came directly from the Lord (1 Cor. 7:10,12). While the canonization of this raises it to a position as a word from Christ, it still reflects the caution that a leader not give his own ideas.

CHECKS ON HUMAN INTERPRETATION AND APPLICATION OF THE TRUTH

Scripture indicates there are several checks on the leadership of the church. The team of *leaders* in a church should *correct each other*. Paul, an apostle, corrected Peter, the leading apostle of the Jews, when he was violating the nature of the gospel that had been revealed by the Word of Christ (cf. Gal. 1:11,12; 2:11ff.). Also, *the people were encouraged* to search the Scriptures to see if the things taught by the apostles were in agreement (Acts 17:11). If a teacher or leader did not conform in life or doctrine to the will of Christ, he was first to be entreated as a father and not to be rebuked without the agreement of two or three witnesses that he was wrong. If a teacher did not agree with the authority and teaching of Christ after appropriate admonition, he was then to be boycotted by the congregation (Rom. 16:17; 2 John 9-11).

FOUR LEVELS FOR APPLICATION OF TRUTH

Congregational. There are four levels at which the Word of God is applied. There is, first, the level of congregational worship, where all the people gather together and where the Scripture is preached by one of the elders. This is the traditional and often the only way in which it has been done in the Protestant churches in recent years in America. A great weakness of this is that those sitting in the pew may say, "This does not apply to me. It applies to John over there, to my wife, or someone else." So he goes away without any specific application, and he does not grow.

Very probably, in the early preaching services, many of the churches were in homes. The group was not so large that they could not interact afterwards to discuss and make more application. Some churches today have a time after the preaching service to interact over the message and to talk with one another about its application. It is good for the father to get the family together on Sunday afternoon or evening to discuss how the message preached to the congregation applies to the lives of each member.

Small groups. A second level is application in small groups. There a leader, who meets regularly with the small group, can more easily see the need and apply the truth to the individual in the particular situation. This may occur by the congregation breaking up into small groups and having fellowship together. Again, through their sharing and exhortation either by the leader or each other, they can better see their own needs and have truth applied to their own lives. This was the way in which the Ruanda revival often operated in Africa. As mentioned, the home is the main small group where the Word is applied.

One to one. Thirdly, there is the one-on-one relationship, whereby when one member of the congregation sees a sin in the life of another he goes to that person. He would show him the Scriptures and say to him, "Brother, I believe you have trespassed against me and I would like to encourage you to repent" (cf. Matt. 18:15-17; Luke 17:3; Gal. 6:1).

Personal Confrontation. The fourth level is probably the most important. That is the level of *the individual* getting alone with God and *meditating on the truth of God*. Obedience ultimately must come down to this. If he has received some application of the Word in the congregation, in the small groups, or from one-to-one contact, he must face that truth in his own life, alone. That is why a daily quiet time is so important for every Christian. This is why our Lord so frequently arose a great while before day, went out, and then prayed (Mark 1:5-38; Luke 4:42).

Psalm 1 was an introduction that was made to *call all people to meditate* on the things written in the psalms that followed. By meditation the people would assimilate and apply the truths that had been made known in the life of David and others. The psalms talk about ''meditating on the law of the Lord day and night.'' Psalm 119 and other great passages speak often of this. Isaiah the prophet talks about the Lord wakening him morning by morning and speaking to him (Isa. 50:4,5). It is in this time of reading, study, memorization, and meditation on the Scriptures that the Holy Spirit then begins to make it real in our lives. All the efforts of others to help us apply the truth to our lives must really come to a focus here.

This is why one of the great tasks of building disciples is to teach men and women to spend time alone with God, to meditate on His Word, and to study the truth of His Word for themselves.

DEVELOPMENT OF THE FOCUS OF OBEDIENCE THROUGHOUT THE SEVEN STEPS OF GROWTH

As Jesus led His disciples through the successive steps of growth in discipleship, there was a change in focus on the area of life to which obedience must be applied. Since the area of knowledge progressively changed, so the focus of obedience changed. Generally speaking, the focus of each step was as follows:

Repentance and Faith. It was shown that man's rebellion against God usually centered in some particular sin that dominated him. That sin (or sins) was but evidence of his sinful nature. The call of God to that person was a call to turn from that particular sin. But the turning actually involved a submitting of his total will to God's will by yielding the point of his highest desire. The woman at the well was challenged to obey by seeking her satisfaction in God rather than in a husband. Nicodemus was called to obey God, trusting the power of God working in him rather than his rabbinical knowledge of religion. The lawyer was called to forsake his prejudice and begin to love his religious enemy, the Samaritan. The rich young ruler was asked to obey God by giving up his idolatrous trust in money for trust in God's eternal provision. The call to obedience for each of these was to yield the focal point of his rebellious human will so that he, the sinner, died to the center of his desires and began to focus on God Himself and His will as the object of his delight.

This step ends in the individual being converted to the attitude of accepting the principle of desiring to obey God. The individual responds to God's love so that he is willing to identify himself as dying with Christ on the cross to serve God henceforth. By the believer's public water baptism he exemplifies his identification with Christ in this principle of obedience. This acceptance of the *principle* of obedience becomes the foundation for *daily practice* of obedience in the later steps.

Enlightenment. The next step was that of coming to understand the greatness of God in Christ so that the disciple would begin to trust Him to lead him in daily obedience to God's will. The disciples had to see that Christ was God's trustworthy leader, so that they would accept Christ's word as the Word of God to be obeyed as they daily followed Him. Today it involves obedience to Christ as the Holy Spirit directs the Christian through the Scriptures and providence. In this step the disciple learns how to be led of Christ into the daily practice of obedience.

Ministry Training. During the step of Ministry Training, Jesus began to call the multitudes to take the step of Repentance and Faith. But His call to His disciples was to obey Him in helping Him confront the world in the ministry of leading the people to repent. They were to obey Him in learning to be fishers of men. This required obedience in actively working with Christ in rescuing men from the power of Satan and bringing them into the kingdom of God. Here the disciples learned of the grace and liberty of being directly and personally under obedience to Christ instead of the dead letter of the law.

Leadership Development. The focus of obedience during this step was on keeping God's commands in relationship with others, in the heart and not just externally. They were taught to obey in accepting the unloved and unwanted, and were shown they must obey God even when there were doubts and opposition from enemies or friends. Most important of all, during this time they were sent out on their own where they were expected to obey Christ even when their leader was absent. He would follow and learn of their work of obedience.

Reevaluation. In this step the disciples were challenged to obey God for eternal rewards rather than for things temporal and to follow Him in obedience even if the world turned away. They were taught to put obedience to the Word of God over human traditions and even to sacrifice their national commitment to that of the eternal kingdom of God. During this time they were told that they must be obedient to their king (Christ) even if it meant physical death. They were told that their commitment to obedience would mean a willingness to lose their life in order to find it again.

Participation and Delegation. This was the time of learning to obey Christ as a part of the body, the church. They had to learn to obey Him in love toward those who questioned and rejected them. They learned to deal lovingly with newer, inexperienced leaders and to forgive the faults of others within the Christian fellowship. They were called to witness in the face of hostile opposition. They were taught to obey for God's honor alone and not to seek respect from men, as the hypocritical Pharisees did.

The Exchanged Life. The final lesson was to obey God in the belief that the kingdom of God was not dependent on the flesh, but entirely on the power of the Holy Spirit. When every evidence of God's presence was absent or destroyed from the fleshly world, He could still give victory to those who obediently trusted Him. This was made clear in the resurrection and in the coming of the Holy Spirit on the day of Pentecost. They learned that by trusting God even to the point of death on a shameful cross, the obedient person would be victorious and be exalted above every enemy. Their life was His life, and His life was eternal and indestructible. They could love as He loved.

THE IMPORTANCE OF OBEDIENCE TO CHRIST, OUR KING

One of Jesus' most important sayings was "He who has an ear, let him hear. . . ." The Hebraic meaning is, "If a man has willing ears to hearken obediently, let him listen" to what God is saying. He warned that the one "who hears these words of mine and does not put them into practice" is like the man who builds his house on the sand and is carried away when a flood comes. But the wise man, the one "who hears these words of mine and puts them into practice," is like a man who builds on a rock foundation that stands amid the storms of life (Matt. 7:24,26). At issue is security or tragedy for all men.

Jesus also showed that the source of blessings in the Christian life is obedience. If a man loves Him and obeys His commandments, he will be given the Spirit of truth as a helper; he will have the love of the Father and the Son; They will disclose their presence with him and live with him; and he will experience the full joy of Christ (John 14:15-17,21,24; 15:10-12). If he lacks love and obedience, he will not receive these things. Christ is not saying love and obedience are the basis of acceptance into His kingdom. John has already indicated the disciples' permanent acceptance by Jesus by saying, "Having loved His own who were in the world, He loved them to the end"

(John 13:1, NASB). Obedience is not a provision for acceptance of a child into the family, but when a beloved son has been disobedient, he is sent to his room away from the father's presence, and all enjoyable gifts are withheld until repentance and confession bring reconciliation. It's a pity that many Christians live in such a condition.

The importance of obedience to Christ is evident in the Great Commission given after the resurrection. They were told to make and baptize disciples, "teaching them to obey everything" He had commanded them (Matt. 28:20). Apparently, when the Lord later commissioned Paul to this same task of making disciples of the nations, He also emphasized that the end product should be obedience (Rom. 1:5; 16:26). Obedience in sacrificial love is still the end product of the church's ministry today.

Notes

[1] Andrew Murray, *The School of Obedience* (Chicago: Moody, n.d.), p. 15.

[2] Ibid., pp. 13ff.

[3] Robert E. Hume, *The World's Living Religions* (New York: Scribner's, 1924), pp. 265-267.

[4] Francis A. Schaeffer, *The Mark of the Christian* (Downers Grove, Ill.: Inter-Varsity Press, 1970).

[5] Murray, *The School of Obedience,* pp. 33,60,61.

[6] Ibid., p. 103.

[7] Ibid., p. 94.

[8] Robert Coleman, *The Master Plan of Evangelism* (New York: Revell, 1963), p. 56.

[9] Norman Grubb, *Continuous Revival* (Philadelphia: Christian Literature Crusade).

18

Conclusion: A Call to Strategy and Dedication

My burden in writing this book is not simply to sell a particular program but to urge the church to establish the government of Christ more completely in the hearts and lives of men. Hopefully it clarifies the direction Scripture indicates we should take in order to accomplish this task. For success we will *need a practical strategy* that wisely applies the biblical approach to discipleship to the circumstances of our present world; we will need unusual dedication to the task; and we will also need a constant vision of the living Christ who is revealed in the Bible, the Word of God.

IMPORTANCE OF A STRATEGY

A man who has a goal, a strategy to reach that goal, and an unrelenting persistence will someday obtain it. The formula: goal + strategy + persistence = achievement. The "how to's" are as important as the goals.

Karl Marx said that philosophers seek to *understand history* but the communists seek *to change history* through the laws of economics. The communists are known for their strategies — their five year plans, their ten year plans, etc. If one plan fails, they make revisions and try another. Through persistent application of their strategies, they have continually extended their control over the world.

We Christians are impatient. Even though we have ideals, we

have little patience for working out the details of a strategy. Some even consider detailed planning to be unspiritual. But God planned His work of redemption in detail before the foundation of the world. He expects us to plan (Prov. 16:3). We are, of course, entirely dependent on Christ to enable us to effect those plans (Prov. 16:9).

To succeed we must adopt a strategy that entails our working with God to achieve His goals. In a sense this whole book deals with strategy — that is, how to build disciples. But we dare not stop short of *a strategy to apply* the New Testament approach to disciple building *to our world*. The consequences are too great, the issue too important. The following guidelines for strategy are brief and broad, but they suggest one way to achieve our goals.

STRATEGY FOR APPLICATION IN THE CHURCHES

The local church is the most obvious place to begin applying the biblical program of disciple building. Jesus will be glorified most when those directly associated with His name (in other words, church members) are fully taught and become like Him. By repentant hearts and faithful commitment to Christ's words the church can be the most dynamic institution on earth. Christ has the power to make it that.

The pastor of the church as well as the other official spiritual leaders are the key to establishing a biblical program of disciple building. If the shepherds do not follow the Chief Shepherd, how will the flock be led? Unless the pastors have the courage and dedication to initiate a change in the way people are taught, nothing will happen. Christ has delegated responsibility to them; they either stimulate or hinder the growth of their people.

What I advocate is for the pastor to effect a persistent determined transformation, not revolution; improved edification, not destruction. Much that many churches are doing is good and can continue useful. But often changes need to be made so that the educational program relates to and develops the individual. Smaller groups need to be established where teaching can be specific, individual attention given, and application made to daily life. But there *must be dialogue* between teacher and disciples, not just lecture. The pastor should initiate the model by selecting a group of people and personally discipling them, just as Jesus did. As they grow, the pastor can train some of them to disciple others. This process can be continued until every willing church member is involved and every father is the leader and teacher in his own home.

Small groups should supplement congregational worship, not displace it. But even in congregational worship the image of one-man leadership needs replacing by team leadership. Why cannot the pastor use other members of his team to speak on Sunday morning or have a different presentation from a lecture? May we avoid treating God with casual familiarity as a buddy, but have Him as a friend; may we worship with dignified freedom, but without lifeless forms.

The pastor must initiate the model with the help of other willing elders and train the first leaders, for if someone else assumes this responsibility, he could easily become a rival for the pastor's leadership. However, he should aim at building a church leadership team to work with him. A pastor can learn how to establish a program for training disciple-builders in a minimum of time. At the same time he will also learn how to meet the needs of his people more effectively. As he sees lives transformed and people growing, he will experience greater satisfaction from his ministry. Some churches that are doing well at reaching many people by one-man leadership and old structures should not be criticized. God may lead them to continue that way, even though they may not minister to their people's needs as well as if they made some changes.

One strategy for the churches. Hopefully, church leaders will use this book as a guideline to help reestablish New Testament models of disciple building. In 1972 I shared this New Testament approach to disciple building with a number of Campus Crusade for Christ staff members who were working under me. Since then, some of the men and women have built models, taking their disciples through the seven steps. One of these has been chosen as a model of the high-school ministry from this large organization.

A businessman who had spent several years training other laymen in personal evangelism attended a Worldwide Discipleship Association conference in December 1974 and then another in August 1975. At the August conference he said that while attending the one in December he gained a vision of the importance of building disciples and what was the biblical approach to this. In the interim he had gathered a group of businessmen to disciple and also had begun to meet with the employees in his plant. He said that he had seen more fruit in the lives of others in those few months than in all his previous efforts. Moreover, it changed the productivity of his plant.

I personally began applying the New Testament method to the men of my church and the leadership is strongly continuing this emphasis. The result has been a vigorous growing congregation in an area where most churches are dying. I am convinced that any Christian worker who faithfully applies this approach of disciple building will experience much success for Christ.

It was to make it easier for leaders to build New Testament models, that I established the Worldwide Discipleship Association, which offers training. My hope is that many denominational and organizational leaders will study this New Testament approach, use it to develop their own training, and establish their own models. Many, I am sure, will be able to improve on what I have written and on the training we offer. My staff and I are available for consultation.

God has led us to the following procedure: First, when a group of pastors express an interest in learning how to institute a disciple-building program, we ask them to invite their friends to meet together for a thorough preliminary orientation, requiring about two hours. As they see the need and how it can be met, most of them express a desire to undergo intense, comprehensive training. We urge them to promote this among still other ministers and church leaders and we offer the training in five days of seminars and lectures. To make the training practical, we include at least one day to help them arrange the calendar of their programs to best initiate such a strategy in their own church. We encourage the pastor to commit himself to trying to carry out the disciple-building program for a year. If the pastor will spend a year applying the New Testament approach to disciple building, he will most probably succeed in establishing the program. It is important that a pastor be strongly committed before starting the program. Otherwise, he might not carry through with it.

We have begun developing seven books to help carry out each of the seven steps. Each has three sections: one on the philosophy and theology involved in that step, a second explaining how practically to do things required in that step, and a third with Bible-study resource materials for that step. The latter includes our guided Bible studies, books to read covering the biblical material, and suggested Scripture to memorize.

These guidelines will be useful to anyone who wishes to reestablish the model of New Testament disciple building. A manual for pastors and church leaders is already in field-test form. It helps them anticipate problems and know how to meet them and it details instructions on carrying out the entire strategy in their churches over a three-year period.

Many outstanding men of God and several outstanding organizations are examining practical ways to improve disciple building.[1] Their insights can be used to implement the program of disciple building outlined in this book. My prayer is that many within the church will devote themselves to this task as quickly as possible. Surely we should give credit where credit is due, but may the Lord deliver us from jealousy and competition. May we share ideas freely and take advantage of the insights the Holy Spirit gives to other members of the body.

It is probable that some may not fully agree with the program for building disciples that I have outlined. But every Christian leader is under obligation to follow *some* program to teach every disciple "to observe *all things*" that Jesus commanded (Matt. 28:19,20). There is room for different approaches, but not for failure to do what our Lord said.

APPLICATION INTERNATIONALLY

In the past the churches in the third world have been greatly influenced by Western models. While these churches are rapidly developing their own way of doing things, they are certainly open to suggestions from any who can give constructive help. Many of them need help in knowing how to train people to build disciples.

In a recent address to the Lausanne Continuation Committee, Dr. Billy Graham suggested that Christians establish a quintuple headquarters for evangelism and missions in Europe, North America, Southeast Asia, Latin America, and East Africa.[2] I hope that these may become the headquarters for missions with the *two divisions* of evangelism *and discipleship,* thereby conforming to the two emphases of the Great Commission as it was given by our Lord. They could then be centers of communication for the disciple-building movement.

STRATEGY FOR APPLICATION TO THE UNIVERSITIES AND PUBLIC EDUCATION

In the opening chapter, I pointed out that most of the institutions of higher education in America (which in turn influence elementary and secondary education) were founded for spiritual purposes by the church. In the mid-eighteenth century approximately 95 percent of the students were studying in schools founded for Christian purposes, whereas today probably 90 percent of the students are taught from a secular, anti-Christian viewpoint. If the church is to effect a change in the modern trend of secularization, we must focus on the intense and comprehensive building of disciples at the university level.

The university level is the source of the church's manpower pool. While in college, men and women decide on their life's work. If the church does not focus its efforts here, secular thought will continue to poison the manpower pool and fewer people will become involved in Christian ministries. Moreover, the poison will continue to affect the church internally by the effect on its membership.

WHERE TO BEGIN IN HIGHER EDUCATION

The Christian college offers the greatest freedom of Christian thought and the easiest place to teach an overall Christian philosophy. In recent years some new Bible colleges and Christian liberal arts colleges have been opened and older ones have expanded. In 1973-1974 the number of students in secular universities fell by 14 percent but enrollment in Bible colleges jumped 7.5 percent.[3] The trend in the secular universities did not continue in 1974-1975. Enrollment in 1975-1976 indicated a 3 percent increase again.

However, for some years it has become increasingly clear that the wisest course of action may be in trying to disciple students who attend secular universities. Somewhere around 1960 Booze, Allen and Hamilton, a Chicago marketing research firm, conducted studies for the Tennessee Baptist Association and for the Texas Baptists. They recommended in each analysis that the Association limit the funds given to small Christian colleges and focus on training students on secular campuses. They stressed the growing costs for private institutions and the fact that the large numbers of students who were Baptists and other church groups attend the secular universities.

Since the Booze, Allen and Hamilton studies, the circumstances have continued to build more support for their conclusions. If the predictions of rising costs are correct (see chapter 1, p. 31), a reversal of the trend of the disintegration of Christian colleges will demand very large sacrificial giving by the churches. Since churches are themselves increasingly being secularized, will they have the will to give what is needed? Also, won't the wealthy be the only ones able to afford a Christian higher education? Will Christian teachers who are being more and more influenced by secular thought be willing to take proportionately lower salaries for work in Christian schools?

Even if the church can establish enough good Christian schools to educate her youth, will she not someday have to attack the Goliath of secular university education who now "taunts the armies of the living God?" (1 Sam. 17:26). On most campuses there are only a few outspoken anti-Christian teachers, but the great bulk of academic teaching exalts man in such a way as to undermine the biblical world view.

The cluster college approach. One approach to using the secular university campus is that of "the cluster college" or "satellite college" — a Christian college (or an extension of one) that operates alongside a secular university campus. A student may enroll in both and get his degree from one or the other. Cluster colleges such as Oxford and Cambridge are old and frequently found in the British Commonwealth countries. Presently, there are at least three Christian cluster colleges in America.[4] Another is to be founded at Lansing by John Wesley College in 1976-1977. While operating differently, they each seek to offer a number of courses from a Christian perspective (for example, Conrad Grebel offers forty courses). Two have faculty, classroom buildings, and residence halls. While less expensive than operating a separate Christian college, these cluster colleges are still costly.[5]

Guest lecture approach. Another approach is to invite visiting Christian professors to a campus for special lectures. Many universities have a Religious Emphasis Week, or the like, during which one or two guest speakers are brought in by the university. Unfortunately, most of these universities invite men who support their secular-humanistic views. Some of the students laughingly call these "Be Kind to God Week." At some schools such as the University of Delaware, significant efforts have been made to utilize opportunities to have guest speakers. There the Inter-Varsity Christian Fellowship sponsors four guest professors who give three lectures in the evening for a week. The Philosophy department even gives credit for attendance.

Probe Ministries of Dallas, Texas, utilizes the guest-lecturer approach to make a significant impact on secular campuses. Under the sponsorship of the evangelical Christian groups on a particular campus and in cooperation with the university, lecturers working with Probe will come for a one-week period and will speak upon request in classrooms. During this week the guest speakers present a Christian perspective of the various academic disciplines to hundreds of students in the classroom. On the following weekend they offer an institute of Christian apologetics for students who show an interest.

The guest-lecturer approach is an excellent way to show students and faculty that Christianity is a viable option, and it is a good pre-evangelism tool. But it obviously is limited in terms of long-range disciple building.

The Fellowship-of-Christian-Learning approach. The Fellowship of Christian Learning (FCL), a ministry conducted by Worldwide Discipleship Association, which I direct, includes aspects of both the "cluster college" and the "guest-lecturer" approach. Full-time staff are employed to work with students on the university campus. The FCL is organized as a student group on the campus, and the students in the group are involved in studying Christian truth.

Instead of seeking to offer courses from a Christian perspective in all the various fields of study, the FCL includes three areas of curriculum.

1. The staff members work with small groups of dedicated students, taking them through *the Steps of Christian Growth*. They

meet with students both on an individual basis and in small groups. This is the most fundamental aspect of the FCL and is the basis of a broader family type fellowship.

2. Because many of the students lack the necessary knowledge of the Bible and church history and in order that they might fully understand the teachings of Christianity, courses are taught that provide them with *biblical background material*. For example, a class in Bible survey helps the student understand the history of the events of the whole Bible.

3. Courses are taught in Christian theistic philosophy as it relates to various academic courses. Students other than those in the small discipleship groups usually attend also. These courses show how the Christian theistic philosophy lends itself to the most meaningful and honest interpretation of the facts about the world. These are *apologetic courses* to give a complete Christian world view.

This third aspect of curriculum aims at showing that the dominating humanistic philosophy in the university has a bias that has distorted the facts, led to fragmentation of thinking in every academic area, is contributing to the breakdown of American morals, and is detrimental to society and to learning. No effort is made to cover all the data taught in the various academic subjects, but only to show *the difference* between Christianity and naturalistic humanism *as philosophies for interpreting and organizing* the data of the various academic subjects.

The courses are given for elective credit whenever acceptable to the university. But the FCL mainly emphasizes small-group personal disciple building with a sense of fellowship as a family in which students center on their relationship to Christ in Christian growth.

One mistake that past efforts to redeem American higher education has fallen into is that of insisting that "cluster colleges" must be staffed only by teachers with Ph.D.'s in order to be intellectually powerful. This overlooks the tremendously important fact that *power lies in the truth* regardless of whether or not the person using it has a Ph.D. Of course, God often uses educated leaders (cf. Moses, Acts 7:22; Paul, Acts 26:24), and people generally should be respected for their degree attainments, and degree programs as such should be encouraged.

But today there are too many people who have wrong motives and cannot be used in an FCL. They have gotten a Ph.D. or other degrees for a status symbol and a ticket to demand a higher salary. Pursuit of knowledge should be to accurately acquire truth with the intent to use it to benefit others. The one with truth should be committed to making it known regardless of the remuneration to self.

The purpose of Christian knowledge of truth should be to use it to make men free unto God (John 8:31,32).

We in WDA have tried to establish a staff training school with these motives in view. These young men and women are taken through the steps of discipleship and are taught the Christian world view as contrasted to humanism. Because they have truth, they are making a mighty impact on university campuses in the FCLs. In a short time we can train many young men and women. Convinced they have the truth, they are willing sacrificially to raise their own support and work tirelessly and enthusiastically to communicate it. Their commitment and enthusiasm is from the Holy Spirit and is contagious.

Students in the FCL are taught how to ask their professors searching questions that might lead to an invitation for FCL staff to come to a class and offer insights from a Christian point of view. The members are made acquainted with helpful books and pamphlets from a Christian perspective. The FCL can either use a "Probe" week or sponsor debates between humanistic university professors and outstanding local or guest Christian professors in the same field. *Thus, the FCL combines the benefits of "cluster colleges" with the "guest-lecturer" approach, and, it also adds an intimate and vital emphasis on disciple building.* Moreover, the FCL offers the strength of Christian fellowship and education without isolating the Christian from the issues of the world, which is sometimes the case in Christian colleges.

The cost of operating an FCL is low, since it involves only a few well-trained staff who also use Christian university professors, guest professors, and qualified local pastors to help teach. Also, no major outlay of funds is needed for buildings. The few basic courses can be taught in rented or borrowed facilities, and the small groups can meet in dorms or other accessable rooms. Recognized student organizations have access to many university facilities, and churches near the campus can also be used. The whole program can be carried on as a cooperative venture with one or more churches at considerable advantage to the church. This means the cost per student is very low and any student from the state can afford to be involved.[6] Some have suggested that the denominational campus ministers be utilized in launching the FCL's. Thus far, this has not proven feasible.[7]

Place for Christian colleges with the FCL. If the church should institute this kind of auxilary school for disciple building on university campuses on a broad scale, it will need to be careful to maintain its Christian colleges. They are the best source for staffing the FCL, and the Christian college is the best place for the conducting of research that thoroughly integrates the Christian philosophy into the various academic disciplines. They are also significant because Christian textbooks can be produced here. This cannot easily be done in the FCL. One or two Christian colleges might become centers for training staff for the FCL's.

To help the financial plight of the Christian colleges, the churches should lobby for tax exemption for those who send their children to Christian schools. This would give much relief to Christian institutions and would be only fair, since tax dollars subsidize the education of students in public universities.

The FCL and separation of church and state. The operation of an auxiliary school like the FCL is within the legal limits of the separation of church and state. Although Thomas Jefferson was a deist and not a Christian, and although he coined the phrase "the wall of separation of church and state," in his views there was a place for an auxiliary use of university facilities. When he established the University of Virginia, he envisioned churches' establishing schools that would be associated with the university, would use its library, and be helped by it in other ways.

Thomas Jefferson's early views are in accord with court rulings that distinguish between *accommodation* of religious teachings and *sponsoring* religious teachings. For instance, Madalyn Murray O'Hair wanted the Federal court in Texas to restrain NASA from allowing astronauts to read the Bible and broadcast religious statements as they did during Apollo 8 and Apollo 11 flights. The court ruled that the government was only accommodating the astronauts and had no establishmentarian purpose. The Fellowship of Christian Learning can be easily operated within the *accommodation* limitations.

Many teachers on university campuses will be threatened by a clear presentation of a Christian theistic view, especially in contrast to humanistic naturalism. But the university should be a place where ideas are freely presented and those that seem most compelling to the mind may be voluntarily accepted without persecution or intimidation. However, it would be naive to think any FCL will escape the opposition of outspoken humanists.

The staff and students of the FCL should positively present the Christian message under the rules of accommodation. But they should also begin to put pressure on the many teachers in the university who are using their platform as teachers to belittle or refute Christian teachings. This is clearly a violation of the neutrality position of the government taught by the Supreme Court (See page 30).

Students should accumulate evidence by tape recording lectures and saving notes made on class papers and tests, and these should be turned over to Christian lawyers who kindly warn professors they are violating the law. Then if this persists, a court case should be made where there is clear violation. While Christians should never be vindictive, but gracious, they should see that the law is upheld (Acts 16:37-39). *Students themselves should not try to correct the errant professor by legal action.*

Drawback to the FCL. The one drawback of the FCL and the cluster-college approach is that additional time is required for regular study, and a poor student, a student with many lab courses, or one who must work may have difficulty, unless the degree work at the university is extended and fewer courses are carried each quarter or semester. But under normal circumstances, the student can do the work and find his fellowship and recreation in the discipleship group. Where the university offers credit for the courses as electives, this also helps.

Effects of the FCL. The disciple-building program on the college campuses has immediate effects. The students and staff begin to influence the thinking of the university. Moreover, the college students who are being discipled can influence the high school youth by working with youth groups in the churches and building disciples there. These high school students then feed into the FCL. College students who graduate and enter the churches are then oriented toward a proper disciple-building ministry.

Also, the students who continue through four years of study in the FCL will be mature Christians, capable of moving into leadership roles in the church. The fourth-year curriculum for them focuses on their running a program of disciple building. Some will go on to seminary and enter the ministry. These can later lead their churches more toward the New Testament model of disciple building. Some can become lay leaders in the churches, some perhaps pastoral assistants and some pastors, helping develop the disciple-building programs. Some will go back on the staff to help expand the operation of the FCL's in other places. There will thus be a cycle furnishing a growing army of young men and women equipped as mature trainers in how to build disciples. They will also clearly understand the difference between the secular humanistic point of view and a theistic one.

It is hoped that as church leaders see the value of the FCL approach, they will not make the mistake of duplicating efforts on the same campuses. The urgency of the situation should compel true believers to unite their forces in one strong associate school on each major campus. Surely the Holy Spirit can lead us into enough unity under our Lord to do this.

Why cannot the FCL incorporate all the best being produced for college work from denominations and interdenominational groups? The literature of Inter-Varsity Christian Fellowship is superb. The Navigators are excellent at discipling men. Campus Crusade has much to offer, as do other groups.

ENOUGH DEDICATION TO ACHIEVE?

Failure in the church today. Our dedication to achieve a goal is based on how fundamental and important we think that goal is and how serious we consider our failures are. The lordship of Christ was fundamental to apostolic thought (cf. Acts 2:36; Rom. 10:9,10, et al.) Today, "teaching men to observe all things," which Jesus commanded, must become the highest priority in our thought and action. Yet how foreign this is to many of the churches and institutions called by His name!

One of the godliest and most influential Christian men of our time, Dr. A. W. Tozer, described the tragic condition of the evangelical churches not long before he died:

> Let me state the cause of my burden. It is this: Jesus Christ has today almost no authority at all among the groups that call themselves by His name.
>
> By these I mean not the Roman Catholics, nor the Liberals, nor the various quasi-Christian cults. I do mean Protestant churches generally, and I include those that protest the loudest that they are in spiritual descent from our Lord and His apostles, namely the evangelicals.
>
> It is a basic doctrine of the New Testament that after His resurrection the Man Jesus was declared by God to be both Lord and Christ, and that He was invested by the Father with absolute Lordship over the church which is His body. All authority is His in heaven and in earth. In His own proper time He will exert it to the full, but during this period in history He allows this authority to be challenged or ignored. And just now it is being challenged by the world and ignored by the church.
>
> The present position of Christ in the gospel churches may be likened to that of a king in a limited, constitutional monarchy. The king (sometimes depersonalized by the term "the Crown") is in such a country no more than a traditional rallying point, a pleasant symbol of unity and loyalty much like a flag or a national anthem. He is lauded, feted and supported, but his real authority is small. Nominally he is head over all, but in every crisis someone else makes the decisions. On formal occasions he appears in his royal attire to deliver the tame, colorless speech put into his mouth by the real rulers of the

country. The whole thing may be no more than good-natured make-believe, but it is rooted in antiquity, it is a lot of fun and no one wants to give it up.

Among the gospel churches Christ is now in fact little more than a beloved symbol. "All Hail the Power of Jesus' Name" is the church's national anthem and the cross is her official flag, but in the week-by-week services of the church and the day-by-day conduct of her members someone else, not Christ, makes the decisions. Under proper circumstances Christ is allowed to say, "Come unto me, all ye that labour and are heavy laden" or "Let not your heart be troubled," but when the speech is finished someone else takes over. Those in actual authority decide the moral standards of the church, as well as all objectives and all methods employed to achieve them. Because of long and meticulous organization it is now possible for the youngest pastor just out of seminary to have more actual authority in a church than Jesus Christ has.

Not only does Christ have little or no authority; His influence also is becoming less and less. I would not say that He has none, only that it is small and diminishing. A fair parallel would be the influence of Abraham Lincoln over the American people. Honest Abe is still the idol of the country. The likeness of his kind, rugged face, so homely that it is beautiful, appears everywhere. It is easy to grow misty-eyed over him. Children are brought up on stories of his love, his honesty and his humility. But after we have gotten control over our tender emotions what have we left? No more than a good example which, as it recedes into the past, becomes more and more unreal and exercises less and less real influence. Every scoundrel is ready to wrap Lincoln's long black coat around him. In the cold light of political facts in the United States the constant appeal to Lincoln by the politicians is a cynical joke.

The Lordship of Jesus is not quite forgotten among Christians, but it has been mostly relegated to the hymnal where all responsibility toward it may be comfortably discharged in a glow of pleasant religious emotion. Or if it is taught as a theory in the classroom it is rarely applied to practical living. The idea that the Man Christ Jesus has absolute and final authority over the whole church and over all of its members in every detail of their lives is simply not now accepted as true by the rank and file of evangelical Christians.[8]

It is a shameful fact that though America is known as a Christian country, the people in many countries not identified as Christian often come nearer living in agreement with the commands of Christ. If the average pastor in the United States will evaluate his membership, he is likely to find many families in which there have been serious moral problems.

Often Christian businessmen have been caught up in covetousness and have overextended themselves financially, and laboring men and women have spent beyond responsible biblical limits. Dedication to the pursuit of money has usurped the time that should have been used with the family or in the Lord's work. The father's absence in pursuit of success or money has left the wife alone and miserable, thus, in part, generating the feminist revolt. Tensions between husband and wife are frequent; divorce is not uncommon; rebellion of children (overt or hidden) plagues even the best of families. Giveaway games on T.V. that stimulate covetousness, filthy and violent motion pictures and television shows, and pornographic literature too often occupy our spare time. Sexual problems involve Christian adults and youth alike. Unfortunately, Christians often do not know what is right or are not motivated to do it.

Few of us lose sleep over this. How often have we wept over our sin or that of others (Acts 20:31)? Most of us do not care that men do not love God or obey Him. We have our own lives and our own ministry and don't want to be bothered, although we would not admit this.

Discipleship to obtain obedience is crucial. The issue at point is crucial — the one that matters most. We do need more "decisions" in evangelism, more effective church management and organization, more money to run the churches, and sometimes we may even need better buildings and facilities. But woe be to us as Christians if we do not see that the greatest need of the hour is to help Christians clearly understand and obey the teachings of Christ. We need to help Christians apply these to their daily lives and to teach them that obedience to His commands is of utmost importance.

Praying a prayer to invite Christ into one's heart, having an emotional experience, testifying for Christ, sharing the "plan of salvation," entering into the fullness of the Holy Spirit, teaching the Bible, and many other Christian acts are valid and good. But they mean nothing, *absolutely nothing,* unless they begin to produce the fruits of righteousness. While salvation is by grace through faith alone, faith without works is *dead,* nonexistent! (James 2:17). I believe I have the mind of Christ when I say that if we have city-wide crusades with thousands of "decisions," hold huge Bible conferences and seminars with outstanding speakers, and enact programs of social and political justice for the poor, it all counts as *nothing* if Jesus is not obeyed in our private lives.

Obedience to the commands of Christ *is* the fulfillment of the law of love (Rom. 13:8-10) and without love *I am nothing* (1 Cor. 13:2). Jesus said:

> Not everyone who says to me, "Lord, Lord," will enter the kingdom of heaven, but only he who does the will of my Father who is in

heaven. Many will say to me on that day, "Lord, Lord, did we not prophesy in your name, and in your name drive out demons and perform many miracles?" Then I will tell them plainly, "I never knew you. Away from me, you evildoers!" (Matt. 7:21-23).

Of all the things evangelical churches might do to forward the cause of Christ, nothing is so important as an audible witness *accompanied by a life obedient to the will of God*.

The power of an obedient church is worth the cost. The New York Ecumenical Missionary Conference of 1900 was one of the most significant conferences to further the Great Commission. The shadow of Simeon H. Calhoun, a brilliant and committed missionary statesman who served in Syria, lay heavy over that meeting. His dying words were written across the conference bulletin: "It is my deep conviction, and I say it again and again, that if the church of Christ were what she ought to be, twenty years would not pass away till the story of the cross would be uttered in the ears of every living man." His statement conveyed the heart of the men who planned and led the convention. During the years that immediately followed, probably more young men and women went forth as missionaries than at any other time in the history of the church.[9]

Many evangelical leaders admit that building disciples and training others to do so is the most important task before the church. However, far too few are willing to pay the price. To break with the status quo brings criticism. To pioneer in new paths requires more work than normal. Are not Christian leaders already too busy to start another program approach? For a person to build disciples who will assume leadership positions over some of his own flock seems to diminish the importance of that leader's role as being the one teacher and administrator of the whole congregation.

At first a pastor or Christian leader will assume added burdens in order to begin a program to train men to build disciples, but it will later liberate him. It will take more time for evangelists to work with churches on assimilating converts and discipling them. The Israelites had to work harder and had to make bricks without straw before they were delivered from bondage and entered the freedom of the promised land.

My great fear is that you who read this book, and the church in general, will agree that building disciples is the top priority, *yet do nothing* about it. When a Christian leader is content with building a superficial work, it may well indicate that he is building a little *kingdom for himself* rather than building the kingdom of Christ. Anything that does not produce obedience to God will prove to be but wood, hay, and stubble when it is tried with fire at the judgment-seat of Christ. My plea is that Christ will not let us rest until we are training disciples to build disciples who will be sacrificially obedient to the Lord — disciples who will reflect His image.

THE SUFFICIENCY OF CHRIST

The failure to proclaim the gospel to all nations is not due to any inadequacy in Jesus Christ. He said, *"All authority in heaven and on earth has been given to me. . . . Therefore go. . . ."* The failure lies in the fact that we have not met the conditions of obedience to receive the power of His presence (John 14:21,23), nor have we been faithful to His goals, especially that of building others so that they know His will and obey Him. Paul reminds us that when Christ was raised and seated at God's right hand, He received power above all principality and powers both in heaven and on earth (Eph. 1:21).

Christ wants the job done soon. He said, "This gospel of the kingdom will be preached in the whole world as a testimony to all nations, and then the end will come" (Matt. 24:14). Let us believe He will do "immeasurably more than all we ask or imagine" (Eph. 3:20), and move immediately to get the task accomplished.

Notes

[1] I am impressed with the work of Chuck Miller, Ray Stedman, R. H. Schuler, Gene Getz, Howard A. Snyder, The Navigators, and others.

[2] Billy Graham, "Our Mandate from Lausanne '74," *Christianity Today,* vol. 19, no. 20 (July 4, 1975): 6 [960].

[3] *The Church Around the World,* vol. 5, no. 3 (February 1975).

[4] Ronald J. Sider, "Christian Cluster Colleges — Off to a Good Start," *Christianity Today,* Vol. 18, no. 17 (May 24, 1974): 12-16. The three of which I am aware are Conrad Grebel College, Ontario; Messiah College, Philadelphia; and Satellite Christian Institute, San Diego.

[5] In 1960-61 I formed plans for a cluster or satellite college concept and came close to implementing it while I was minister for the Campus Christian Life program for the Presbyterian Synod of Appalachia at East Tennessee University. Shortly thereafter the Rev. Robert Henderson who was also serving the Presbyterian Church in North Carolina separately offered a similar idea. A few years later the Rev. Jody Dillow drew up a similar plan while working with Campus Crusade for Christ. In 1967 John W. Snyder, dean of the Junior Division of Indiana University, Bloomington, advocated the "cluster college" idea in some detail. He presented it to a consultation on higher Christian education held on the campus of Indiana University. It was also reported in *Christianity Today* (vol. 11, no. 10 [February 17, 1967]: 14 [494]). Two years later the John Wesley Foundation announced hopes to sponsor twenty-five satellite schools in the next five years. Plans were to begin with the first Wesley College in Detroit. Dr. Kenneth Armstrong, Nazarene pastor, was the one seeking to spearhead this. They hope to get their first satellite school started at Michigan State University, East Lansing, in 1976 or 1977. This will be sponsored by

John Wesley College of Owosso, Michigan. Also shortly after Dr. Snyder's suggestions appeared in *Christianity Today* the three cluster colleges mentioned above were started. Doubtless there were others who thought of this idea during that period of time when Christians were wrestling with the problem of the rapidly growing secular universities. Dr. Carl Henry's concept of a Christian university was another option offered at that time.

[6] Worldwide Discipleship Association plans to establish a Fellowship of Christian Learning on one major university campus in every state of the United States by 1985. Our objective is to have one major center on a university campus in each of the nine major regions of the United States by 1980. We now have ministries in four cities, with more than fifty staff members.

[7] For two reasons, I have deliberately sidestepped the idea of using denominational campus ministers to help implement a campus disciple-building program. First, in most of my contacts with many of the men serving in that role on university campuses, I have found the great majority of them are humanistic in orientation rather than theistic. There are exceptions, of course. Generally speaking, they do not accept the Bible as the Word of God as did Jesus, and they reject Jesus Christ as God incarnate. A house built on such sand for a foundation cannot long stand and certainly will not help the church toward obedience of faith. Second, ecclesiastical red tape makes it very difficult and slow to get things done. Many pastors are zealous to protect their old alma maters and contend with each other within the denominational organization to get the FCL located where they can personally benefit.

[8] A. W. Tozer, *God Tells the Man Who Cares* (Harrisburg, Pennsylvania: Christian Publications, Inc., 1970). Used by permission.

[9] J. Edwin Orr, *Campus Aflame* (Glendale, California: Regal Books, 1971), p. 95.

IV

Study Questions

Study Questions

This book, *With Christ in the School of Disciple Building*, is written more for those who want to learn how to build disciples than for those who want to grow as disciples. No doubt those who use it will experience growth, but that is not its primary purpose. These study questions have been prepared to help the reader better grasp the content of the book. For best results, the book should be read through thoroughly at least once. Then each chapter should be read through again as the study questions are used.

The goals of these study questions are as follows:

1. To cause you to check the Scriptures to see if the overall philosophy in the book is founded on a sound biblical base. This should give you greater confidence in and a greater commitment to what you are learning.
2. To help you see the overall picture of Jesus' ministry so that it is no longer a mass of disjointed facts and events, but an overall meaningful strategy.
3. To help you see some of the basic principles involved in building disciples and help you think through how you would apply these so as to avoid errors and have a successful discipling ministry.
4. To aid your growth in Christ and deepen your commitment to Him as you more effectively serve Him.
5. To enable you to teach these concepts more easily to others

and so help multiply disciple building, thereby forwarding the work of the churches.

One should have a notebook to record chronologically the answers to questions. A complete Bible is needed, since frequent references are made to the Old Testament as well as to the New Testament. The quotations in the book are from the *New International Version* (New Testament) and the *New American Standard Bible* (Old Testament) unless otherwise indicated. This study assumes the use of discipleship groups of ten to twelve people that can be broken up into smaller groups of three, four, or five.

I suggest the following procedure be followed in using the study questions:

1. Read through the chapter in the book. For chapters four through eleven that cover the seven steps, trace the material in the outline available from Worldwide Discipleship Association, Inc., Suite 315, 1001 Virginia Avenue, Atlanta, Georgia 30354.
2. Answer the questions on content.
3. Assign four or five people to meet in small groups to cover the discussion questions and perhaps interact over the research projects and their results. Each individual should read through the questions and think through the answers before the group meets. If there is time, report some of the findings in the class or larger discipleship groups of ten or twelve.
4. Answer the achievement questions and pray over your answers. If you feel that you, your discipleship group, or your church is not achieving the desired goals, prayerfully seek God's help in making plans to do what seems necessary to improve.
5. Use the research suggestions in the following way: If the suggestion recommends a project, divide it up among those in one small group so that it can be accomplished in a shorter period of time. Otherwise there will not be enough time to do the things suggested. Then compile the materials in a meeting of the small group. When there is time, share the results in the larger group or class. The research questions are designed more for use as projects in seminary or Bible school classes than in a normal discipleship group.

Chapter 1

The Need for a New Approach to Disciple Building

CONTENT QUESTIONS:

1. What factors led to the decline of disciple building in the early Christian church?
2. Secular humanism has been defined as the view of life that puts ultimate value on man and temporal and material benefits apart from God and the eternal. What primary factors led to the ascendance of these views in American thought and life?
3. What trends within the church have made it difficult for the pastor to have a personal association with his people close enough to make practical application of the Word of God to their lives?
4. Give two reasons why evangelism is likely to decline if efforts at building disciples are inadequate.
5. What are the two functional dimensions or aspects in which God works to build and develop His church?

THOUGHT QUESTIONS FOR THE INDIVIDUAL OR FOR GROUP DISCUSSION:

1. Why would the predominance of secular humanism in men's thoughts destroy respect for God's moral laws?
2. What evidence is there that American society is degenerating? How would obedience to the commands of Christ change this?
3. What evidence is there that education and politics alone cannot solve the problem of the degeneration of American society?
4. In your opinion, do most American churches have one man, namely the pastor, who does most of the work in leading and ministering in the church? To what extent have you observed churches in which small groups operate where the leader has dialogue with the members of the group?

ACHIEVEMENT QUESTIONS:

1. How would you rate your church in its ability to build disciples who live in daily obedience to Christ?
   Good   1   2   3   4   5   Poor
2. Has anyone ever spent time helping you personally understand and apply the truth of Scripture to your life? What would be some advantages in having a person more mature than yourself do this?

RESEARCH SUGGESTIONS:

1. Check with the teachers of your church school and see which of the following they do:

  a. Teach mainly by lecture.
  b. Teach by lecture and dialogue.
  c. Teach by discussion only.
  d. Spend time outside of class with the students.
2. Phone pastors in your community to see if they have a group of leaders in their church whom they are training to disciple others. Find out what kind of procedure they use in leading the group and what kind of resource materials they use in teaching.

Chapter 2

The Relationship of Disciple Building to Other Goals

CONTENT QUESTIONS:

1. Name in chronological order the five primary goals of God's kingdom.
2. What are some of the indications in Scripture that God wants the world evangelized?
3. Give evidence from Scripture that Christ and His apostles aimed at founding a church or churches.
4. What does the word *disciple* mean? What word seems to replace it in the Epistles?
5. Name the principle for growth involved in evangelizing and building disciples that is missing in evangelism alone.
6. What is the qualitative goal of disciple building?
7. What is the ultimate and final goal for all ministry?

THOUGHT QUESTIONS FOR THE INDIVIDUAL OR FOR GROUP DISCUSSION:

1. Why is it important to see all the primary goals of God's plan before evaluating and discussing any one of them?
2. What are some of the worldwide implications of the five primary goals?
3. Why is disciple building important for the qualitative goal of renewing man in the image of Christ?
4. In what ways can a ministry be perverted if one focuses only on evangelism? on church building? on disciple building? on producing Christlike people?
5. What are some of the benefits of a ministry with all the goals in proper focus? Would this benefit a person even though he has the gift of evangelism? of teaching?

ACHIEVEMENT QUESTIONS:

1. How well do you feel you have kept sight of all the goals in your ministry?
2. What plans can you make to help you get and keep a proper focus?

RESEARCH SUGGESTIONS:

1. Study a few books on management in your local library and find out how important a proper understanding of goals is to successful achievement. Make observations as to how this relates to this chapter.
2. Make a cursory study of the book of Acts and note the references and implications there concerning each of these goals in the apostolic church.

Chapter 3

The Biblical Approach to Disciple Building

CONTENT QUESTIONS:

1. What are two incomplete or inadequate views of building disciples?
2. Define briefly the New Testament concept of disciple building.
3. Give in chronological order from memory the names of the seven steps of discipleship.
4. What reasons are there to believe the apostle Paul followed in general the disciple building model of Jesus?

THOUGHT QUESTIONS FOR THE INDIVIDUAL OR FOR GROUP DISCUSSION:

1. After reading through the Harmony of the Gospels and using the outline, did you feel the progressive emphasis was properly interpreted and divided?
2. Do you feel the seven steps are the logical progression for Christian development? Switch positions of some of the steps and discuss some of the weaknesses such a switch offers compared to the way they occur. (E.g., place step four before step three. Weakness is that one could not lead others in a ministry he had never learned to do himself.)
3. What would you do if you had some disciples who are more advanced than others? Would you keep them in the same group if you didn't have enough for two groups? Do you think Jesus probably faced this problem, too? What is the advantage of taking

them through all the steps? How could you meet the needs of these more advanced people as well as the slower ones?

ACHIEVEMENT QUESTIONS:

1. Where would you place yourself in the seven steps of growth?
2. If you are still in the seven steps, seek someone whom you would like to help you grow and solicit his teaching and personal supervision.

RESEARCH SUGGESTIONS:

1. Use the bibliography and your nearest Christian library and check for books that suggest any kind of chronology for growth and compare with the seven steps.
2. Get books used by organizations for follow-up and see if there is a correlation of the material in them to the seven steps (e.g., "Ten Basic Steps of Campus Crusade for Christ" and your denominational material for youth).

Chapter 4

Repentance and Faith

CONTENT QUESTIONS:

1. What is the meaning of the Greek work that is most frequently translated "repent"?
2. What is the objective of the step of Repentance?
3. Who was instrumental in initiating the repentance and faith in the disciples who were Jesus' first followers in His movement?
4. What doctrines should be preached to promote repentance and faith?
5. What was the message that Paul said he initially preached in a community?
6. What is the key to the way of salvation?

THOUGHT QUESTIONS FOR THE INDIVIDUAL OR FOR GROUP DISCUSSION:

1. Why is it important for a person to have genuinely repented and to have been converted to Christ before being involved in a discipleship group?
2. How does the first step of Repentance and Faith relate to the other steps of growth in the life of a disciple?
3. In what way does preaching sin and judgment lead one to repent? What does preaching the forgiveness and love of God do to promote repentance?

ACHIEVEMENT QUESTIONS:

1. Did you experience real repentance and faith leading to conversion at the time of your first public profession of Christ?
2. Have your evangelistic efforts included an adequate message to enable people to repent fully so they are desirous of being taught God's will?
3. Evaluate your past evangelistic presentation to see if you should change it so that it will be more effective in leading others to repent.

RESEARCH SUGGESTIONS:

1. Get a book of messages by some outstanding evangelists and evaluate the content in the light of this chapter.
2. Prepare an evangelistic message of your own that meets the standards of Scripture as presented in this chapter.

Chapter 5

Enlightenment and Guidance

CONTENT QUESTIONS:

1. What is the objective of the step of Enlightenment?
2. Indicate which statements are true and which are false about the period of Enlightenment:
   a. Jesus was preaching to large crowds most of the time.
   b. Jesus talked most about how human He was during most of this time.
   c. It is wrong to say Jesus did not reveal His messiahship until the middle of His ministry, because He taught His first disciples that He was the Messiah.
   d. John the Baptist clearly affirmed that Jesus was the Messiah.
3. What was the purpose of the miracle of changing water to wine? Of the healing of the nobleman's son?
4. Match the following messianic claims of Christ with the person or persons involved:

   a. The temple leaders _____ 1. The promised prophet like Moses

   b. The woman of _____ 2. The one who gives a new
   Samaria birth to eternal life

   c. Nicodemus _____ 3. The one anointed to bring in the eternal jubilee

d. The people of the synagogue in Nazareth	____ 4. The one on whom the angels will ascend and descend
e. Philip	____ 5. The Messiah who by prophetic power will reveal all things
f. Nathanael	____ 6. The coming of God, the King, to purge the sons of Levi

5. Name some differences in the step of Enlightenment after Christ's resurrection.

THOUGHT QUESTIONS FOR THE INDIVIDUAL AND FOR GROUP DISCUSSION:

1. Is there still a need for God to demonstrate the supernatural power of Christ to men today?
   Why do you think this?
2. Is it important to see that Jesus was conscious of His heavenly origin and of His messiahship?
   If so, why is it important? (Check note 6, p. 99.)
3. Name some of the ways that Jesus linked His messianic claims to the Old Testament Scriptures and discuss the meaning of these.
4. What are some reasons a new convert needs to be taught and enlightened to the greatness of the person of Christ?
5. Could the truth of the greatness of Christ be taught as meaningfully and appropriately after the step of Ministry Training or Leadership Training as right after conversion? Why or why not?
6. What does the apostle Paul mean when he says that though we once regarded Christ from a worldly point of view, we do so no longer? (2 Cor. 5:16).

ACHIEVEMENT QUESTIONS:

1. Before you read this chapter, did you think of Christ more as having a human nature or as having a heavenly nature? Did you think of Him as a teacher in Galilee or as the Lord from heaven? What new things did you learn if any?
2. Do you understand the way in which Christ leads a person through the indwelling Holy Spirit?
3. If you sin against Christ your Lord, what assurance do you have that you will not be rejected by Him? On what is this based?
4. What ways can you improve your teaching to new converts?

RESEARCH SUGGESTIONS:

1. Read and study some of the following passages and consider the

implications about who Christ is: Exodus 3:1-15; Ezekiel 1:1-3,25-28; Daniel 10:5-10; Matthew 17:1-6; Revelation 1:12-18.
2. Make a list of other Scriptures that especially disclose the heavenly nature and origin of Jesus.
3. Read Geerhardus Vos, *The Self-Disclosure of Jesus* (Grand Rapids: Eerdmans, 1954), pp. 13-36, 105-254.

Chapter 6

Ministry Training and Appreciation of Benefits

CONTENT QUESTIONS:

1. Why was it appropriate for Jesus to begin training some men to share His ministry at this time?
2. List five reasons why training men to have a public ministry is difficult.
3. What are some of the things Jesus did to help the disciples overcome obstacles to having a ministry with Him?
4. What kind of ministry did Jesus emphasize when He called His men?
5. What three main benefits did Jesus teach and demonstrate that He came to give?

THOUGHT QUESTIONS FOR THE INDIVIDUAL OR FOR GROUP DISCUSSION:

1. Why did Jesus contend most against the laws of the Sabbath while Paul was most concerned about the law of circumcision? Are there any laws Christians have set today that are misused like these were? What are they? Explain why you feel they are in the same category.
2. Why did the Jews get angry about Jesus' claim to be able to forgive sin? Why were they angry about His claims in regards to the Sabbath day?
3. How would you use some of the same principles that Jesus used to get a group of people to become involved in your ministry?
4. What simple but important method did Jesus use to teach His disciples to have a ministry? Is it still valid today?
5. Is ministry training relevant to leadership development? Why? Why will any ministry cease to grow at a certain point unless others are trained to have a ministry?
6. In the steps of Repentance and of Ministry Training one is taught about forgiveness of sin, liberty through the Holy Spirit, and deliverance from the physical consequences of sin through Jesus

Christ. What is the difference in the way these things are taught at each of the different steps?

ACHIEVEMENT QUESTIONS:

1. In evaluating your disciples, how many of them do you feel would be willing to give up their jobs and future plans to learn how to reach and build men?
2. Prayerfully look to the Lord for ways to show your disciples how much more important the kingdom of God is than anything else they can invest their time in. Write out the ways you feel God would have you challenge them. Seek to make the plan for challenging them relevant to their situation. Example: If one is a high school teacher, challenge him to seek to start a pre-school prayer meeting at school and begin it by sharing his testimony with the students who attend.
3. How would you train a disciple to share his faith with someone personally? to hold a home evangelistic meeting? to give an evangelistic message to a group meeting of about fifty people?

RESEARCH SUGGESTIONS:

1. If you have not had much biblical training, read Gordon Bridger's *A Day That Changed the World* (Downer's Grove, Illinois: Inter-Varsity Press, 1975), 96 pages. For a consideration of the meaning of salvation in contrast to false views being taught, I suggest you read J. Gresham Machen's *Christianity and Liberalism* (Grand Rapids: Eerdmans, 1923, reprinted 1974), pp. 117-156. For those with more technical biblical training I suggest you read and study James Denney's *The Death of Christ* (Downers Grove, Illinois: Inter-Varsity Press) listed in their 1976 catalogue, paperback, 207 pages (originally printed by Hodder and Stoughton, London, 1902, 2nd ed.) or Leon Morris' *The Apostolic Preaching of the Cross* (Grand Rapids: Eerdmans, 1955), 280 pages.

Chapter 7

Leadership Development and Government Under God

CONTENT QUESTIONS:

1. What was the event that seems to have led to Jesus' withdrawal from Capernaum, the appointment of leaders, and the organization of His kingdom?
2. What Old Testament event was Jesus probably copying when He

came down on the plain, appointed twelve leaders, and gave the Sermon on the Mount?

3. What were some of the conditions that called for new and additional leadership?
4. What are some of the factors that should be involved in choosing new leaders?
5. Why did Jesus choose twelve men instead of ten or thirteen?
6. What are some of the reasons for a public ordination or recognition service for appointing new leaders?
7. Jesus drew strong contrasts between the religious acts of the Pharisees and the acts His disciples should exhibit. List as many of these contrasts as you can.
8. Who are the leaders of the two conflicting kingdoms? Who is the victor and how did this occur?
9. In what way did Jesus demonstrate His power as King? Name some of His credentials of authority.
10. What were some of the missionary principles that Jesus taught His disciples before sending them out?
11. What event occurred at the end of this step of Leadership that made it even more important to have the twelve new leaders?

THOUGHT QUESTIONS FOR THE INDIVIDUAL OR FOR GROUP DISCUSSION:

1. Can you think of leaders in modern times who have led whole nations to commit atrocities and evil? Who are two men in the Bible by whom all people have been affected? Name some leaders in the Bible who led others into evil. Name some who led them to obey God.
2. Is God just in charging the leaders with the fundamental responsibility for the direction of moral action that the people take? Why do you feel this way?
3. Why is there a relationship between a father's leadership of his home and an ability to be a leader in a church? How important is spiritual maturity to being an effective leader? What was the difference in the women leaders and the men?
4. What are some of the reasons God might use a team of leaders rather than just one person? Do you know any churches that function with a team leadership?
5. What is the danger of waiting too long to appoint leaders? What is the danger of appointing them too soon? What are some conditions that indicate it is time to appoint additional new leaders?

ACHIEVEMENT QUESTIONS:

1. In evaluating your disciples, how well have they learned to have a

ministry and how ready are they for being appointed leaders? Have they learned to do personal evangelism? To speak to a group? To lead a small group Bible study?

2. Have you and your disciples personally experienced spiritual combat against Satan and his kingdom? In what ways? What power is it that enables you and your disciples to overcome Satan?

3. Are you seeing your disciples overcome the power of Satan in their lives? Give examples.

RESEARCH SUGGESTIONS:

1. Have the members of small discipleship groups read J. Oswald Sanders, *Spiritual Leadership* (Chicago: Moody, 1967). Select and assign certain chapters and ask each member of the group to compare Sanders's ideas of leadership with Christ's concepts of leadership presented in chapter 7 on Leadership Development and Government Under God.

2. Have the members of the discipleship group take select chapters of Harold Lindsell's *The World, the Flesh, and the Devil* (Minneapolis: Worldwide Publications, 1973) and evaluate the spiritual conflict presented there with the conflict between Christ and Satan in the Gospels.

Chapter 8

Reevaluation and Separation

CONTENT QUESTIONS:

1. Give reasons why it was time for Jesus to challenge His disciples to put eternal values over temporal values.

2. In what way did Jesus prepare His men to accept the claim that He came to establish an eternal kingdom?

3. Why did Jesus feed the five thousand with earthly bread and then tell them not to labor for that but for eternal sustenance? Why did He heal many with extreme diseases but not all? In what way were these miracles, done to a limited number of people, intended to point to something greater?

4. What event in Jesus' ministry caused the crowds to be offended and turn away from Him?

5. In what way had the Pharisees transgressed God's law by following the traditional law of Corban?

6. What did Jesus do that threatened the narrow Jewish nationalism of His day?

7. What is the meaning of the phrase "gates of hades" in Greek

writings? What did Jesus mean when He used this phrase? What is meant by saying "If a person seeks to save his life he will lose it, but if he loses his life for Christ, he will find it again"?

8. In what way did the disciples get a preview of what eternal life would look like?
9. What experience taught the apostles that satanic forces could be overcome only by the power of the Holy Spirit?

THOUGHT QUESTIONS:

1. Name some ways that Christian values should differ from non-Christian values.
2. What is the basic reason for the separation between Christians and the world?
3. Do people deliberately let human traditions, rather than God's Word, control them, or do they usually just follow along with what is traditionally considered right?
4. How significant is the matter of following human tradition rather than divine revelation?
5. Does human tradition usually support and promote heavenly or temporal values? Why? Why would obeying God's Word support heavenly values rather than temporal ones?
6. In what way does greed for temporal things contribute to the economic problems of the West? How would the Christian example of putting eternal values first affect these problems?

ACHIEVEMENT QUESTIONS:

1. Have you ever faced a situation in life when you had to choose eternal over temporal values (for example, give up job security to pursue Christ's will, forsake a person you love for Christ's sake, etc.)? Would you be willing to forsake anything if Christ called you to do so for His sake?
2. In what ways might you practically challenge your disciples to put eternal things over the temporal, God's kingdom over man's?

RESEARCH QUESTIONS:

1. Make a list of things you do in your church that you can clearly show were done in the same way in the New Testament church. Make another list of things you do in your church that were not done in the New Testament church. Do any of the differences violate the Word of God in letter or spirit?
2. How many modern preachers, movements, or groups with which you are acquainted are emphasizing present temporal values rather than eternal ones? Study to learn more about various sects in this regard.

Chapter 9

Participation and Delegation

CONTENT QUESTIONS:

1. What is the objective of the step of Participation and Delegation?
2. What developments in Christ's movement led to the need to teach His followers how to conduct themselves as a body now distinct from the world?
3. Why did Christ appoint the Seventy?
4. What are some of the problems that Jesus gave His church guidelines to meet?
5. How did Jesus meet those who openly opposed Him and were hostile to Him?
6. What conditions today indicate the church in the United States and the Western world may soon face open hostility as never before?
7. What were some of the things Jesus publicly claimed when He was in Jerusalem at the Feast of Tabernacles about the time He sent the Seventy out to minister?
8. What Jewish prejudices did Jesus correct at this time?
9. What were the primary errors of the religion of Jesus' time? Do these same errors exist in other forms today?
10. In what way did Jesus demonstrate His authority over death?

THOUGHT QUESTIONS:

1. Why is it easier for us to trust Christ to work in us than to trust Him to work in others? What would happen if we learned to trust Him to work in others?
2. If we could learn to trust Christ to work in others, how would it affect specific relationships between a husband and his wife, between parents and their children, between an employer and his employees, and between church leaders and the members?
3. How would you apply the teachings of Christ to the following situations:
   a. Your church has put you in charge of its daily vacation Bible school. You and the committee in charge, working with the pastor, decided to use some study materials you feel are better for your purposes than those printed by the church's denomination. You are criticized by one or two members for being disloyal. What will you say? What will you do?
   b. One of the younger members of your church is challenging the leadership of an officially appointed leader. This younger

member is obviously eager to become the leader. What should he be taught?

c. You are youth advisor for your church. An interdenominational youth movement has begun meetings in a home in your community. They seem to love Christ and want to honor Him. What should your attitude toward this movement be?

d. A new pastor comes to your church and begins teaching things that don't agree with Scripture and dishonor Christ. What will you do?

e. A young man from your church moves in to live with a young divorcee. How should he be corrected?

f. Your business partner repeatedly gets angry with you for little things but repeatedly repents and asks for forgiveness. How long should you go on taking this?

g. You are doing interdenominational evangelistic work in a community and the pastor of a denomination tells his youth not to cooperate with your ministry. What should be your attitude toward that pastor?

4. You are attending a small college and start a Christian group on the campus. Some men in the administration say your teaching is antiquated and anti-intellectual, how should you meet their criticism?

ACHIEVEMENT QUESTIONS:

1. Consider how many instances and what circumstances there have been in which you have acted so as to trust Christ in other Christians.

2. Plan ways in which you can begin to trust Christ to use others in the ways you are not trusting Him at present.

3. Do you know what gift or gifts God has given you to serve in the church?

4. Do you consider your gift or gifts from the Lord to be more important than the gifts of others? Do you feel you have a gift everyone should have?

5. Plan ways in which you can use your gifts to help others.

RESEARCH QUESTIONS:

1. Get a good book on management and compare the principles of delegation used by Jesus with those found there; e.g., Louis A. Allen's *The Management Profession* (New York: McGraw, 1964), pp. 198-216.

2. Study the outline on discipleship, using A. T. Robertson's *A Harmony of the Gospels for Students of the Life of Christ* (New York: Harper & Row, 1950), pp. 131-136. See how many reli-

gious errors Jesus mentioned there that exist today in some form within the church.

Chapter 10

The Exchanged Life and Worldwide Challenge

CONTENT QUESTIONS:

1. Indicate if the following questions are true or false:
   a. The working of the Holy Spirit was talked about and evident from the beginning of Christ's ministry.
   b. The disciples still saw themselves as important to the kingdom.
   c. Jesus didn't know He would die at Jerusalem but planned to set up an earthly kingdom when He rode into Jerusalem.
   d. Jesus clearly foresaw that Israel as a nation would be set aside for a new people made up of all nations.
2. In the final moments when Jesus was with them in Gethsemane what did He teach Peter, James, and John about the flesh?
3. Enumerate the ways in which the experience of the Holy Spirit in the lives of the Twelve was the same and the ways it was different from that of all Christians since.
4. What was unique about the coming of the Holy Spirit on the day of Pentecost?
5. Indicate if the following questions are true or false about the exchanged life:
   a. A person becomes sinless.
   b. A person will perhaps fail or get depressed but he will know why and he will know how to return immediately to victory.
   c. A person will rest in the adequacy of Christ through the Holy Spirit.
   d. A person will no longer feel he must have a miracle every day to be sure God is with him.

THOUGHT QUESTIONS:

1. Why is learning the complete adequacy of the Spirit of the risen Christ usually the last step or final test before severing one's teaching relationship to a disciple?
2. Why did Jesus link the challenge of carrying the gospel and His teachings of the kingdom to the whole world to the step of resting in the adequacy of his power?
3. Do most disciples today tend to identify their earthly ministry with the ultimate kingdom of God and therefore give far too much

value to their efforts and accomplishments? Do we tend to build our own little kingdoms and think it is the kingdom of God? How can we avoid this?

4. What are the indications that a person who has been an effective Christian leader is in need of learning the lesson of the exchanged life?

5. In what ways might you help your disciples to experience the exchanged life?

ACHIEVEMENT QUESTIONS:

1. Is the working of the Spirit in our lives like a river of water giving life everywhere, or like a dripping faucet? What did Jesus say was the key to the working of the Spirit (John 7:37-39)? Have you learned to rest in the sufficiency of the Spirit?

2. Are there times when you feel God is a thousand miles away when you wish you could feel His presence? Have you ever become professional in your ministry for Him and done things in your own ability without looking to Him?

RESEARCH QUESTION:

1. Read V. Raymond Edman, ed., *They Found the Secret* (Grand Rapids: Zondervan, 1960) 159 pp., or *Crisis Experiences* (Minneapolis: Bethany Fellowship) 96 pp., and evaluate these testimonies as to whether they describe the step of the Exchanged Life.

Chapter 11

Association for Communication

CONTENT QUESTIONS:

1. Match the step with the characteristics that describe the relationship:

   a. Step One   ____1. Helping the leader direct a larger new group of leaders.

   b. Step Two   ____2. Being weaned from direct personal association to a dependence only on the Spirit.

   c. Step Three   ____3. A small intimate select group, without others being selected and added.

d. Step Four _____4. An open, small group that is
  and   growing, with people
 Step Five   coming and going.

e. Step Six   _____5. Casual association to reach
        the most people.

f. Step Seven _____6. A select group of twelve,
        closed to others.

2. Indicate which are true and which are false:
   a. Jesus began with a casual relationship to a group of men from whom He selected some who became more and more intimately involved in a growing movement.
   b. Jesus waited until He had a large group of intimate followers and then all at once gave them the responsibility of leadership.
   c. Jesus had different relationships to several different groups of people at the same time.
   d. One associates in the same way at each step of discipleship training.
3. List the unique values of a small-group association.
4. What are some of the things Jesus did to find opportunity to associate more closely with His men?
5. Name some things that indicate Jesus' close association with His men.

THOUGHT QUESTIONS:
1. Why is the principle of moving with the interested people so important? Why do most churches fail to follow this principle?
2. The old-line denominational churches often use small-group Sunday school classes that are not very effective. What is often the missing factor in these small groups?
3. Why is development of middle management so important in order to multiply a close association for a growing number of disciples?

ACHIEVEMENT QUESTIONS:
1. Have you established the right kind of association to communicate best with your disciples at their state of development?
2. What things did Jesus do that you aren't doing with your disciples that might enable you to communicate better?
3. Try to recall the times you have met individually with each of your disciples. Plan a schedule to meet with each of them personally.
4. Is your small-group association one of lecture-type teaching or is there opportunity for dialogue?

RESEARCH SUGGESTIONS:

1. Examine the history of a number of organizations and see if close association by the leader was the key to its original growth.
   a. Religions: Buddhism, Mohammedanism, Sikhism, et al.
   b. Businesses: General Electric Co., J. C. Penney Co., et al.
2. Survey some of the people you know who are effective Christian laymen and see if a close personal relationship with a more mature Christian was an important element in their growth.

Chapter 12

Fellowship for Discipleship

CONTENT QUESTIONS:

1. Circle the letters of the statements that apply to *Christian* fellowship:
   a. Fellowship always occurs when Christians meet together.
   b. Fellowship involves a two-dimensional relationship; first, vertically with God and, second, horizontally with men.
   c. Fellowship with Christ is maintained daily by the Holy Spirit through the written Word of God.
   d. The word "fellowship" means "sharing."
2. List five Christian virtues or character qualities that help produce the kind of fellowship conducive to helping a Christian grow.
3. What are the reasons small groups are conducive to promoting vital fellowship?
4. What part should spiritual gifts play in promoting fellowship?
5. In what ways should the pastor or leader of a group take the initiative in establishing the right kind of fellowship?

THOUGHT QUESTIONS:

1. Why is a person's ability to receive teaching from another related to his trust in the person teaching him? How do each of the Christian virtues mentioned in your answer to Content Question no. 2 affect this ability to trust and receive teaching?
2. How do each of these Christian virtues affect a person's ability to share with others?
3. Why is hospitality often a key point for opening up sharing or fellowship in regard to spiritual and personal things? Why does eating together at church not stimulate fellowship as much as if a leader of the church invites a group into his home and provides food for them?

ACHIEVEMENT QUESTIONS:

1. List specific ways and times you feel you have manifested each of the virtues or characteristics that help produce fellowship conducive to growth. Plan ways you can improve in these.
2. Do you feel you show hospitality toward others? Plan ways you can improve in this.
3. Do your small-group meetings have a free sharing of the members with each other? How can this be improved?

RESEARCH SUGGESTIONS:

1. Evaluate the following as to how much sharing they allow the people to do:
   a. The way study is conducted in your discipleship group.
   b. The way various churches of your community are organized and function.
2. Read John R. W. Stott's book, *One People* (Downers Grove, Illinois: Inter-Varsity Press, 1968), and discuss principles of fellowship exhibited in the book.

Chapter 13

Involvement and Disciple Building

CONTENT QUESTIONS:

1. Indicate whether each statement is true or false:
   a. The proper motive for involving individuals in a ministry is to help the individual develop, be useful, and bring glory to God.
   b. It is good to get people involved in Christ's work as much as possible any way you can.
   c. Everyone needs to become involved and grow in involvement according to the progress of his maturity.
   d. The Twelve developed their ability to handle responsibility as their responsibility grew over a three-year period.
2. Match the appropriate involvement with the step:

   a. Repentance and Faith _____ 1. Do simple tasks, e.g., buy food.

   b. Enlightenment _____ 2. Stand with Jesus when many forsake Him.

   c. Ministry Training _____ 3. Conduct public baptism.

   d. Leadership Development _____ 4. Learn how to delegate authority to others.

   e. Reevaluation and Separation _____ 5. Show how to conduct an evangelistic tour.

f. Participation and _____ 6. Conduct a ministry alone
    Delegation   without personal
                             supervision.

g. Exchanged Life _____ 7. Have authority to go on a
                             tour alone for Christ.

3. List the four steps involved in transferring responsibility.

THOUGHT QUESTIONS:

1. Name some of the ways Christians can abuse the use of others in a Christian ministry.
2. In the following situation, what would be proper?
   A prominent student body leader from a non-Christian home has become a Christian; he has grown very rapidly and has the confidence of his fellow Christian students. Would you or would you not begin to let him take a leadership position after a few weeks? What would be the consequences for the student and for those in the group, in both alternatives?
3. Can you conceive of situations where it would be best to limit a person's involvement? If so, state them and explain why.

ACHIEVEMENT QUESTIONS:

1. Can you trace an increasing involvement of yourself in Christ's work, especially in recent months?
2. What disciples do you have that need more involvement or a different kind of involvement? Plan ways to correct these.

RESEARCH SUGGESTIONS:

1. Interview several persons as to how their involvement in ministry has affected their growth rate. Did they grow more rapidly when more involved, or grow less? What kinds of involvement affect growth most?
2. Read a short biography of a Christian and see if you can trace the evidences of growth in maturity to his ministry involvement; e.g., Isabel Kuhn, Dwight L. Moody, Hudson Taylor.

Chapter 14

Motivation and Momentum

CONTENT QUESTIONS:

1. Define the following:
   motivation
   momentum

intrinsic motivation
extrinsic motivation
sustained momentum
2. Explain the relationship between motivation and momentum as they relate to the individuals and the movement.
3. How are motivation and momentum related to growth of the individual and of the movement?
4. What is the relationship between quantity and quality in regard to momentum?
5. What are the four elements essential to motivating people to achieve a sustained momentum?
6. Name ten ways Jesus motivated people in order to gain momentum in His movement.

THOUGHT QUESTIONS FOR INDIVIDUALS AND FOR GROUP DISCUSSION:

1. Picture a situation in which great emotion might be risky or even dangerous. Describe a situation in which some emotion might be healthy and helpful.
2. Review ministry experiences you know about in which quick momentum was created but did not last long. Analyze these and seek to determine as well as possible why the momentum was not sustained. Suggest things that might have been done to continue the momentum.
3. Which is more important in Christian work, growth in quantity or in quality?
4. Think of situations in the past in which you have seen or heard of a lack of unity among Christians. What might have been done in these situations to promote Christian unity?
5. Make up reasonable ministry situations and decide which emphases you would use to motivate a disciple in those situations.

ACHIEVEMENT QUESTIONS:

1. How would you evaluate your level of motivation?
   Poor   1   2   3   4   5   Good
   If your motivation is not very good, what do you feel are the reasons for this? Plan ways to improve.
2. How much sustained momentum have you had in your ministry? If momentum is not good and your disciples are not motivated, what can you do to improve this?

RESEARCH SUGGESTIONS:

1. Read the biographies of missionaries or the history of certain movements and evaluate the means used by the leaders to moti-

vate the people and create momentum in their work; e.g., Hudson Taylor, Dwight L. Moody, C. T. Studd, Bill Bright, Billy Graham.

2. Work with someone else who is leading a ministry (such as a pastor) to evaluate momentum and motivation. Then discuss with them the things that cause the momentum if it is good, or things that could be done to improve the momentum if it is poor. Watch the efforts to make improvement and evaluate them.

Chapter 15

Evangelism and Discipleship

CONTENT QUESTIONS:

1. Name the three forms of evangelism in which Jesus trained His men.
2. In addition to learning how to share one's faith with individuals, what else is needed before personal evangelism will occur?
3. What are the benefits of party or home evangelism?
4. What are the unique benefits of mass evangelism?
5. How many waves of alternating evangelism and disciple building did Jesus conduct?
6. Historically, how and when did the division between evangelism and disciple building begin?
7. Who was the liberal scholar who revived an interest in Christian nurture?

THOUGHT QUESTIONS FOR INDIVIDUALS AND FOR GROUP DISCUSSION:

1. Why does personal witnessing enable a disciple to grow?
2. In what ways can each different form of evangelism help or support the others?
3. In what ways are evangelism and building disciples interrelated?
4. Why is there a growing tension between evangelism and disciple building? How can this be averted?

ACHIEVEMENT QUESTIONS:

1. Do you have a good balance of evangelism and disciple building in your life and ministry? How can you plan to achieve a better balance?
2. Have you trained your disciples to use and appreciate all forms of evangelism so that they can practice them effectively?
3. What can you do to help reunify the efforts of evangelism and disciple building?

RESEARCH SUGGESTIONS:

1. Write to some of the largest evangelistic organizations and inquire how they formulated their strategy for church cooperation. Especially ask how many active pastors were involved in planning the strategy. Also, inquire into what is being done by these organizations to cooperate with the churches so that their converts are effectively assimilated into the churches. Inquire into what efforts they have made to discover how many of their converts continue to be active in the churches six months or a year later.
2. Scan some of the current books on evangelism and evaluate them as to their understanding and emphasis on building disciples; e.g., D. James Kennedy, *Evangelism Explosion* (Wheaton: Tyndale, 1970), Mendall Taylor, *Exploring Evangelism* (Kansas City, Missouri: Beacon Hill, 1964).

Chapter 16

Prayer

CONTENT QUESTIONS:

1. Name some of the ways Scripture emphasizes the importance of prayer.
   a. generally
   b. in the life of Christ
   c. in the early church
   d. in the Epistles
2. List four reasons why we *must* pray.
3. Match each of the following steps with the prayers that would be most emphasized at that step.
   a. Repentance and Faith
   b. Enlightenment and Guidance
   c. Ministry Training
   d. Leadership Development
   e. Reevaluation and Separation
   f. Participation and Delegation
   g. Exchanged Life

   _____ 1. for sanctification by the truth and keeping from the evil one
   _____ 2. for intercession for other members of the body
   _____ 3. for an open door to preach and for boldness
   _____ 4. for the disciples to choose to live for the eternal rather than the temporal
   _____ 5. for the Spirit to draw disciples to you and open their eyes to see the greatness of Christ

_____ 6. for guidance in choosing initial leaders

_____ 7. for God to show select disciples that to fish for men is more important than their vocations

THOUGHT QUESTIONS FOR INDIVIDUALS AND FOR GROUP DISCUSSION:

1. Why may one do everything else right in building disciples and still fail if he does not pray?
2. Why does it usually seem easier to carry out a program of activities than it does to have a consistent prayer ministry?
3. If one of your disciples is being tempted by Satan, are there biblical grounds for believing God will protect or restore him if you pray for him?
4. On what basis can you believe that God will answer clear objective prayer, thereby giving His endorsement to the biblical teaching you give your disciples?

ACHIEVEMENT QUESTIONS:

1. How faithful are you to spend time daily praying for your disciples? To what would you attribute your success or failure? What specific steps can you take to correct any failure in this regard?
2. What can you do to help motivate your disciples to pray more?

RESEARCH SUGGESTIONS:

1. Study the passages in the Pauline Epistles that relate Paul's prayers for his disciples in the churches (cf. pp. 225ff.). List the different things he prayed for on their behalf. Consider how these should influence your prayers and those of your disciples.
2. Read Andrew Murray, *The Ministry of Intercession* (New York: Revell, 1898). Make a list of ideas you learn that you feel will help you in your life of intercession for your disciples.

Chapter 17

Application of Truth to Obtain Obedience

CONTENT QUESTIONS:

1. What was the inherent danger in the Reformation and why? Why is this especially crucial for today?
2. What danger should we guard against in correcting the error mentioned in the first question?
3. Why are the efforts of all ministry frustrated if obedience is not attained? Explain.

4. Who bears the chief responsibility before God of obedience or disobedience among His people?

5. What was the agreement of the people of Israel in the old covenant?

6. What is the agreement of Jesus' disciples in the new covenant?

7. Indicate which of the following statements are correct by listing their letters and omitting those that are incorrect:

   a. The dispensation of the old covenant ended with John the Baptist.

   b. The old covenant required outward obedience to the letter of the law, while the new covenant requires an attitude of obedience in the heart to the spirit of the Law.

   c. The new does away with the commands of the old.

   d. The violations of the old covenant are punished by the sacrifice made for the new.

   e. The old covenant focused on obedience to laws before men while the new covenant focuses on pleasing the Lawgiver personally.

   f. The old covenant is summarized in requiring the members to love others even to the giving of themselves.

   g. The old covenant promises judgment, while the new offers grace and forgiveness.

   h. The old covenant pertains to God's reign over Israel in earthly life, while the new covenant pertains to God's kingdom of eternal life.

   i. The old covenant looks to blessings under the old creation, while the new covenant has hope based on the resurrection and the new creation.

8. What is the meaning of the "principle of obedience" and of the "practice of obedience?" In what step is the "principle of obedience" accepted and how does it relate to the "practice of obedience"?

9. What is the motive of obedience?

10. Name three errors in regard to obedience.

11. How should truth be applied if obedience is to be achieved?

12. Name five ways to communicate truth so as to apply it and obtain obedience.

13. At what point does a human teacher make himself a judge and step between the Lord and His subjects?

14. What are some of the ways interpretations and practices by leaders can be kept within the boundaries of the clear teachings of Christ?

15. What are the four levels for application of the truth? Which is the

most open to rationalization? Which is most important as the place where truth is ultimately applied?

16. Tell why obedience to Christ is important to every person. Why is it important for the Christian?

THOUGHT QUESTIONS FOR THE INDIVIDUAL OR FOR GROUP DISCUSSION:

1. What is one error to which many evangelical Bible colleges and seminaries are likely to be vulnerable in regard to obedience? What are some things that could be done to help minimize this?
2. In seeking to promote a revival of obedience to Christ, what group should be first addressed as responsible for the present situation and for changing it? How would you advise them to go about effecting the change?
3. Why will a person's obedience to Christ's command to love as He loved enable all men to know he is His disciple? How well are church members doing this today?
4. What truth about God would you emphasize most if you wished to motivate people to obey Christ?
5. What part does Christ's example or the example of Christian leaders play in promoting obedience, and what is the part of the Holy Spirit?

ACHIEVEMENT QUESTIONS:

1. Have you been aware that as a Christian your covenant responsibility is to die to self, to love God and others sacrificially?
2. Are you willing to trust Christ through His Holy Spirit to love others sacrificially through you? Is there anything you would not give up or do for Christ?

RESEARCH QUESTIONS:

1. Make a study of a church or several churches and see what part communicating the ways of applying truth are used. For example, how often do the leaders urge the people to follow their example or the example of Christ? How much public sharing is done by the people so as to allow identification? How often are people publicly or privately commanded to do the will of Christ? How much actual exhorting, reproving, or rebuking is done?
2. Have every member of the group read Andrew Murray's *The School of Obedience* (Chicago: Moody, n.d.) and keep notes on ways you are failing to do and teach obedience. Compare these.

Chapter 18

Conclusion: A Call to Strategy and Dedication

CONTENT QUESTIONS:

1. How important is a practical strategy for implementing the New Testament method of disciple building? Illustrate.
2. Why should our strategy begin with the church?
3. Who should be responsible for initiating a program of disciple building in a church?
4. Why must the program include dialogue between disciples and leader as well as lectures?
5. How can this program of training in disciple building be transferred to many in the churches through the pastors?
6. What seems the wisest approach to reinstituting disciple building at the university level? Why are the universities important?
7. Why should disciple building be the basic thing in the curriculum, with apologetics only a supplement?
8. Why should Christians take care not to be anti-intellectual but at the same time not put a strong emphasis on degree honors? Should teachers be favored or disdained because they have earned degrees?
9. Indicate which statements are true and which are false:
   a. The F.C.L. can combine the benefits of the "cluster college" and the "guest-lecture" approach.
   b. Christian colleges should be neglected because they are not as important as reaching the secular campuses.
   c. The F.C.L. cannot operate within legal limits of the U.S. Constitution, but F.C.L.s should be established anyway.
   d. Secular professors who attack religious views cannot legally be stopped from doing this.
   e. A drawback of the F.C.L. is that it requires additional study time that some students cannot give.
10. What good will reading this book and even agreeing with it accomplish if *you* do nothing to train men to be disciple builders?

THOUGHT QUESTIONS FOR INDIVIDUALS AND FOR GROUP DISCUSSION:

1. Considering all the facts about the conditions in our modern world, do you feel the strategy advocated in this book makes sense? How would you improve on it? What can you do to help effect it?

2. In your estimation, is it possible that God the Holy Spirit could lead different evangelical groups and leaders of organizations to cooperate in carrying out such a strategy? What would have to be done for this to occur? Would you be willing to pray for this?
3. Could a local university near you profit by having an F.C.L. located there? What could you do to help get one going?
4. Would God likely restrain His hand of judgment against America if He saw the church leaders become serious about implementing a strategy to build disciples that would seek to "teach them to observe all things" that Christ commanded?

ACHIEVEMENT QUESTIONS:

1. How concerned are you about the way God is dishonored in some churches and in America?
2. Are you willing to pay the price to do something about these conditions for Christ? Are you willing to be questioned and perhaps looked down on for cooperating outside your group or denomination? Are you willing to work harder and receive less? What steps are you ready to take *now?*

RESEARCH SUGGESTIONS:

Write to several organizations that you feel might help you implement an effective disciple-building program in your church, your school, your place of work. Evaluate what they offer you and begin to implement what you think is best.

Addenda

1. Report on Current Evangelistic Expansion

In the twentieth century there has been an evangelism explosion throughout the world. David Barrett has compiled statistics on the growth of Christianity in Africa, using information from the Protestant, Roman Catholic, and African Independent groups. In 1900 approximately 3 percent of the African population were Christian. By 1970, however, the percentage of African Christians had increased to 28 percent. Mr. Barrett predicts that at the present rate 46 percent of the continent will be Christian by the year 2000.

On the basis of this report he predicts that Christianity will become the major religion of Africa in the not-too-distant future. While divisions and diversity of thought do exist, there is no question but that the evangelization of Africa is proceeding at an unprecedented speed.

Clyde Taylor has pointed out that the same growth is occurring in Asia. Billy Graham has stated that the church is growing four times faster than the population in South Korea. At the one-week Billy Graham crusade in Seoul, Korea (1973), 75,000 people accepted Jesus Christ. South Korea hosted Explo '74 (sponsored by Campus Crusade for Christ), where 325,000 people were trained to share their faith. It was anticipated that every person in the nation of South Korea would be confronted with the gospel by 1976. In the Philippines 12,500 teams have been trained by the "Christ-the-Only-Way" movement to evangelize the country. The evangelistic teams are made up of laymen. In northeast India, Christians now form a majority of the population. There has been an amazing revival in Indonesia. Multitudes have become Christians in the last decade in this predominately Moslem nation.

South America is experiencing a similar evangelism "explosion." According to Ralph Winters, the Christian population of Chile is doubling every four years. In Brazil, it is doubling every seven years, whereas the population itself doubles every twenty years.

Billy Graham said to the delegates at the World Congress on Evangelization (1974), "In North America, especially the United States, there has been a remarkable upsurge of interest in the gospel in the last decade, especially among youth.'' In 1972 the *U.S. News and World Report* published a book entitled *The Religious Reawakening in America,* which featured an evangelistic expansion among the Jesus People, the Catholic Pentecostals, and many other groups.

Recently, Campus Crusade for Christ has begun to work with churches to help committees and to serve as a resource in order to evangelize all of the major population centers of the nation. Its plans in 1975 included an anticipated 50,000 decisions for Christ in Nashville, and over 100,000 in Atlanta. Campus Crusade for Christ has planned, in time, to have similar city-wide campaigns in every population center of the country under the banner name, ''Here's Life, America.'' The Billy Graham organization continues to have a dynamic impact on many of the cities of this country. Also Pentecostal groups and other evangelistic groups are presently growing at a rapid rate.

2. Frustrations of Pastors

Many pastors have been trained in the seminaries that teach humanistic and antisupernatural views. They have been taught that they are the hand-maids who will usher in a modern utopia by their preaching and social reforms. As a result, there has been considerable disillusionment among these contemporary pastors.

Modern history has exposed the false optimism in human nature, and many of the basic programs of social reforms have not been successful. The movement toward racial equality and racial integration has now found itself at a point with no answer. As early as 1965 the black leaders of the racial movement pushed the liberal, social-gospel leaders out of the racial fore-front and out of the black organizations. The Supreme Court edicts and pressure from the federal government have not helped close the gap between the economic status of the white and the black. Neither has mob violence succeeded. Moreover, the successful integration of southern school systems has not changed matters a great deal. The reaction of the northern com-munities (such as in Boston) to social integration has shown that the ''white'' south is not the chief culprit in matters of racial prejudice but that there exists a basic failure in human nature that those with an antibiblical bias have not been willing to take into account.

The student thrust of the liberal movement began to show a lack of power during and especially following World War II, as the Student Volun-teer Movement phased out. It came to an end on the national level in the United States in 1969 when the University Christian Movement was closed down as an ecumenical structure. In the following years, the students of the national and international meetings sponsored by the churches of the World Council of Churches rejected the traditional Christian position and took a very radical stance. The radical extremes to which the student campus movements went in the Students for a Democratic Society and its successors shocked even the liberal adult leadership, which was often thrust aside and scorned.

When the International Missionary Council and the World Council of Churches merged in recent years as a result of the ecumenical movement, the resultant World Council of Churches organization virtually gave up the mission of the church as that of evangelistic preaching of the gospel and discipling the converts and substituted helping satisfy human physical needs. The movement to unify the churches has come to a stalemate because of an impasse in the debate over the necessity of apostolic succession and the contrary position of the Reformed churches. The latter hold that faith and a personal call by God and the contemporary churches are adequate credentials for ordination.

In addition to these problems, man's intellectual achievements in the areas of science, psychology, and sociology seem to have failed him, for pollution and economic insecurity threaten his very existence.

Hence, men's faith in the ability of man to build his own utopia has begun to falter, and many pastors who have been trained in the social gospel with an aim to build the "secular city" have nothing to preach. Thus, their theology has very little attraction today. For this reason, many of the old-line denominational seminaries have begun to dwindle and even to close.

Frustrations of the Evangelical Pastors

Even in evangelical groups (who draw their men from evangelical seminaries) there is tremendous frustration for the pastor in trying to lead a church. The trends that are discussed in the first chapter have placed the pastor in the position of a lecturer and an administrator who seldom sees anyone obey his preaching. Moreover, he is often the target of criticism. He finds himself faced with many people who have little biblical knowledge or understanding or willingness to respond to the truth. Generally speaking, even many laymen with evangelical views are too busy in business and pleasure to do the work of the church.

In recent years there has been a refreshing revival of personal evangelism among laymen. Laymen have learned something about the Scriptures and are especially excited about the basic message of the gospel. In many cases the clergy have found themselves threatened by the laymen who have learned from other sources how to communicate their faith. These laymen are often critical of the pastor because he is not personally involved in training them or sharing his faith. These laymen often do not understand the problems of the pastorate. Although well-meaning, they add to the frustrations of the pastor. They need to be trained so they can share all the pastor's burdens with him. Moreover, they need to be discipled by the pastor himself so they will continue to follow his leading.

The harvest of the years of the Jesus Movement is beginning to be felt in the seminaries, producing an 11-percent rise in enrollment from the fall of 1974 to 1975. Generally, the more evangelical the school, the higher the increase of enrollment has been. The number of new men entering the ministry is not as great as it appears by this, because much of the increase is in post-basic studies. This itself *may* indicate a dissatisfaction with ministry in the churches. In 1969, registrations for basic studies accounted for 79.5

percent, whereas in 1975-1976 it was only 63.3 percent. (See *Christianity Today,* May 21, 1976, vol. 20, no. 17, pp. 34,35.)

3. Evaluation of the Theory of a Four-Year-Ministry

Johnston M. Cheney's *The Life of Christ in Stereo* (Portland, Oregon: Western Baptist Seminary Press, 1969), is a valuable contribution to a study of the material in the Gospels. However, I have not taken seriously his claim for a four-and-a-quarter-year ministry of Christ. He bases this on "new material" that he claims he has found in doing this work. His two basic arguments are these: (1) There is too much material and there are too many events in the ministry of the Seventy to the thirty-five cities to put in the brief time usually attributed to this. (2) The parable of the fig tree (Luke 13:6-9) indicates four years.

Most students of the life of Christ and most of the composers of harmonies before Cheney have seen the same difficulties in the chronology and the large amount of material in Luke 9:51–19:27. Moreover, Cheney overlooks certain statements in Luke that indicate this *was a brief period* and that Christ did go rapidly through the cities evangelized by the Seventy. Luke 9:51 itself says, "As the time approached for him to be taken up to heaven, Jesus resolutely set out for Jerusalem." If the days for the ascension had been more than a year off, Luke would hardly have indicated they were approaching. Moreover, Luke 13:22 indicates that Jesus was rapidly going through the cities of the Seventy.

On the surface the passage about the fig tree does seem to indicate a four-year ministry. But when one understands the fig tree's pattern of bearing in Palestine, the parable really favors a three-and-a-quarter-year ministry. The fig tree there bears two crops each season. The first ripe figs appear on the old wood in April and finish in June; the second crop appears on the new wood in August (cf. E. W. G. Masterman, "Fig, Fig Tree," *International Standard Bible Encyclopedia* [Grand Rapids: Eerdmans, 1939] 2: 1108,1109). John the Baptist would probably have been thirty years old in June, so the time for him to begin his priestly ministry would have been about July. Cheney himself quotes John the Baptist's threat to the fig tree of Israel (Matt. 3:10; Luke 3:9) as the first time the husbandman was ready to chop it down (cf. Cheney, p. 235). John's ministry began right at the conclusion of the first bearing of the fig tree nearly six months before Jesus' ministry began. Therefore, Jesus' cursing of the fig tree for refusing to bear in April, just before His death three years later, would have constituted the fourth fruitless season.

Cheney's effort to find another Passover in the collection of the temple tax (Matt. 17:24) and in the cruel death of Galileans by Pilate (Luke 13:1) is not persuasive. While the temple tax was collected in Palestine, especially in Judea, before the Passover, it was not collected from foreigners until Pentecost and for some, at the Feast of Tabernacles. Since it took some time to collect the tax, it is perfectly possible that it was being collected in December from Jews in Galilee. This is not new information, but was known by Edersheim and other Gospel scholars. Also, it is very unlikely that Pilate would have cruelly killed the group of Jewish Galileans at a big feast where a large crowd was present. Pilate feared the people too much for that (Matt. 27:24; Mark 15:15; Luke 23:24). Galileans were in Jerusalem constantly for business and other reasons and they and others were constantly offering their sin and trespass offering at the temple. To make a case for a Passover from this is unwarranted (cf. Cheney, p. 233).

4. Paul's Exposure to, and Use of, the Three-Year Discipleship Program

Paul seems to have stayed in Corinth approximately three years. He arrived in Corinth right after Emperor Claudius issued a decree for all Jews to leave Rome (Acts 18:2). This occurred in the ninth year of his office or in A.D. 49 (Orosius says it was then, cf. Adv. paganos VII, 6, 15; along with statements of Suetonius, chapter 25; and DioCassius). We also know that Paul appeared before Gallio for a court trial from which he escaped without a conviction (Acts 18:12-17). From Roman records and the Delphic inscription we know that Gallio's one year as proconsul of Achaia was A.D. July 51 - June 52. Paul, therefore, would have been in Corinth two to three years, probably about two and a half. Following the trial, Luke the historian says Paul "stayed for some time" and then took his leave. Generally, if a time span is more than a year, Luke states it in years. This gives a total of about three years.

The time in Corinth may be estimated in another way; namely, the time implied by the events and references to time (cf. Acts 18:1-18):

1. Paul arrived in Corinth, met and established friendship with Aquila and Priscilla, moved into their house and established a business where he worked daily with them (18:3). During this period he reasoned in the synagogue "every Sabbath" (18:4).

2. After his co-workers came from Macedonia, apparently bringing money, Paul stopped tentmaking and "began devoting himself *completely* to the Word" (18:5). During the time of these first two periods the leader of the synagogue, Crispus, and a large number of others were converted.

3. After much resistance and accusation of blasphemy, Paul caused *a schism* and led the Christians out of the synagogue and began to meet next door in the House of Titus Justus. Paul was the victim of many hostile threats, perhaps because of the conversion of the synagogue leader.

4. Paul taught for a year and a half in the house of Titus Justus after a vision from the Lord assured him he would not be harmed (18:7,11). During this time the new leader of the synagogue, Sosthenes, became a believer. This led to Paul's trial before Gallio. The hostility toward Sosthenes indicates that the conversion of this second synagogue leader precipitated the trial.

5. After the trial Paul "stayed for some time" before he left.

The time for these events may be estimated as follows:

1. Tent making and part-time preaching for several weeks plus the period of full-time preaching that led up to the schism — six months to a year.
2. One year and a half teaching in house of Titus Justus, leading to the conversion of second synagogue leader and trial before Gallio.
3. "Some time" (18:18) after the trial. Time of less than a year.

Paul first worked with Barnabas in Antioch. A year after they had begun to minister there (Acts 11:25,26), a prophet named Agabus predicted that there would be a famine (11:28). For the next several months (or approximately a year) Paul and Barnabas helped direct the collection of an offering to help the Jerusalem church (cf. 1 Cor. 16:1-3; 2 Cor. 8:1-9; and, especially, 9:2). After going to Jerusalem, Paul and Barnabas returned to Antioch for a short time (Acts 11:29,30; 12:25–13:4). On the whole they spent more than two years and probably three years there.

After Paul had begun his ministry in Rome, he rented quarters and stayed for two full years (cf. Acts 28:16-30, especially 30).

How did the apostle Paul learn the three-year program that Jesus used for building disciples? The answer is that he went through the model under the leadership of Barnabas and also perhaps had been made familiar with the total ministry of Jesus from those who had followed Him.

Barnabas was born in Cyprus but he owned land in Judea and probably lived there (Acts 4:36). Most likely he was one of the seventy apostles trained by Jesus. The Twelve required other leaders in the early church to be familiar with, and to be experienced in, the entire ministry of Christ (cf. Acts 1:21,22). Barnabas was one who had easy access to, and the confidence of, the Twelve (cf. Acts 9:26,27). He is one of the few men specified as an apostle other than the Twelve (Acts 14:14). It is unthinkable that the Twelve would have sent any man who was not intimately acquainted with Christ's ministry and teaching to guide the very delicate and strategic ministry with the Gentiles in Antioch.

There is much evidence to suggest that Paul was intimately acquainted with Christ's earthly ministry in other ways than through Barnabas. Soon after his conversion Paul went to Arabia. This is probably when he first learned what and how Jesus taught His disciples. In Galatians 1:11,12 Paul stated that he did not get his gospel from men but had received it by a direct revelation from Jesus Christ. This revelation would not have precluded his study of the available information about Jesus Christ's earthly life and death, and he certainly would have studied the methods Jesus used.

Ananias of Damascus is said simply to have been instructed to lay hands on Paul that he might be filled with the Spirit and have his call confirmed. But it would have been strange, indeed, if Ananias had not also begun to supply Paul with considerable information about Jesus' earthly ministry. Luke recorded in Acts 9:19,20, "Saul spent several days with the disciples in Damascus. At once he began to preach in the synagogues that Jesus is the Son of God.'' It is possible that Paul studied this information while in Arabia.

Within a few years after his conversion Paul had become acquainted with other apostles (some of whom were probably part of the Seventy) (cf. Acts 9:26,27 and Galatians 1:18,19). In Romans 16:7 Paul said that his kinsmen, Andronicus and Junias, who were in Christ before he was, were ''outstanding among the apostles.''

Luke began his Gospel in this way: ''Many have undertaken to draw up an account of the things that have been fulfilled among us, just as they were handed down to us by those who from the first were eyewitnesses and servants of the word.'' The implication is that those who had been with Christ during His ministry immediately began to recount the things that took place in the life of Jesus Christ. A man with the ability and scholarship of Paul would certainly have gathered all possible data on the life and teachings of Jesus Christ. Since Luke traveled with him, he would have been a major source. Thus, Paul would have been intimately familiar with the events in the life of Christ.

Many of Paul's actions and teachings reveal a knowledge of Christ's ministry. For example, when he and Barnabas were rejected in a city, they ''shook the dust from their feet,'' doing exactly what Jesus had told His early disciples to do (cf. Matt. 10:14; Luke 9:5; Acts 13:51; 18:6; cf. also Mark 7:27; Rom. 1:16; 2:9,10; cf. also Matt. 16:24; Luke 14:27; Gal. 2:20).

While one cannot be dogmatic about Paul's acquaintance with Jesus' ministry, it is a fact that he limited his ministry to approximately three years, just as Jesus had done. And he certainly was exposed to the model under Barnabas at Antioch.

Bibliography

I. Biblical Foundations for Disciple Building

Bruce, A. B. *The Training of the Twelve*. Grand Rapids: Kregel, 1971. The classic study of Jesus' ministry with His disciples.

Chamblin, Knox. *Following Jesus According to the New Testament*. Unpublished Th.M. dissertation, Columbia Theological Seminary, 1967. Chamblin, a professor at Belhaven, believes that, in the Gospels, "to follow" Jesus is the best phrase for describing what is involved in being His disciple; he examines all the implications of this in the New Testament and provides many useful insights for contemporary discipling.

Coleman, Robert. *The Master Plan of Evangelism*. Westwood, N. J.: Revell, 1964. This professor at Asbury argues convincingly that Jesus' ultimate objective on earth was to build the truth of Himself into twelve men who would then do likewise; eight aspects of that discipling process are explained in a practical and challenging fashion.

Kittel, Gerhard, general editor. *Theological Dictionary of the New Testament*. 9 volumes. Translated by Geoffrey Bromiley. Grand Rapids, Michigan: Eerdmans, 1964. Vol. IV, pp. 415-461, *"Mathētēs"* by K. H. Rengstorf. Scholarly study of the historical meanings of the Greek word for "disciple"; the final fifteen pages are particularly helpful.

Pentecost, J. Dwight. *Design for Discipleship*. Grand Rapids: Zondervan, 1971. A series of expository sermons in which this Dallas professor surveys the New Testament's teaching on discipleship.

Robertson, A. T. *A Harmony of the Gospels*. New York: Harper & Row, 1922. An eminent New Testament scholar arranges the content of all four Gospels in chronological order, enabling the reader to observe first-hand the flow of Jesus' discipling ministry.

Rogers, Cleon. "The Great Commission" in *Bibliotheca Sacra*. July, 1973. Study of how Jesus' discipling ministry compares and contrasts with the teaching methodology of the Hebrew rabbis of His day.

II. Disciple Building and the Local Church

Baumann, Daniel. *All Originality Makes a Dull Church*. Santa Ana, Calif.: Vision House, 1976. A look at the distinctive features of several of today's great churches.

Getz, Gene. *Sharpening the Focus of the Church.* Chicago: Moody, 1974. This Dallas professor and successful pastor draws lessons from Scripture, history, and culture to develop a contemporary strategy for the church.

Girard, Robert. *Brethren, Hang Loose.* Grand Rapids: Zondervan, 1972. The success story of Our Heritage Church in Scottsdale, Arizona. Girard includes many practical suggestions for developing an "ideal" church.

Halverson, Richard. *How I Changed My Thinking About the Church.* Grand Rapids: Zondervan, 1972. The pastor of Washington, D.C.'s Fourth Presbyterian Church explains his commitment to focusing his ministry on the few.

Jenson, Ron. *Gearing the Local Church for Discipleship.* Unpublished doctoral dissertation, Western Conservative Baptist Seminary. After visiting 175 top churches in America, the author sets forth his excellent ideas for developing a church into a total discipling organism.

Ortiz, Juan Carlos. *Call to Discipleship.* Plainfield, N.J.: Logos, 1975. Vision-expanding account of how this Buenos Aires pastor transformed his congregation from an "orphanage" to a family by discipleship.

Richards, Larry. *A Theology of Christian Education.* Grand Rapids: Zondervan, 1975. A well-known Christian educator shows how, according to Scriptures, the fundamental purpose of the church is discipling; he then thoroughly works out the implications of this for Christian education in the church.

Smith, Bob. *When All Else Fails, Read the Directions.* Waco: Word, 1974. An associate of Ray Stedman provides a fresh look at New Testament principles for church organization.

Snyder, Howard. *The Problem of Wineskins.* Downers Grove: Inter-Varsity Press, 1975. Perhaps the most thorough of the many "church renewal" books, taking more of an historical perspective and stressing that we "should not only discover and apply New Testament principles, but also New Testament structure."

III.   "How To's" of Disciple Building

Collins, Gary R. *How to Be a People Helper.* Santa Ana, Calif.: Vision House, 1976. Practical, biblical volume from a Trinity Evangelical Divinity School professor who discusses counseling with a view to building disciples.

Henrichson, Walter. *Disciples Are Made, Not Born.* Wheaton: Victor Books, 1974. Navigators' executive provides a thorough and very useful handbook for "how to make disciples out of Christians."

Kuhne, Gary. *The Dynamics of Personal Follow-up.* Grand Rapids: Zondervan, 1976. A former Campus Crusader stresses follow-up as the first stage of discipling, with discussions of the worker's attitude, problems he will face, and ten follow-up appointments.

Moore, Waylon. *New Testament Follow-up.* Grand Rapids: Eerdmans, 1963. Similar to Kuhne's book, but written from the perspective of the pastor of a local church.

IV.   Training Disciples to Be Leaders

Eims, LeRoy. *Be the Leader You Were Meant to Be.* Wheaton: Victor Books, 1975. The director of evangelism for the Navigators provides a down-to-earth presentation of biblical leadership principles.

Gangel, Kenneth. *Competent to Lead*. Chicago: Moody Press, 1974. He has
   explored biblical and secular organizational studies and sought to present a
   comprehensive view of the church's leadership, especially with the
   perspective of solving the problem of human relations in the church.

Hyde, Douglas. *Dedication and Leadership*. South Bend, Ind.: University of
   Notre Dame, 1964. Converted Communist applies proven techniques to
   Christian leadership.

Sanders, Oswald. *Spiritual Leadership*. Chicago: Moody Press, 1974. God's
   design for His leaders and how to conform to that design is the focus of this
   excellent volume.

Author Index

Subject Index

Abraham, 86, 92, 112, 123, 149, 158, 161, 235, 237

Absolutism, scientific, 41

Acceptance by God daily, 64, 97, 188, 258, 259

Acts, 13, 51, 54, 72, 203, 225, 226

Adam, 18, 48, 53, 56, 107, 242, 246
the second, 46, 159, 160

Adonijah, 156

Aenon, 90, 149, 150, 214

Anabaptist movement, 39

Ananias and Sapphira, 121

Andrew, 92, 173, 175, 212

Antioch, 69, 118, 216

Antisupernaturalism, 146, 147, 219

Apologetics, 20, 42

Apostles, 117. See also Twelve, the

Apostolic repetition
of Christ's kingly power, 125. See also Authority
of Christ's teaching, 83-86, 96, 108, 109, 117, 121-123, 126, 127, 139, 145, 148, 151, 157, 163

Ascension of Christ, 97, 116, 157, 159, 212, 252, 275

Association, 67, 72, 80, 90, 108, 114-117, 171-183, 195, 248

Atonement, 56, 220. See also Death of Christ

Authority, 19-24, 64, 116, 119, 143, 227, 252
biblical, 11, 12, 23, 30, 41-43, 57, 75, 113, 136, 146, 253
of Christ, 90, 94, 106-108, 123-125, 146, 150, 155, 207, 240, 252-255, 271, 272 See also Deity of Christ

Baptism, 20, 52, 81, 85, 86, 94, 161, 162, 195, 196, 198, 257
of Jesus, 90, 91, 116, 153, 173, 202, 212, 224, 228

Barnabas, 50, 69, 75, 118, 197, 215, 226, 312-314

Beatitudes, the, 116, 120

Bethany, 150

Bethesda, pool of, 108

Biblical authority. See Authority

Body life movement, 23, 40, 64, 66, 71, 191

Body of Christ. See Church

Booze, Allen and Hamilton, Inc., 265

Bread of life, 132, 138, 142, 224, 236

Campus Crusade for Christ, 40, 98, 212, 215, 262, 271, 308

Cana, 93, 96, 216

Canon, New Testament, 19, 75

Capernaum, 90, 96, 100, 105, 111, 113, 124, 148, 216, 217, 229, 230

Charismatic movement, 23, 24, 36, 37, 98, 252

Child of God, 48, 80, 81, 108, 123, 206, 232

Christ. See Jesus Christ

Christian liberty, 107, 108, 110, 144, 188, 242. See also Legalism

Christianity Today, poll, 38

Chronology of Christ's ministry, 11, 13, 61-65, 310, 311

Church
body of Christ, 11, 23, 64, 70, 103, 141-151, 187, 191, 252, 258, 271
Christ the head, 11, 136, 141, 159, 162, 191, 252-254, 271, 272
early post-apostolic, 19-22
establishment and edification of local church groups, 50, 51, 65-68, 91, 92, 116, 124, 125, 142, 143, 162, 173, 184, 208, 210, 215, 216, 250, 251
failures, 246, 271-274
functional dimensions, 38-40
today, 18, 22-25, 37-40, 65-68, 71, 261-264. See also Education, Evangelism, Kingdom of God, Leadership, Obedience, Prayer, Clergy-laity separation

Churches Alive, 180

Circumcision, 109

Claudius, 311

Cleansing the temple, 74, 75, 93, 94, 157

Scripture Index